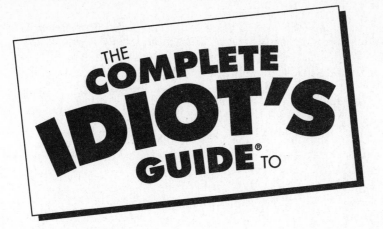

THE COMPLETE IDIOT'S GUIDE® TO

Cashing In On Your Inventions

Second Edition

by Richard C. Levy

ALPHA

A member of Penguin Group (USA) Inc.

Fairy tales do come true. I dedicate this book to Sheryl and Bettie, the bright and beautiful women who continue to enrich and illuminate my life and keep me young at heart. I'll love you forever and always. It doesn't get any better. Mwah!

A special call out to Julie and Mr. Bumble for keeping Team Levy real.

ALPHA BOOKS

Published by the Penguin Group

Penguin Group (USA) Inc., 375 Hudson Street, New York, New York 10014, USA

Penguin Group (Canada), 90 Eglinton Avenue East, Suite 700, Toronto, Ontario M4P 2Y3, Canada (a division of Pearson Penguin Canada Inc.)

Penguin Books Ltd., 80 Strand, London WC2R 0RL, England

Penguin Ireland, 25 St. Stephen's Green, Dublin 2, Ireland (a division of Penguin Books Ltd.)

Penguin Group (Australia), 250 Camberwell Road, Camberwell, Victoria 3124, Australia (a division of Pearson Australia Group Pty. Ltd.)

Penguin Books India Pvt. Ltd., 11 Community Centre, Panchsheel Park, New Delhi—110 017, India

Penguin Group (NZ), 67 Apollo Drive, Rosedale, North Shore, Auckland 1311, New Zealand (a division of Pearson New Zealand Ltd.)

Penguin Books (South Africa) (Pty.) Ltd., 24 Sturdee Avenue, Rosebank, Johannesburg 2196, South Africa

Penguin Books Ltd., Registered Offices: 80 Strand, London WC2R 0RL, England

International Standard Book Number: 978-1-61564-007-2
Library of Congress Catalog Card Number: 2009941617

12 11 10   8 7 6 5 4 3 2 1

Interpretation of the printing code: The rightmost number of the first series of numbers is the year of the book's printing; the rightmost number of the second series of numbers is the number of the book's printing. For example, a printing code of 10-1 shows that the first printing occurred in 2010.

Printed in the United States of America

Note: This publication contains the opinions and ideas of its author. It is intended to provide helpful and informative material on the subject matter covered. It is sold with the understanding that the author and publisher are not engaged in rendering professional services in the book. If the reader requires personal assistance or advice, a competent professional should be consulted.

The author and publisher specifically disclaim any responsibility for any liability, loss, or risk, personal or otherwise, which is incurred as a consequence, directly or indirectly, of the use and application of any of the contents of this book.

Most Alpha books are available at special quantity discounts for bulk purchases for sales promotions, premiums, fundraising, or educational use. Special books, or book excerpts, can also be created to fit specific needs.

For details, write: Special Markets, Alpha Books, 375 Hudson Street, New York, NY 10014.

Publisher: *Marie Butler-Knight*
Associate Publisher/Acquiring Editor: *Mike Sanders*
Senior Managing Editor: *Billy Fields*
Senior Development Editor: *Christy Wagner*
Senior Production Editor: *Megan Douglass*
Copy Editor: *Krista Hansing Editorial Services, Inc.*

Cover Designer: *Kurt Owens*
Book Designer: *Trina Wurst*
Indexer: *Heather McNeill*
Layout: *Ayanna Lacey*
Proofreader: *John Etchison*

Contents at a Glance

Contents

Appendixes

Introduction

The next time you access the Internet through your mobile phone, warm a frozen pizza in your microwave or ride an elevator in a high-rise office building, thank an independent inventor. In fact, nearly every modern convenience we have today owes its origins to a thinker, a dreamer, a creator—an independent inventor. These are society's dreamers, doers, risk takers, and makers of things. And they are heroes who continue to shape and enrich our lives.

—Mike Drummond, editor-in-chief, *Inventor's Digest*

Of the more than 7.5 million patents granted in the United States since 1790, a few have had enormous impact on our lives while at the same time bringing fame and fortune to their inventors. The electric lamp, the transistor radio, the internal combustion engine, and the telephone come to mind quickly. Some inventions have had little or no impact on our lives, such as the Pet Rock and Cabbage Patch Kids, but have brought fame and fortune to their inventors. But the vast majority of inventions dreamed up during the last 200 plus years have created no recognition or financial gain for their inventors. Why? Because these concepts were never commercialized. They have left no trace. You can bet that when the inventors applied for their patents, the inventions seemed like terrific ideas. But then something happened—or, more accurately, *didn't* happen.

What didn't happen was the sale, and nothing happens until something is sold. Just as invention begins with resistance, so does the sale. When resistance is overcome, the idea finds a successful structure and the sale is made. *The Complete Idiot's Guide to Cashing In On Your Inventions*, now in its second edition, is about overcoming resistance, at myriad levels.

In this book, you learn how to …

- ◆ Recognize your own potential.

- ◆ Avoid invention marketing rip-off schemes.

- ◆ Protect your invention through patents, trademarks, and/or copyrights.

- ◆ Pitch and license your concepts to manufacturers.

- ◆ Have prototypes made professionally.

- ◆ Make the best deal: a win-win.

- ◆ Dramatically reduce your legal expenses.

- ◆ Find expert advice and support via associations, publications, and the Internet.

In addition to learning how to license and protect your inventions, it is my hope that *The Complete Idiot's Guide to Cashing In On Your Inventions* encourages you to …

♦ Trust yourself more and recognize, accept, and take responsibility for the mutuality of events.

♦ Forbid yourself to be deterred by poor odds just because your mind has calculated that the opposition is too great. Remember, if Edison had stopped at, say, 30 filaments, we might still be in the dark.

♦ Do not fear the winds of hard times. Kites rise against the wind, not with it.

♦ Take your chances, not someone else's chances. The rewards are greater.

♦ Ask questions. If you don't ask a question, the answer is an automatic "no."

♦ Have the courage to make mistakes. Mistakes are the by-product of experimentation.

♦ The best hitters fail 65 percent of the time.

♦ Resist the herd instinct. Be yourself and be faithful to your own muse. Never give up your individuality.

♦ Look for opportunities, not guarantees.

♦ See rejection as rehearsal before the big event. There can be no success without failure.

♦ Learn the value of teamwork and how much people contribute to each other's success. There's no *i* in *team*.

♦ Pay attention to what author James Burke calls the *web of change*. Through it we are all linked to each other and to the future. No individual acts without causing the web to change. He calls this phenomenon the Pinball Effect.

♦ Do not fear pressure deadlines and situations. After all, diamonds are made under pressure.

♦ Create change. Change is inevitable, except from vending machines.

♦ Enjoy the hunt. For it is here, in the moment of transition, in the rushing to a goal, that power resides.

The book you hold in your hands is written for the ordinary person with the extraordinary idea and the yen to turn it into royalty income. It's a classic American landscape: real fortunes being made by plain folks with an itch, courage, indefatigable entrepreneurial spirit, and, of course, the better idea.

Look upon this book as a chart, superimpose your own lines on it, and use it to navigate the stormy and hazardous waters of protecting, licensing, and commercializing your inventions.

One important note: The chapters on the protection of your intellectual property are provided as a primer. Intellectual property laws, regulations, filing fees, and so forth are in a constant state of change, pushed and pulled by technologies, marketplaces, and special interests. These chapters are not designed to take the place of competent legal counsel, which I encourage you to seek.

It's a requirement today that you have the full gamut of tools, e.g., a computer (PC and/or laptop) with high-speed Internet connection, e-mail accounts, BlackBerry or other smartphone, multiple-line phones for conferencing, voicemail/answer service, scanner/copier/fax, and so on. This way, you'll be able to keep pace with industry.

From August 23 through September 26, 2008, my wife and I took a 10,616-mile road trip from the Eastern seaboard, north to Canada, across the TransCan from Thunder Bay to Vancouver, and then back East. Between our BlackBerry and FedEx, our business didn't miss a beat. Such tools allowed us to combine business and pleasure and never lose touch with the pulse of our enterprise. Get wired!

Some Notes on Terminology and Credits

If you've researched inventors and inventions, you know that discrepancies, especially over inventorship, come with the territory. More than 100 years ago, Ralph Waldo Emerson realized this, too. He explained it like this:

> 'Tis frivolous to fix pedantically the date of particular inventions. They have all been invented over and over fifty times.

I choose to use the terms *inventor, developer,* and *creator* interchangeably, as does the industry, to signify one or more of the independent creative forces behind an invention, usually a signatory to a patent application and a license agreement and, as such, a participant in any advances and royalties.

John Melius, president of Inventor's Network of the Capital Area (INCA), prefers to refer to himself as a *product developer.* He feels this designation puts him closer mentally to commercialized product. An inventor is typically dealing with something that's not a complete product ready for sale. It's an interesting approach.

Many inventors quoted in this book are extremely prolific. To be fair to everyone, including my editors, who need to deal with space considerations, I decided to list only one invention credit per inventor. The exception is A. Eddy Goldfarb, the dean of independent toy inventors, who has licensed more than 600 inventions since he left the Silent Service after World War II.

The process of invention and innovation isn't easy to analyze. Therefore, I did not even attempt to list co-inventing credits. Anyone who knows this business understands that it would be an impossible task. Therefore, if you see more than one person credited with the invention of a product, there's probably a good reason for it.

While my book focuses mostly on the independent inventor, this is not to imply that there's a lack of creativity or inventiveness at the corporate level. It is just the opposite. Many outstanding concepts come from in-house. Furthermore, the contributions made by R&D and marketing executives to outside submissions often make the difference between success and failure. This has surely been the case with my products.

It is my most sincere hope that this book will intrigue, inform, entertain, and turn on a light bulb or two for even the most seasoned inventor.

This book is highly organized. But you're an inventor, and when things are too organized, well, you get the picture. So go ahead; just plunge in and browse around.

I'm sure I have missed a few things here and there, but as Goethe noted, "Incompleteness stimulates."

Curtain up. Light the lights.

Richard

How This Book Is Organized

This book is designed to be a quick-access resource companion to accompany you throughout your journey from "What if?" to the deal and, hopefully, to riches (although financial reward must not be the only thing that drives you). The sequence is a step-by-step blueprint for overcoming your fears, building your confidence, taking pride in your ideas, adapting to change, taking risks, and taking control.

Part 1, "How to Get Your Great Ideas on the Road," shares America's greatest traditions and visions as a center of innovation and free enterprise, home to the world's most prolific, daring, and successful inventors and entrepreneurs. Through all the wit, color, and home-spun truth I could muster, it asks you to look at yourself and realize that, on any given day, your dream can come true. But for this to happen, you must have the "Dare to Go," know where to go, and what to do when you get there.

The most important part of this book appears in Part 1. Here I instruct you how to avoid being ripped off by carrion birds who toil under the guise of reputable invention marketing services. Further along in Part 1, you analyze whether it is better to license your invention or seek "adventure capital" and build a business.

Part 2, "How to Build 'Em and Make 'Em," explains the various types of models and prototypes and how to get them made, if you don't have golden hands. The second chapter in Part 2 addresses how to set up manufacturing. This information is invaluable whether you make a product yourself or license your invention.

Part 3, "Getting High Marks," assumes you have opted to go the licensing route. (If you want to establish your own manufacturing and marketing operation, take a giant step to Part 4.) Part 3 explains how to find the right company for your invention, get through its door, pitch the idea, and make a deal if you're fortunate enough to be afforded an opportunity. It's all about the hunt!

Part 4, "Goin' for the Gold," takes you to the U.S. Patent and Trademark Office (USPTO). Learn what makes the USPTO tick and how you can take advantage of its invaluable services. You'll also learn ways to conduct a patent search. It wraps on a very important issue—how to hire competent patent counsel.

Part 5, "Uncle Sam Wants (to Protect) YOU!" explains the different kinds of intellectual property (ip) protection—e.g., utility patent, plant patent, design patent, trademark, copyright, and trade secret. The information is designed as a primer, not to take the place of a patent counsel. The final chapter in Part 5 takes you behind the scenes at the U.S. Patent and Trademark Office for a look at how your application is handled.

In **Part 6, "People Who Share, People Who Dare,"** you see how Uncle Sam has gone from being a principal customer of technology to wanting to share technologies with private industry and build partnerships. There's a smorgasbord of delicious opportunities for you, and Chapter 21 is the appetizer.

Chapter 22 is a primer on the toy industry, one of the last great frontiers for the entrepreneurial inventor.

After the chapters come the appendixes. And while I can do nothing to alleviate patent fees, I can help reduce your legal expenses. I've provided a confidential nondisclosure form (NDA) and licensing agreements for inventions and trademarks, respectively, that you can use as templates for your own transactions, potentially saving your lawyer hours of work and you thousands of dollars in legal fees.

Extras

To add some perspective, inspiration, and a bit of off-road mental adventure, I've peppered six different types of collateral information throughout:

Bright Ideas

These boxes give you inspirational and frequently entertaining stories behind well-known inventions and their frequently not-so-well-known inventors.

Notable Quotables

These boxes provide inspirational nuggets and pearls of wisdom I've collected over the years, as well as advice from successful inventors.

411

Here you'll find important phone numbers, addresses, websites, and other vital information.

Fast Facts

This box offers a potpourri of factoids and assorted trivia that will contribute to your greater understanding of the invention business.

---

def•i•ni•tion

What do you call a dictionary for inventors? How about an *inventionary*? Well, whatever you call it, in this box you will find buzzwords, terms, and expressions used by inventors.

Inventions Wanted

Many invention contests and companies invite submissions. I cannot vouch for even a small fraction of them. Many require up-front fees and are questionable. But check these boxes for some opportunities I've discovered.

Acknowledgments

The Complete Idiot's Guide to Cashing In On Your Inventions, Second Edition, is built on the foundation established through the generous contributions of those people thanked in the first edition released in 2002. Their warm reception, hospitality, expertise, and good cheer made the experience one I'll always remember fondly. However,

I must thank again the officials at the USPTO for their outstanding cooperation when the time came to fact-check this edition. Also my deep appreciation goes to my friends, extraordinary ip attorneys Dinesh Agarwal, Howard R. Fine, and Roberta Jacobs Meadway for their unselfish and invaluable contributions.

Ronald O. Weingartner, thanks for allowing me to pull material from our book, *The Toy and Game Inventor's Handbook*.

At Alpha Books, heaps of gratitude to my editors: Mike Sanders, for his continued belief in this book, his friendship, sound judgment, and for compassionately taking my calls; Christy Wagner and Megan Douglass, for their sharp editorial skills; and the rest of their stellar team. A special shout out to Dawn Werk, Alpha's talented marketing maven for keeping me in the loop and getting out my words.

There's no way to repay my wife, Sheryl, for her oceanic patience, personal sacrifice, daily inspiration, and enduring those 18-hour stretches of time when words were my only world. But as with every project I take on, she provided unqualified and unwavering support and wise counsel and kept our lives and business on track until the book gods again released me from their grasp.

A special mention to Bettie, the love of our lives; The Beck and SZL, who set the examples by which I lead my life and whose footprints are forever in my heart; Uncle Mike, for my love of words; Nana and TRA, for showing me the world; The Chick in Hudson, because she's THE CHICK; The J-Man in Hotlanta for this book's cover photo and thousands of snapshots over the years; Montez in Boston for his friendship and humor and Haig der Marderosian (wherever you are).

The Beck rules!

Trademarks

All terms mentioned in this book that are known to be or are suspected of being trademarks or service marks have been appropriately capitalized. Alpha Books and Penguin Group (USA) Inc. cannot attest to the accuracy of this information. Use of a term in this book should not be regarded as affecting the validity of any trademark or service mark.

Part 1

How to Get Your Great Ideas on the Road

There's nothing more difficult, more risky, or more uncertain than to be a change-ready individual. Change makes people nervous. It brings in elements of the unknown. I call uncompromising people the *Gottas*. *Gotta* do it this way. *Gotta* do it that way. Well, this section is, in part, about how not to let the *Gottas* get you.

These chapters are designed to tighten your mental bolts, fill your tanks with verbal fuel, and rev your self-confidence until it redlines and sends you out full throttle to meet and win over strangers—and build lasting relationships.

Along the way, you can expect to be ambushed by road pirates who attempt to pull you over and steal your money and intellectual property. Part 1 shows you how to avoid them.

Finally, you will learn the advantages and disadvantages of licensing your invention, vis-à-vis seeking venture capital to commercialize it.

Ready? Engine purring? If so, buckle up, release the brake, and prepare yourself for an exciting ride.

How to Realize Your Full Potential

In This Chapter

◆ Makin' it happen

◆ Proving the naysayers wrong

◆ America, start your engines

◆ Genius, insight, and passion

◆ 10 Commandments of Success

> Nothing in the world can take the place of persistence. Talent will not; nothing is more common than unsuccessful men with talent. Genius will not; unrewarded genius is almost a proverb. Education will not; the world is full of educated derelicts. Persistence and determination alone are omnipotent. The slogan, "Press on," has solved and always will solve the problems of the human race.
>
> —President Calvin Coolidge

Heavier-than-air flying machines are impossible, the well-known British mathematician and physicist William Kelvin assured everyone in 1895. Man can never tap the power of the atom, said Nobel Laureate and physicist

Robert Andrews Millikan, credited with being the first to isolate the electron and measure its charge. Everything that can be invented has been invented, stated another man of vision, Charles H. Duell, director of the U.S. Patent Office in 1899.

TRW, Inc., the global technology, manufacturing, and service company, listed these observations in a *Wall Street Journal* ad tagged with these lines: "There's no future in believing something can't be done. The future is in making it happen."

What Kelvin, Millikan, and Duell didn't understand, quite obviously, is what inventors in everything from high-tech labs to basement workshops across America are proving each day:

♦ There is no future in the word *impossible.*

♦ Results first. Theory second.

♦ Alert optimism beats conservative skepticism.

♦ Failure breeds success. Celebrate it!

Pessimism arrests growth and sensitivity. It has the same effect on you that leaving the cap off a bottle of Coke has on the pop—you go flat. What you need in order to have any chance at success is tons of energy (or, in soda terms, high carbonation). You'll never reach your limits without being fully charged.

Overcoming Naysayers

In his first three years in business, Henry Ford went broke three times. Dr. Seuss's first children's book was rejected by 23 publishers. The twenty-fourth publisher sold 6 million copies. In 1902, a young poet's poems were rejected by *Atlantic Monthly* as being "too vigorous," but Robert Frost persevered. Michael Jordan was cut from his high school basketball team. The University of Bern rejected a Ph.D. dissertation, saying it was irrelevant and fanciful. Albert Einstein was disappointed but not down for the count.

Richard Hooker's book *M*A*S*H* was turned down by 21 publishers. Then Morrow released it in 1968, and it became a barn-burning best-seller, a movie, and one of the most popular television series of all time.

> **Notable Quotables**
>
> Far better it is to dare mighty things, to win glorious triumphs, even though checkered by failure, than to take rank with those poor spirits who neither enjoy much nor suffer much, because they live in the gray twilight that knows not victory nor defeat.
>
> —Theodore Roosevelt

In 1931, Pearl Buck received a rejection letter for *The Good Earth* that went like this: "Regret the American public is not interested in anything on China." In 1932, she won the Pulitzer for this work. Sir William Golding, author of *Lord of the Flies*, was told, in 1954, "It does not seem to us that you have been wholly successful in working out an admittedly promising idea."

In each of these instances, innovation, innovators, and positive thinking met, challenged, and overcame negative and myopic people—the type who go through life blocking light and avoiding anything that sounds iffy. Not every idea deserves to be supported. But I'm driven to total distraction when ideas are blown off because they don't follow a well-known business model, scientific or engineering principle, or proven pattern, or are flippantly labeled as not being feasible by people who are experts in keeping up with the art of yesterday.

My friend Ceil Hughes, of blessed memory, up in northeastern Pennsylvania had the right idea. She approached life every day knowing there are no guarantees, no matter how many yesterdays proved something to be right or wrong. She wore a small gold scroll locket on a necklace. Inside, a piece of paper read: "Yesterday is history. Tomorrow is a mystery."

The First Pitch

Before pitching an idea, realize it will be shot down by at least a few companies, if not all of them. Like batters in baseball, many executives don't swing at the first pitch. Only once or twice in my career has a concept sold to the first looker.

Bright Ideas
Tired of the stains made by his fountain pen, Hungarian journalist, painter, and inventor Laszlo Biro (1899–1985) and his brother, George, developed a pen with a ball point that wrote without leaving ink blotches. Laszlo is credited as the pen's inventor, although he was not the inventor of the first ballpoint pen—or the best design. During World War II, the ballpoint pen became standard equipment in military aircraft because it worked at high altitudes—and with this capability came recognition for this innovative writing instrument. In 1945, a New York City department store introduced a ballpoint pen and sold 10,000 units in one day at $12.50 each. Today billions are sold worldwide, many for pennies apiece.

In the late 1980s, our Adver*teasing* board game was rejected by Milton Bradley, Parker Brothers, and too many other companies to list before Cadaco, a small, family-owned publisher from Chicago, licensed it. The game requires players to recall advertising slogans, jingles, and trivia. Introduced in 1988, it has sold over 1 million units to date and is still on the market. Two companies rejected the concept for our animatronic Furby before we pitched it to the courageous mavericks at Tiger Electronics. Furby, now marketed by Hasbro, has sold 50 million units since its debut in early October 1998.

In the early 1980s, not a single publisher was willing to take on *Richard C. Levy's Secrets of Selling Inventions,* so I self-published the 200-page, soft-cover book and sold it by mail order for $45 plus $4.50 shipping/handling. (There was no Internet at that time) Once the book had proven itself, earning about $120,000, an enhanced edition was licensed to Gale Research. That book ultimately morphed into the first edition of this book, the proposal for which was seen by no less than a dozen publishers before Mike Sanders at Alpha Books saw its potential. He and his colleagues put their tray tables and seat backs into the upright position, fastened their seat belts, and signed on for the ride.

These are just a few of more than a few hundred such instances in my own career across multiple disciplines; film, television, publishing, journalism, toys and games. The moral? Never give up. Be persistent and consistent. Follow the light of faith. It alone can trample underfoot the status quo, smite yes-but-isms, and devitalize onslaughts of skepticism and negativism.

> **Fast Facts**
>
> In fiscal year 2008, inventors from California were issued 22,122 patents, making it number one out of the 50 states in patent awards. The fewest patents, 28, were issued to residents of Alaska. Four patents were awarded to inventors living in the U.S. Pacific Islands, including American Samoa, Guam, and miscellaneous U.S. Pacific Islands.

America, the Land of Opportunity

We Americans invented free enterprise. Nowhere in the world do people have more freedom and encouragement to innovate and be different than from sea to shining sea. A visitor to this country in the late 1820s observed that the moment an American hears the word *invention,* he pricks up his ears.

It is said that we Americans are men and women with "new eras in our brains." Our history is replete with examples of independent and courageous individuals who succeeded by doing things differently, people who believed in themselves and their ideas.

> **411**
>
> *Inventor's Digest,* America's only inventors' magazine, first appeared in 1985. This excellent publication delivers information and encouragement by the shovel load. Check it out at www.inventorsdigest.com.

Alexis de Tocqueville, a French writer who visited America in 1831, wrote this about Americans:

> They have all a lively faith in the perfectibility of man, they judge that the diffusion of knowledge must necessarily be advantageous, and the consequences of ignorance fatal; they all consider society as a body in a state of improvement, humanity as a changing scene, in which nothing is, or ought to be, permanent; and they admit that what appears to them today to be good, may be superseded by something better tomorrow. America is a land of wonders in which everything is in constant motion and every change seems an improvement. The idea of novelty is there indissolubly connected with the idea of amelioration. No natural boundary seems to be set to the efforts of man; and in his eyes what is not yet done is only what he has not yet attempted to do.

On the occasion of the 150th anniversary of the Patent Act of 1836, then vice president George H. W. Bush, speaking at the National Museum of American History, said this:

> It takes a special kind of independence to invent something. You put yourself and your ideas on the line. And maybe some people will say that you're crazy or that you're impractical, but for [over] two centuries, millions of Americans have ignored the ridicule. They've worked on ideas. From those ideas, they've started businesses. And many of those businesses have grown and are our greatest industrial companies, companies like Xerox, Ford Motor Company, American Telephone and Telegraph, and Apple Computer. Think of what America would be like if the skeptics had silenced the inventors.

This independence was never truer than in the cases of the following inventive Americans, people who dared to be different and refused to swap incentive for security. Many of their names have become well known.

Towering Examples of American Ingenuity

In 1923, Clarence "Bob" Birdseye, the father of frozen food, got a patent on quick freezing. Dr. William "Billy" Scholl patented his first arch support in 1904 at the age of 22. Beginning in 1896 and during a 47-year career, one-time slave George Washington Carver developed more than 300 products from peanuts alone. On a cold day in January 1839, Charles Goodyear vulcanized rubber. Yankee tinker Eli Whitney transformed the South with the cotton gin he invented in 1792. New Englander Edwin H. Land demonstrated his first instant cameras in 1947.

Many inventors are known for more than one product. William Lear, best known for the Learjet, also received a patent on the first car radio and the eight-track tape system. His company eventually became Motorola. In 1845, Peter Cooper, inventor of the famous locomotive Tom Thumb, was awarded the first patent for a gelatin dessert, which became known as Jell-O. George Westinghouse not only invented air brakes for railroad cars, but is also credited with a type of gas meter and a pipeline system that safely conducted natural gas into homes. Bell Telephone was named for Alexander Graham Bell, a former Boston University professor, who received his first patent for the telephone and a telephone system in 1876.

> **Notable Quotables**
>
> An invasion of armies can be resisted, but not an idea whose time has come.
>
> —Victor Hugo, French author

Other Fields of Dreams, and Dreamers from Other Fields

Some well-known Americans are famous for something other than their inventions. Actress Hedy Lamarr patented a sophisticated antijamming device to foil Nazi radar during World War II. After the patent expired, Sylvania adapted the invention, and it is still used in satellite communication. Author Samuel L. Clemens (a.k.a. Mark Twain) patented a pair of suspenders. Zeppo Marx patented a wrist-worn heart alarm. Novelist John Dos Passos is listed as co-inventor of a toy pistol that blows bubbles. Actress Julie Newmar patented a type of pantyhose. Singer Edie Adams patented a ring-shaped cigarette and cigar holder. Confederate General James E. B. Stuart patented a method of attaching sabers to belts. Escape artist Harry Houdini held a patent on a diver's suit that permitted escape. Bette Nesmith, mother of Michael Nesmith of The Monkees, invented Liquid Paper typewriter correction fluid.

Who's Whitcomb L. Judson?

Other Americans are not as well known as their inventions. In 1893, Whitcomb L. Judson of Chicago filed the first patent on a slide fastener for shoes ("Clasp Locker Or Unlocker For Shoes"), better known today as the zipper. During the Civil War, Martha Coston invented a safety flare for which the U.S. government paid her $20,000. Northam Warren, after graduating from Detroit College of Pharmacy, originated the first liquid cuticle remover (Cutex) in 1911. Newspaper editor Carlton Magee invented the parking meter in Oklahoma City in 1932. Walter Hunt patented the safety pin in 1849. Joseph F. Glidden protected his idea for barbed wire in 1874. Alonzo D. Phillios struck a bright idea in 1836 when he patented the friction match.

Not all inventions are so conventional. Two virtually unknown American inventors, Philip Leder of Chestnut Hill, Massachusetts, and Timothy A. Stewart of San Francisco, California, made history on April 12, 1988, when U.S. Patent No. 4,736,866, titled "Transgenic Non-Human Mammals," was issued. The Harvard University researchers were awarded the first patent covering an animal. Their technique introduced activated cancer genes into early stage mice embryos. The resulting mice were born with activated cancer genes in all their cells. These mice, extremely sensitive to cancer-causing chemicals, developed tumors quickly if exposed to small amounts of such chemicals. The resulting value to medical and scientific research is considerable.

Let's not forget the plant inventors, an example of whose work is covered by U.S. Patent No. 4,092,145. John Wesley Willard Sr. protected a method of prolonging the life or beauty of cut flowers. The patent abstract reads, in part: "Cut flowers are intimately contacted with water containing a catalytically effective amount of a novel catalyst to prolong their life or beauty. In a preferred variant, the water may also contain water soluble catalyst treated lignite." This invention has 22 claims in its patent.

How well do you know your inventors? Check out www.prongo.com/station/index.html for a fun quiz. Although designed for kids, it's fun for all ages.

> **Fast Facts**
>
> A kill fee is a negotiated payment made to an inventor by a manufacturer if an agreement is prematurely terminated prior to the start of production and through no fault of the inventor.

Answering the Call

As diverse as the aforementioned inventions are, the inventors share many things in common—characteristics you, too, need to fulfill your aspirations and see your inventions patented, licensed, manufactured, and commercialized. Perhaps the most important characteristic these people share is that, while others reflected on their ideas, these inventors answered the call.

Investing in Your Invention

The biggest barrier facing you is not the amount of money in your bank account. To quote Arnold Bennett, an English novelist, "Much ingenuity with a little money is vastly more profitable and amusing than much money without ingenuity." What you do need is time to invest. Don't think that just because you read this book you'll prepare a proposal, walk in with a prototype, pitch it, magically get a deal, and start cashing advance and royalty checks. This is a long, tough road that's always under construction. You've heard this old saw by Thomas Edison before, but it's worth repeating: "Genius is 1 percent inspiration and 99 percent perspiration."

Whether you're a clerk, plumber, psychologist, sailor, lawyer, dentist, priest, or university president, if you're the best at what you do, it has taken your full-time focus and hands-on experience. You didn't reach the heights of your career working part-time. Nothing great was ever achieved without blood, sweat, and tears.

Two common denominators that appear in the stories of each and every successful individual are sacrifice and risk. People who have reached the top of their game didn't do so by standing back, shivering and contemplating the cold waters of uncertainty. They jumped in with both feet and scrambled through as best they could.

Bud Grant, a former head coach of the Minnesota Vikings, said that you practice hard all week long so that when the ball bounces your way on Sunday afternoon, you will know what to do with it. It's no different for you. You'll play as you practice.

I'm not suggesting that you give up your day job tomorrow, but prepare yourself for a change of attitude, pace, and routine. If you work hard enough, even if you're not the most inventive person, you'll position yourself within the lightning strike zone. As you can tell by now, I love quotes, and one from Woody Allen seems appropriate here. He said that 90 percent of success is showing up.

Bright Ideas

In May 1849, Abraham Lincoln received Patent No. 6,469 for "A Device for Buoying Vessels over Shoals." It consisted of a set of bellows attached to the hull of a ship just below the waterline. On reaching a shallow place, the bellows were inflated, and the ship, thus buoyed, was expected to float clear. Lincoln whittled the prototype of the invention with his own hands.

Lincoln's appreciation of inventions was later to be of great service to the nation. John Ericcson's *Monitor*, the ironclad ship that defeated the *Merrimac*, would never have been built except for Lincoln's insistence, nor would the Spencer repeating rifle have been adopted for use by the Army.

Education Isn't Everything

Thomas Alva Edison received 1,093 patents, 4 posthumously. Perhaps the greatest inventor in history, Edison was a grammar-school dropout who had just three months of formal education. Edwin H. Land, inventor of the Polaroid camera; Bill Gates, founder of Microsoft and one of the nation's richest individuals; and R. Buckminster Fuller, social theorist, all dropped out of Harvard. Henry Ford never went to high school.

The fact that you don't have a formal education shouldn't stop you. The world is full of intelligent people who haven't had the benefit of a formal education. Conversely, you may have graduated from a top university, but I wouldn't put too much emphasis on it. When my dad, a former assistant attorney general for the Commonwealth of Pennsylvania, interviewed job candidates, he would remind them that he wasn't impressed just because they graduated from Harvard, Yale, or another prestigious law school. He would tell the young lawyers, "I'll be impressed when the school brags about you."

Stanford psychologist Nevitt Sanford has said, "Leaving college may leave a student with a sense of unfinished business that will, in some cases, provide motivation for learning for the rest of his life."

An exceptionally high IQ could mean something in some fields, but studies show that the threshold for creativity is an IQ of about 130. After that, *Business Week* reports, IQ doesn't make much difference—such nonintellectual traits, such as values and personality, become more important. In the end, product is king.

My own philosophical and social wiring were installed primarily by three people: Daddy, who was bright, well reasoned, honest, and cool under fire; and Mother and Nana, two strong, savvy, and creative liberated ladies. Their taste and social skills had no equal. In college, my wrestling coach, Jim Peckham, taught me that to win was not enough; one had to "earn the right to win." Add to this the gifts bestowed upon me by my wife, Sheryl, and I was good to go the distance. I was always encouraged to try things, even at the risk of failure. I was brought up to believe that I could accomplish anything I put my mind to doing.

Bright Ideas

On December 19, 1871, Mark Twain received Patent No. 121,992 for "An Improvement in Adjustable and Detachable Straps for Garments," otherwise known as suspenders. Twain, who later lost a fortune investing in the inventions of others, actually received three U.S. patents: the second was in 1873 on his famous *Mark Twain's Self-Pasting Scrapbook,* and the third was in 1885 for a game to help people remember important historical dates.

Levy's 10 Commandments for Success

Succeeding in the exciting, frequently gut-wrenching enterprise of product development and commercialization takes a lot more than a good idea, a strong patent, and luck. In fact, the idea is about 10 percent of the equation. If you want to beat what can sometimes seem like insurmountable odds, study the following concepts:

1. *Don't take yourself too seriously.* Don't take your idea too seriously, either. The world will probably survive without your idea. Industry will probably survive without your idea. You may need it to survive, but no one else does.

2. *The race is not always to the swift, but to those who keep running.* It's a mistake to think anything is made overnight other than baked goods and newspapers. My first corollary is: *Nothing is as easy as it looks.* My second corollary is: *Everything takes longer than you think.* You win some, you lose some, and some are rained out, but always suit up for the game and stick with it.

Inventions Wanted

General Mills has launched a search for innovation through its General Mills Worldwide Innovation Network (G-Win). CEO Ken Powell invites submissions: "We believe that there is a great opportunity for us to enhance and accelerate our innovation efforts by teaming up with world-class innovators from outside of our company." All submissions must be covered by an existing patent or have a pending patent application. For information, go to www.generalmills.com/win.

When the Convair Company couldn't find a way to stop San Diego's night fog from rusting the Atlas missile parts it manufactured, it put out a public plea for assistance. Norm Larsen, a local chemist, responded with 39 formulas. But it was his fortieth that held the answer, producing a petroleum-based chemical that gets under water and displaces it through the pores of metal. Larsen's invention became WD-40; sales for this product top $100 million. (By the way, *WD-40* stands for Water Displacement—40th formula.)

It's not speed that separates winners from losers; it's perseverance. It's the salesperson driving 30 miles at 4:15 P.M. to make one last sales call before 5 P.M. It's the actor auditioning for the hundredth time. It's the writer facing a keyboard every day creating 25 pages to get 4 or 5 that are keepers. And it's the athlete never quitting the team. These all show perseverance. That's the quality required to hit the heights of personal achievement.

3. *You can't do it all yourself.* My success continues to be the result of unselfish, highly talented, and creative partners and associates willing to face the frustrations, rejections, and seemingly open-ended time frames inherent to any product development and licensing exercise. I've also been lucky to meet and work with very creative, understanding, and courageous corporate executives willing to believe in me and gamble on our concepts. When we all work well together, nothing can stop this combo. The cross-pollination and subsequent synergism of these two forces result in success in which all parties share. For if any link in this complex and often serpentine chain breaks, an entire project could flag.

A good way to put it all into perspective is to sit through the credit crawl that runs following a television show or feature film. It becomes immediately evident how many more people than the stars and/or a celebrated director were involved to get the show on the air or screen.

David Berko, partner in East West Innovations, LLC, has a great response when asked if he's ever upset not to receive credit for his work on a particular product. "I don't care about the credit—I take cash," he quips, referring to royalties.

While not disclaiming the telephone, Alexander Graham Bell noted that "great discoveries and improvements invariably involve the cooperation of many minds. I may be given credit for having blazed the trail, but when I look at the subsequent developments, I feel the credit is due to others rather than myself."

Bright Ideas

In 1867, Alfred Nobel, a Swedish chemist and industrialist, patented the dynamite stick while trying to find a way to make nitroglycerin safe to handle. He combined the powerful liquid with a fine, chalky powder and packed it into a paper cylinder. The term *dynamite* is derived from the Greek word meaning "power." The Nobel Prizes were established using money from the sales of his chemical explosives.

It's perhaps summed up best by advertising industry legend Bill Bernbach, who said an idea can turn to dust or magic, depending on the talent that rubs against it.

4. *Keep your ego under control.* Creative and inventive people, according to profile, hate to be rejected or criticized for any reason. They're usually critical of others. They are also extremely defensive where their creations are concerned.

An out-of-control ego kills more opportunities than anything. While we inventors need a healthy ego to serve as our body armor, it can quickly get out of hand and become arrogance if not tempered. Great mistakes are made when we feel we're beyond questioning.

I've always found that my ideas are enhanced by the right touch. Working together or in competition, others contribute time and time again to making an idea more useful or marketable. Share an idea, and get back a better one.

I've worked with many egomaniacs, and most ended up as lonely as the survivors of the Titanic. Unchecked egocentricity can be a major source of failure. Arrogance has no place in the process. So if ego is a problem, check it here and now.

5. *You will always miss 100 percent of the shots you don't take.* Don't be afraid to make mistakes. If you don't put forth the effort, you won't fail, but you won't succeed, either. Inaction will keep opportunities from coming your way.

Nobel Prize–winner William Shockley, known as the father of the transistor, described the process of inventing the transistor at Bell Labs as "creative failure methodology."

Trust yourself. Don't allow yourself to be deterred by poor odds because your mind has calculated that the opposition is too great. I once asked Dr. Erno Rubik, inventor of Rubik's Cube, why children are so good at solving his puzzles and adults often don't even try. "Because no one has told the children that they cannot do it," he explained.

6. *Don't invent just for the financial rewards.* We all want to make money. That's only natural. It is what we are taught from the earliest age. But you should be motivated by the gamesmanship as well. It may sound trite, but people who do things just for money usually come up shortchanged. To put it another way, pigs get fat, while hogs get slaughtered.

Although I've negotiated and received seven-figure advance and guarantee packages, other times I took a small advance against higher royalties and earned seven figures on the other end. And sometimes I didn't earn anything.

As important as money is, you need to use common sense and judge cases on their own merits. Each industry has its own standards you can use as a baseline.

From time to time, I do paid consulting. I charge by the hour plus out-of-pocket expenses. I insist on first-class travel, top-of-the-line hotels, and so on. On the other hand, I don't charge the licensees of my products for my time if it involves a product of mine. I just ask for out-of-pocket costs. I look at it as a marketing expense. I analyze everything in terms of risk and reward. But most of the time, I see it as my obligation and pleasure to do what it takes. If successful, I will benefit on the other end through royalties and more business, hopefully.

Bright Ideas

In 1948, George de Mestral, a Swiss engineer, took a hunting trip into the Alps. As he picked burrs off his socks and pants, de Mestral wondered why they stuck to his clothing. When he looked closely at the burrs, he saw that they contained tiny hooks that caught on thread loops in his clothing. A light bulb went off in de Mestral's head. Eight years later, Velcro was born. The patent on Velcro has expired, but the trademark is alive and the technology is used in all kinds of applications, from shoes to space suits.

I believe one of the shortcomings of the independent inventor is that he or she insists on being paid for every hour of labor. If you feel this way, get over it. Look at the bigger picture. Learn to trade short-term security for long-term goals. Except when I worked in the kitchen and bookstore at college, I cannot recall ever being paid by the hour. My corporate and government jobs were not based on hourly rates. Executives are not paid by the hour.

If all you want to do is make money, and take no risk, Will Rogers has some advice: "The quickest way to double your money is to fold it over and put it back in your pocket."

7. *If you bite the bullet, be prepared to taste gunpowder.* Not every idea or decision works. So often do I find myself victimized by the Law of Unintended Consequences. One day you get the gold mine; another day you get the shaft. It's easy for people who live by their creative wits to go from drinking wine to picking grapes. But I find the risks and gambles are what I love most about a career with no safety net. Knowing how hard the business of invention development and licensing is keeps my feet moving and me on the *qui vive*.

For every action, there is always a criticism. Odds are, you'll encounter far more criticism than acceptance. This is simply the way it is. Don't whine about mistakes. Learn from them. Don't blame someone else. Take responsibility for your actions. Fix the problem, not the blame.

8. *Learn to take rejection.* Don't be turned off by the word "No," because you'll hear it often, as in, "No, we're not looking for that at this time." "No, you will have to do better than that for us to consider it." "No, your idea isn't original."

Rejection can be positive if it's turned into constructive growth. Don't let rejection shake your confidence. My experience is that products get better the more times they're presented. Rejection is a rehearsal before the big event. I define "No" to mean "Not yet." It's the shakedown period, similar to the practice of taking a play out of town before it opens on Broadway. Remember that the finest steel goes through the hottest fire.

Bright Ideas

NASA Ames scientists developed a padding concept for a better airplane seat. Today it has all kinds of additional applications, including wheelchairs, x-ray table pads, off-road vehicle seats, ski boots, and football helmet liners. The material is open-cell polyurethane silicone plastic foam that takes the shape of impressed objects but returns to its original shape even after 90 percent compression and absorbs sudden impacts without shock or bounce. The manufacturer claims a 3-inch-thick pad can absorb all the energy from a 10-foot fall by an adult.

I rarely license a product to the first person that sees it. And for every product I've licensed, many more never made it off the drawing board, and probably shouldn't have.

Bottom line: rejection of ideas is part of the invention licensing business. If you're going to live by the crystal ball, sometimes you have to eat glass.

9. *Believe in yourself.* One of the first steps toward success is learning to detect and follow that gleam of light Emerson says flashes across the mind from within. We tend to dismiss our own thoughts without notice because they're *ours*. In every work of genius, we recognize our own rejected thoughts; they come back at us with a certain alienated majesty. It's critical that you learn to abide by your own spontaneous impression. Allow nothing to affect the integrity of your mind.

Fast Facts

The terms *patent pending* and *patent applied for* are used by a manufacturer or seller of an article to inform the public that an application for patent on that article is on file in the Patent and Trademark Office. The law imposes a fine on those who use these terms falsely to deceive the public.

If you stand for something, you'll always find some people for you and some against you. If you stand for nothing, you'll find nobody against you and nobody for you. Take your choice.

Remember the advice of Winston Churchill: "Never, never, never, never, never give in—except to dictates of conscience and duty."

10. *Sell yourself before you sell your ideas.* Be concerned how you're perceived. You may be capable of dreaming up ideas, but if you cannot command the respect and attention of corporate executives, associates, and investors, your product will never get off the mark, and you may not be invited back for an encore.

Ideas come, and ideas go. Know how much to push. Know when to disappear. Don't wear out your welcome. (Some people suffer from *sellitus!*) You can't put a dollar value on access to a corporate executive's valuable space and time. I cannot tell you how hard I have worked over the years to gain and maintain access.

Independent inventors who have corporate experience understand the fragility of ideas much better than people who have never worked inside. Former corporate types realize the pressures of such work, and people without this experience don't have a clue. There's an unwritten code of conduct. Inventors with corporate experience understand that there are territorial imperatives, lines one must not cross, manners that must be displayed. Alas, many great ideas never see the light of day because their inventors blow-up on the launch pad.

And for good measure, let's add …

11. *Know your market.* Identify your market—both consumer and manufacturer—and know it backward and forward. One of the inventor's greatest downfalls is inventing in a vacuum and not in the marketplace.

Nothing beats good preparation. It will help equalize your position *vis-à-vis* the professionals to whom you are pitching. The more you know your product and its market, the more confident you will become and the more you'll be able to handle people who may attack your positions. A residual benefit of confidence is that it tends to be contagious. You want to make believers out of everyone. You want to enlist in-house champions for your concepts, people who will support it when you're no longer on the front line.

Bright Ideas

Elijah McCoy, son of runaway slaves, invented the oil lubricator. Born in Canada, he studied engineering in Scotland and then worked for a railroad in Michigan as an oil-man. Back then, trains had to stop at regular intervals to be lubricated. Crews would run around squirting oil between the train's moving parts. Without periodic lubrication, parts would rub together, overheat, and come to a halt. It was expensive and wasteful to stop the train every time it needed lubrication. So in 1872, McCoy invented the oil lubricator, a device that oiled engine parts while the train was under power. McCoy designed lubricators for lots of machines. People insisted on McCoy lubricators—they wanted *the real McCoy.*

---

12. *The paranoids are chasing me!* There are two kinds of amateur inventors, the paranoid and the more paranoid. If you're worried about getting ripped off by licensees,

don't deal with them. Better yet, if you're worried about being ripped off, go into another business.

The quickest turnoff is when a company feels that the inventor is distrustful of it. We've all heard about inventors who were ripped off by major corporations. Remember the Sears wrench and the hidden windshield wiper stories? But there are far more stories about honorable executives and great win/win deals. Instead of going in paranoid, I follow the advice of former president Ronald Reagan, who, when asked what it was like to work with the USSR, counseled, "Trust, but verify."

There's simply no way to avoid the ache and pain of hard work. Longfellow put it well when he wrote in *The Ladder of St. Augustine,* "The heights by great men reached and kept, were not attained by sudden flight, but they, while their companions slept, were toiling upward in the night."

The Least You Need to Know

- Trust yourself and your instincts. They are anchors in a storm.

- Realize that what you can accomplish is truly amazing if you keep your feet on the ground and your eyes on the stars.

- Don't be afraid to make mistakes. The price of never being wrong is never being right.

- Don't simply follow where the path leads; rather, go where there is no path and leave a trail.

- Enjoy what you do!

Chapter 2

Beware of Invention Marketing Flimflam Artists

In This Chapter

- Forewarned is forearmed
- Killer patent attorneys
- Fraud fighters: the Federal Trade Commission
- What to do if you are victimized
- Finding the good, avoiding the bad

My rule is simple. Never deal with invention marketing firms, *patent trolls*, or agents that reach you through TV, radio, newspaper, magazine ads, unsolicited direct mail appeals or e-mail. It is as simple as that. No ifs, ands, or buts. You can remember it like this: ad equals bad.

—Richard C. Levy

This is the most important chapter because this phase of your invention commercialization adventure is a real minefield for rookies. It is here that you're most vulnerable to having your intellectual and physical pockets picked. At this point, you are apt to be swindled by smooth-talking flimflammers in the guise of marketing services, disreputable agents, and even patent attorneys who overcharge. The scams are many. Unprincipled attorneys are fewer but are nonetheless pernicious to your business and bank account.

What do advertised invention marketing services and some patent attorneys share in common? Both take advantage of your inexperience. The advertised marketing services charge up-front fees and have no skill or track record in product placement. The business model for such companies is based entirely on fees and not royalty income. In other words, they'll do slipshod market research, marketing plans, patent searches, patent applications, and/or other assorted initiatives that rarely result in product placement. In fact, invention services that cater to non-industry-specific inventors rarely make an effort at licensing. They leave you with a pile of worthless paper—and you'll be a lot poorer for all of it.

Who Are These Parasites?

About 80 percent of all people claiming to help inventors build a business, market their product, or raise capital are con men, beggars, thieves, or incompetents, cautions Professor Mark A. Spikell, co-founder of the Entrepreneurship Center at the School of Business Administration of George Mason University.

def•i•ni•tion

A **patent troll** is a shakedown artist, a person or company that procures active patents from their inventors and uses the patents to bleed money from businesses through lawsuits or the threat of lawsuits for patent infringement.

Alan A. Tratner, founder of the nonprofit Inventor's Workshop International Educational Foundation (IWIEF), describes most invention marketing companies as cancers on the inventing community and a disease that needs to be eradicated immediately. Too often inventors lose large amounts of money and are derailed by the unfulfilled promises and come-ons of these companies, he says.

Dave Thomas created an improved joystick for video games. His wife, Susan, saw an ad in *USA Today:* "Have an invention? Need help?" They responded to the ad, and the company, located in Boston, was excited about promoting the device. There was just one hitch: it would take $10,000 to get it off the ground.

Then Susan's brother-in-law, who believed in the invention, was killed in an auto accident. His widow provided the needed $10,000 from the insurance settlement.

Dave and Susan flew to Boston. The account representative wined and dined them. They signed a contract and handed over a $10,000 cashier's check. And then? The account representative disappeared. The Massachusetts Attorney General's Office didn't have any record of the company.

Dave and Susan are now $10,000 wiser.

The Numbers Reveal the Truth

Let's look at a typical example of an invention *marketing* company. There's an outfit called Davison Design and Development, Inc., in Pittsburgh, Pennsylvania. (It was previously known as Davison and Associates, but that's another story for later in this chapter.) Davison, in compliance with the American Inventor's Protection Act of 1999, 35 United States Code § 297, and as ordered by the court, reveals on its website affirmative disclosure to consumers that includes its success record in commercializing inventions. This information was current as of June 2009:

Number of people who submitted new product ideas during the past five years: 522,772

Number of people offered a predevelopment agreement (or similar contract for research services): 308,412

Number of people offered a contingency agreement (or other contract for licensing representation): 308,412

Number of people who purchased a predevelopment agreement or similar contract for research services: 49,255

> ## def•i•ni•tion
>
> **Marketing** is the process of selling or offering something for sale based on a plan.

Number of people who signed a contingency agreement or other licensing representation agreement: 49,255

Number of people offered a new product sample agreement (or any other contract for design services for a virtual or a product sample): 37,201

Number of consumers who signed a new product sample agreement or similar agreement: 13,425

Number of consumers who obtained a license agreement with a company not affiliated with Davison: 314

Number of consumers in the last five years who made more money in royalties than they paid, in total, under any and all agreements with Davison: 10

Percentage of Davison's income that came from royalties generated by licenses of consumers' products (drum roll, please): .001 percent

Clearly, this company makes its money from fees. The successful inventors it has represented are few and far between. Furthermore, these numbers cover only business conducted within the United States. Davison, and other invention marketing companies, sign up people from all over the world. There's no way to regulate or calculate their offshore business. But it seems fair to assume that Davison's rate of success is no greater for offshore inventors than it is for American inventors.

Patent attorneys, on the other hand, can deliver a very valuable service, as you learn in Part 4. Alas, the occasional bad egg overcharges and builds false expectations. You must be ever vigilant. Don't assume advanced law degrees on the wall mean you have nothing to worry about.

Attack of the Killer Patent Attorney

I recall speaking to a novice inventor a few years ago who was excited about four design patents she was awarded for a juvenile health–related product. I explained the difference between a design patent and a utility patent. Based on the design patents, I told her I thought the chances of a major player licensing them were slim to none, although the patents might help attract and impress an unsophisticated investor.

She took the news well. Then something she mumbled about her patent attorney prompted me to ask how much she was charged for the design patents.

"He charged me $7,500 each, plus some fees," she responded.

Arrrgh! I almost came unglued. Her total legal bill for the four design patents ran around $30,000. Design patents can be done for a lot cheaper by inventors themselves (i.e., *pro se*) or a less opportunistic patent attorney (see Part 5), so you can understand my reaction. This is the worst instance of overcharging I've heard of. It's far from typical of most patent attorneys. I include it as an example because it is so dramatic.

Had she filed for the design patents herself, she would have paid the U.S. Patent and Trademark Office (USPTO) a filing fee of $160 per patent (today $190) as a Small Entity. Add to this an issue fee of $220 per patent (today $265), and the USPTO gets $380 each. The subtotal is $1,520. Let's say the drawings cost $100 each, although

I have a hunch the cost would have been less. (If you'd rather submit high-quality photographs in lieu of drawings, this is now acceptable; see Part 5. And you might be able to shoot the photos yourself.) In any event, a rough-and-tough estimate for all this work is $1,920—nowhere near $30,000.

The next day, I called my patent searcher, George Harvill, president of Greentree Information Service in Bethesda, Maryland. I shared her story and patiently waited for his reaction, pen in hand. There was a long pause. Then he said: "Each?! Holy moley. That's unconscionable. I can't believe it. That's thievery."

The following day, I called patent attorney Richard Besha at Nixon and Vanderhye, in Alexandria, Virginia. His reaction went like this: "Each?! It's been a while since I have done a design patent, but that's gouging. She got [expletive deleted]." Dick's fee for a design patent was $650 plus USPTO fees, drawings, etc.

And for good measure, I spoke to another patent attorney, Dinesh Agarwal of Alexandria, Virginia: "Each?! I guess that attorney doesn't need too many clients with fees like that."

Again, this is an extreme example meant to be a wake-up call to each and every one of you to be vigilant.

Rogues Unlimited

After hearing an ad calling inventors to action and a toll-free number (something like 1-800-GET-RICH), in the spirit of investigative reporting, I decided to give the invention marketing company a call. I told the voice on the other end of the line that my idea was for a way to keep individual strands of spaghetti fresh. My invention was a clear plastic tube capped off at both ends. "No pasta lover will be able live without it," I bragged.

"Terrific. Lots of potential," I was assured in a voice reminiscent of a carnival barker. All I had to do was pay $400 for an initial assessment. As he explained it, my investment gradually increased into the many thousands of dollars if I bought into various stages of the company's patenting and marketing program. Having had worms for breakfast, I obviously didn't go for the one on that hook.

The minute someone starts asking you for money, it's time to run for the hills. Money talks, and if you give it to these kinds of companies, you'll hear it tell you "Good-bye."

Fast Facts _____

The Federal Trade Commission (FTC) has a total of 1,149 full-time employees in fiscal year (FY) 2010. Its budget for FY 2010 is $287.2 million. Cases involving invention marketing fraud originate in the Bureau of Consumer Protection's Division of Marketing Practices or one of the FTC's regional offices. Enforcement actions and monitoring for cases that have already been litigated or settled fall under the purview of the Bureau of Consumer Protection's Enforcement Division. No single office is dedicated to invention marketing fraud. The FTC's Enforcement Division actively monitors compliance with all federal court orders obtained in FTC consumer protection actions.

Know When to Walk Away

Most invention promotion firms claim—falsely—that they can turn almost any idea into cash. Here's how to follow up if you hear the following lines from these unblushing liars:

"We think your idea has great market potential." If a company fails to disclose that investing in your idea is a high-risk venture, and that most ideas never make any money, you cannot hang up fast enough.

"Our company has licensed a lot of invention ideas successfully." Ask for a list of its successful clients and their phone numbers. If the company refuses, it means they've not had any success. A reputable company would brag about its good fortunes.

"You need to hurry and patent your idea before someone else does." Be wary of high-pressure sales tactics. Simply patenting an idea does *not* mean you'll ever make any money from it. This is just an attempt to drain you of industry and seize your treasure.

"Congratulations! We've done a patent search on your idea, and we have some great news—there's nothing like it out there!" Patent searches by fraudulent invention-promotion firms usually are incomplete, incompetent, conducted in the wrong categories, or unaccompanied by competent legal opinion on the results of the search from a patent attorney. Because unprincipled firms promote virtually any concept without regard to its patentability or efficacy, they may sign an idea for which someone already has a valid, unexpired patent. In that case, you may be the subject of a patent infringement lawsuit—even if the promotional efforts on your invention are successful.

"Our research department, engineers, and patent attorneys have evaluated your idea. We definitely want to move forward." Hogwash. This is claptrap. Many questionable firms do not perform any evaluation. In fact, many do not have the "professional" staff they claim to employ.

"Our company has evaluated your idea and now wants to prepare a more in-depth research report. It'll cost you several hundred dollars." If the company's initial evaluation is positive, ask why the company isn't willing to cover the cost of researching your idea further. Run for the hills.

"Our company makes most of its money from the royalties. Of course, we need some money from you before we get started." If a firm tells you this but asks you to pay a fee up front of any amount or to agree to make credit payments, ask why they're not willing to help you on a contingency basis.

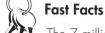

Fast Facts

The 7 millionth patent was awarded to John P. O'Brien and assigned to E. I. du Pont de Nemours and Company on February 14, 2006.

Speaking of which, now is a good time to revisit Davison ….

The Untold Story

I spoke to Elizabeth Tucci, senior trial attorney, Division of Enforcement, Bureau of Consumer Protection, Federal Trade Commission (FTC), about Davison after finding its website and its claim to be in compliance with the American Inventor's Protection Act of 1999 35 U.S.C. § 297. Here's a story not told on the company's current website (www.davison.com):

In July 2008, the FTC reached a settlement with Davison Design and Development, Inc., formerly known as Davison & Associates, Inc., and related defendants, requiring them to pay $10 million to settle charges that they deceived consumers nationwide, charging consumers up to $12,000 each to evaluate and promote their inventions. The defendants enticed consumers with false claims about their selectivity in choosing products to promote, their track record in turning inventions into profitable products, and their relationships with manufacturers. They also deceptively claimed that their income was derived from sharing royalties with inventors rather than from the fees the inventors paid to Davison.

The Davison settlement, entered as a federal court order, followed a trial in the U.S. District Court for the Western District of Pennsylvania in which the court found defendants had defrauded consumers and violated the FTC Act.

If you want all the details, I refer you to *FTC* v. *Davison & Associates, Inc., et al.*, Case No. 2:97-cv-01278-GLL, Civil Action No. 97-1278 [W.D. Pa.].

Did I mention that on the day I visited Davison's website, this quote from the company's founder appeared at the top of the website's main page: "When you want the best for your invention, we're the company that partners with you to protect, produce, and promote your idea into the marketplace."

The Same Old Song and Dance

I asked Attorney Tucci if she could give me other examples of invention scams that the FTC had taken to court.

In 2007, following a successful civil contempt action by the FTC, a federal judge ordered Patent and Trademark Institute, Julian Gumpel, and related defendants to pay $60 million for violating a 1998 court order and operating what a judge called "one grand con game to take money away from consumers." The judge also shut down the business and banned Gumpel and other individual defendants from working in invention promotion.

In a press release issued at the time, Lydia Parnes, director of the FTC's Bureau of Consumer Protection, said, "By changing the name of their company, these individuals thought they could continue to make false promises and take inventors' money, but they didn't get away with it. This scam should also remind inventors to question the assurances of promotion firms. No one can guarantee an invention's commercial success."

Under the 1998 order, Julian Gumpel, Darrell Mormando, Michael Fleisher, and Greg Wilson were barred from misrepresenting the services they offered to inventors, but they revived their scam under a new name, the Patent and Trademark Institute (PTI). For a fee of $895 to $1,295, PTI promised to evaluate marketability and patentability of inventors' ideas, but its evaluations were almost always positive and were not meaningful, according to the FTC. For a fee of anywhere from $5,000 to $45,000, PTI's clients were offered legal protection and assistance to obtain commercial licenses for their inventions. They also were told that PTI would help them earn substantial royalties from their inventions. But PTI did not help consumers license their inventions, and clients did not earn royalties.

In January 2007, the FTC charged the defendants with civil contempt and obtained a temporary asset freeze against PTI and its owner, Gumpel, and the appointment of a receiver over PTI. In March, the FTC added Fleisher, Mormando, and Wilson as contempt defendants, alleging that they had participated in the order violations as managers and salesmen.

On May 3, 2007, after a 4-day hearing, U.S. District Court Judge Gerald Bruce Lee held the defendants in contempt, finding, among other things, that PTI had failed to disclose to consumers that none of its clients had successfully marketed an invention. The judge concluded that consumers were defrauded of $61 million through "lies and misstatements."

On July 12, 2007, the court permanently banned Gumpel, Mormando, and Wilson from engaging, in any way, in the marketing of invention-promotion services. The court did not enter a ban against Fleisher because he had not signed the original order, although the court found that he had known about it and was subject to it. On August 27, 2007, the court entered an order holding PTI and Gumpel jointly liable for a $61 million judgment, and holding Fleisher, Mormando, and Wilson jointly and severally liable for the judgment to the extent of $59,682,958.

PTI operated through several corporate entities, including original defendants Azure Communications, Inc., and London Communications, Inc., and through United Licensing Corp.; International Patent Advisors, Inc.; Datatech Consulting, Inc.; International Product Marketing, Inc.; and Unicorp Consulting, Inc. These companies also were held in contempt and ordered to pay $61 million.

The FTC is in the process of seeking to collect on the judgment and hopes to conduct partial redress to consumers soon.

In 2008, the FTC brought a separate action against Michael Fleisher, who operated as second-in-command at PTI, seeking to ban him from the invention promotion business as well. In the 1997 contempt action, Fleisher had been held jointly and severally liable for $59,682,958 in damages, but he was not subject to ban because he was not a signatory to the original 1998 order.

As a result of the 2008 action against Fleisher, he entered into a federal court order that permanently bans him from marketing invention-promotion services and required him to dismiss his appeal of the prior contempt judgment and stipulate that his $59 million liability from the contempt action cannot be voided through bankruptcy.

If these examples are not enough to put you on guard, consider Googling American Inventors Corporation (AIC). Its management was indicted for mail fraud, money laundering, and tax evasion for allegedly bilking more than 34,000 inventors out of nearly $60 million.

These companies "morph" from one entity into another. For example, AIC had already set up the American Institute for Research and Development when the hammer came down on it. Furthermore, in Florida in late 1994, these guys had something called Washington Financial Group ready to go in case they had to close their doors up north.

When I asked William M. Welch, an Assistant U.S. Attorney for the District of Massachusetts, whether AIC had ever licensed any inventor product, he told me a part of the scam that was totally new to me. AIC would go to a manufacturer, but rather than pitch the product as a royalty license, it would offer to give the so-called licensee *X* number of dollars that the licensee would pay back to the inventor as royalties. This way, AIC could defend itself if claims were made that its inventors were not making any royalties. An example he cited involved a night sight for a gun that was sold to a company. AIC gave the company $20,000 to channel back to the inventor. Unfortunately, the company went Chapter 11.

I cannot say it strongly enough: *avoid invention marketing firms.* Their principals get rich and buy big homes and fast cars on *your* money. They are slot machines that don't pay off.

Project Mousetrap and Other Sweeps

Project Mousetrap was a law enforcement sweep that attacked misrepresentations by invention promotion firms. While individual cases announced during the sweep may have been settled or litigated later, the sweep itself was carried out in 1997. The FTC, which brought five of the cases, said the defendants in its actions generated in excess of $90 million for their own pockets by exploiting the ideas, hopes, and dreams of tens of thousands of consumers. For details, I encourage you to visit www.ftc.gov/opa/1997/07/mouse.shtm.

411

It's hard enough to control these polecats at home, but it's impossible overseas. Through foreign advertising campaigns, American invention marketing companies attract unsuspecting inventors from around the world, and these vultures really get away with murder. The long arm of American justice cannot reach that far.

The FTC conducts sweeps when it determines that a particular type of scam is causing a high degree of consumer injury. Many factors influence whether the FTC will conduct a sweep. For example, the FTC monitors consumer complaints filed with its Consumer Response Center. The FTC also receives information from and confers with industry watchdog groups, state law enforcement agencies, and foreign governments.

"The FTC's goal is to remain nimble and flexible so that it can respond to changing market conditions and the effect these changes have on consumers," says Elizabeth Lordan of the FTC's Public Affairs Office.

The Price Is Not Always Right

"Necessity may be the mother of invention, but some of these marketing companies are nothing more than deadbeat dads," remarked U.S. Senator Joe Lieberman (I-CT), a former Connecticut attorney general who chaired a hearing on invention marketing scams in 1994, the last Congressional hearing to date on the subject.

Lieberman told those attending the Government Affairs Subcommittee on Regulation and Government Information ...

> They praise all inventions, even those that stand no chance of being brought to market. They paint a rosy picture of huge profits, then do little or nothing to make that dream come true. They say they will make their money from royalties off the sale of the invention, when in reality their profits come from the inventor's up-front fee. And just when the inventor thinks the company is going to get rolling on their behalf, he or she has just been rolled, and the company has moved on to the next victim.

A Step in the Right Direction

The American Inventors Protection Act of 1999 was signed into law (P.L. 106–113) on November 29, 1999. It contains two key provisions:

- The title requires invention promoters to disclose in writing the number of positive and negative evaluations of inventions they have given over a five-year period and their customers' success in receiving net financial profit and license agreements as a direct result of the invention promotion services.

- Customers injured by failure to disclose the required information or by any material false or fraudulent representation by the invention promoter can bring a civil action to recover statutory damages up to $5,000 or actual damages. Damages of up to three times the amount awarded are available for intentional or willful violations.

If you have a complaint about operators of invention promotion companies, file it at the FTC by visiting www.ftc.gov. Or call toll-free, 1-877-FTC-HELP (1-877-382-4357). At the USPTO, the toll-free number for complaints about invention promotion firms is 1-866-767-3848.

Another option for filing a complaint is your state attorney general and the attorney general in the state(s) where the invention marketing company operates. The attorney general is the chief legal officer of a state. If you're going to file a complaint, it's a good idea to include the attorney general along with the FTC and Better Business Bureau (BBB). Go for a full-court press! To find your state attorney general's name and contact data, go to www.naag.org/attorneys_general.php.

Heads Up!

If you're interested in buying the services of an invention promotion firm, here's some information from the FTC that can help you avoid making a costly mistake:

Many fraudulent invention promotion firms offer inventors two services in a two-step process: one involves a research report or market evaluation of your idea that can cost you hundreds of dollars. The other involves patenting or marketing and licensing services, which can cost you several thousand dollars. Early in your discussion with a promotion firm, ask for the total cost of its services, from the "research" about your invention through the marketing and licensing. Walk away if the salesperson hesitates to answer.

Many fraudulent companies offer to provide invention assistance or marketing services in exchange for advance fees that can range from $5,000 to $10,000. Reputable licensing services rarely rely on large up-front fees.

Unscrupulous invention promotion firms tell all inventors that their ideas are among the relative few that have market potential. The truth is that most ideas do not make any money.

Many questionable invention promotion firms claim to have a great record licensing their clients' inventions successfully. Ask the firm to disclose its success rate, as well as the names and telephone numbers of their recent clients. Success rates show the number of clients who made more money from their inventions than they paid to the firm. Check the references. In several states, disclosing the success rate is the law.

Ask an invention promotion firm for its rejection rate—the percentage of all ideas or inventions that the invention promotion firm finds unacceptable. Legitimate firms generally have high rejection rates.

Fraudulent invention promotion firms may promise to register your idea with the U.S. Patent and Trademark Office's Disclosure Document Program. Many scam artists charge high fees to do this. Well, here's a heads-up: the USPTO's Disclosure Document Program was discontinued on February 1, 2007.

If someone tells you that a provisional application allows you to enforce patent rights, don't believe them. The provisional is an application only. It won't be examined on its merits, and it goes away in 12 months from its filing date. A provisional patent establishes an early priority date for what follows, a nonprovisional application.

Fishy firms often promise to exhibit your idea at trade shows. Few companies attend such shows looking for inventive ideas. And exposing your idea at a trade show before you've made application for a U.S. patent can jeopardize your ability to get one.

Bright Ideas

In 1906, Ole Evinrude took his neighbor, Bess Cary, by rowboat in 90° heat to picnic on an island in his favorite Wisconsin lake. As he rowed, he watched their ice cream melt and wished he had a faster way to get to the island. At that moment, Evinrude realized that a car was not the only vehicle that could benefit from a gasoline engine. The next summer, he conducted field tests of the first outboard motor, a 1½-horsepower, 62-pound iron engine.

Many deceitful firms agree in their contracts to identify manufacturers by coding your idea with the U.S. Bureau of Standard Industrial Code (SIC). Lists of manufacturers that come from classifying your idea with the SIC usually are of limited value.

Before You Contract for Services ...

Here are some things to do before you sign on with an invention marketer or agent:

- ◆ Question any claims and assurances that your invention will make money. No one can guarantee your invention's success.

- ◆ Investigate the company before you commit. Call the BBB, the USPTO, and the attorney general in your state and in the state where the company is headquartered. Ask if there are any unresolved consumer complaints about the firm. According to Elizabeth Tucci, senior trial attorney for the FTC's Division of Enforcement, Bureau of Consumer Protection, any complaints filed with the FTC are maintained in a confidential database used for law enforcement purposes.

- ◆ Be sure your contract contains all the terms you agreed to—verbal and written— before you sign. Hire an attorney to review the agreement.

Remember, once a dishonest company has your money, you'll likely never see it again.

411

The BBB has a cooperative agreement with the FTC. To find the closest BBB where you can file a complaint against a local invention marketing company, go to www.bbb.org. Or contact the Council of Better Business Bureaus, 4200 Wilson Boulevard Blvd., Suite 800, Arlington, VA 22203-1838; 703-276-0100; fax: 703-525-8277. In Canada, contact the Canadian Council of Better Business Bureaus, 2 St. Clair Avenue, East Toronto, ON M4T 2T5.

How to Tell the Pros from the Cons

Separating the legitimate invention marketing companies and agents from the bad ones isn't easy. The image the fly-by-nights portray through false and misleading advertising in legitimate media and on websites is compelling. Messages are tagged with toll-free numbers, paid actors deliver confidence-building call-to-action pitches, and slick four-color brochures picture well-known inventions the invention marketer had absolutely nothing to do with (e.g., the tricycle, ballpoint pen, zipper, teddy bear, or radio) and retail logos that imply distribution and sales. Often in print too small to read, it will say "These products are not intended to represent success for inventors who have worked with our firm."

Does advertising ever show evidence of the company's own product placement? Rarely. And if it does, you won't recognize the product, and inventor testimonials—if any—will be signed with a name and state only. Nothing is offered that would help you contact the inventor for a reference.

Here's the bottom line: there's no way any one company or individual could have enough meaningful contacts or expertise in enough fields of invention to find a home for the numbers of products that come in as a result of shotgun, mass-media advertising.

I specialize in the toy industry. It takes every bit of energy, and most of my waking hours, to keep up with the intercompany and intracompany movements of research and development and marketing executives, and to stay ahead of what's in and what's out in terms of product trends. There's no way I could track a multitude of industries simultaneously. No one could. The business of invention licensing depends too much on personal relationships, not unlike every business. Success is a combination of "know how" and "know who."

Here's how you can tell if a company is run by pros or cons:

Up-front fees. Reputable invention marketing services and agents do *not* require up-front fees. You invested your ingenuity, time, and money to create and protect your invention. The marketer is obligated, in turn, to invest whatever it takes to find the invention a home. What's fairer than that? The moment you pay for services, the carrot is removed. With nothing to lose and your deposit in hand, the broker has little reason to display incentive.

Track record. A reputable firm or agent will demonstrate a track record of successful product placement and a list of satisfied clients. A reputable company will crow about its accomplishments and urge you to call its clients and references.

Bright Ideas

King of pop Michael Jackson and Dennis Tompkins are joint inventors of U.S. Patent 5,255,452, issued on October 26, 1993. It covers a method and means for creating an antigravity illusion. Remember the Michael Jackson "Smooth Criminal" video where he and his fellow dancers dramatically lean forward beyond their centers of gravity? Look up the patent at www.uspto.gov to see how they did it.

A New Twist to an Old Scheme

Here's a novel way of getting money from inventors. A letter or website banner offers the inventor a free booklet on how to sell inventions. It invites a visit to the company's offices "… just to chat and to see what we look like." It's made clear that there's no obligation whatsoever.

The booklet is given away for free because, the letter states, "… inventions are our business." A visit is encouraged because "some inventors are reluctant to entrust their invention to people they have never seen and I [a company executive] cannot blame them for being cautious." A prepaid response card is enclosed.

The company goes on to build your confidence by separating itself from invention marketing companies. It claims not to neglect inventors after they pay a fee or to steal or mishandle their invention. Some companies put seals of approval on their website and literature. It claims to stick to what it does best, *preparing invention descriptions and compiling lists of manufacturers.*

An employment agreement is proffered through which you are asked to buy into the company's "technique" for writing descriptive material, preparing folios, and selecting manufacturers it "believes" may "potentially" be interested in your invention. It asks for no rights to your invention. It does not seek to legally bind you or your invention in any way. The descriptive materials it sells you become your property.

The agreement states that you understand "the company does no developing, promoting, or brokering." Its services are "strictly" to prepare invention descriptions and compile lists of manufacturers. It further claims to offer "no evaluation of the merits, practicability, feasibility, potential salability" of the invention.

Fast Facts

The Patent and Trademark Office can assist you in the marketing of your patent by publishing, at your request, a notice in the *Official Gazette* that the patent is available for licensing or sale. The fee for this is $25.

What does it cost for this company to do a write-up of your invention and provide names of potential manufacturers? $589.50.

While I can see nothing dishonest in the service offered, the question you must ask yourself is, what is its value? In my opinion, it's a lot of money to pay for a technique in writing descriptive material, preparing folios, and selecting manufacturers that *might* be interested in your invention. The company exhibits neither "know how" nor "know who" in a particular field of enterprise.

How Do They Get Your Name?

Odds are, if you've been awarded a patent, you've received an unsolicited letter that began with the fateful words, "Dear Inventor: A number of manufacturers have invited us to send them descriptions of your invention."

I can always tell when a patent is about to issue. Mailers from invention marketing companies flood my post office box. Often three or four will come from the same company on the same day. They are a harbinger of a new patent much as the robin is of spring.

Bright Ideas

Patent leather got its name because the process of applying a polished black finish to leather was patented.

When a patent issues, notice of it is automatically carried in the *Official Gazette* of the U.S. Patent and Trademark Office. This publication has come out weekly since 1872. It's mailed to subscribers and put on sale every Tuesday. The *Official Gazette* tells its readers the name, city, and state of residence of the applicant, with the mailing address in the case of unassigned patents, the patent number, title of invention, and lots of other information. The invention marketing companies use this information to help them appear to have given great consideration to your invention.

What to Do If You Are a Victim

If you think you've been victimized by a fraudulent invention marketing company, first contact the firm in writing and attempt to get your money back. If you are unsuccessful, report the problem to the FTC at www.ftc.gov, your local consumer protection agency, the BBB, and the attorney general (Consumer Protection Division) in your state and the state where the company is located. Also contact any media you think might be interested in following up on your story.

If the invention marketing company is national, you might want to tell your story to reporters who cover the consumer beat at network-level news-gathering operations, national daily newspapers, weekly and/or specialized magazines, and radio programs. Maybe begin with local media just to get the story in play.

Depending on the amount of money owed, small claims court may be an option if the invention marketing company is local.

States (Inventor) Rights

More states are passing legislation that protects inventors. Among them are California, Connecticut, Illinois, Iowa, Kansas, Massachusetts, Minnesota, Nebraska, North Carolina, North Dakota, Ohio, Oklahoma, South Dakota, Tennessee, Texas, Utah, Virginia, Washington, and Wisconsin. Unfortunately, most inventors who get ripped off by the paracreative, parasitic sluggards who operate under the guise of invention marketing services do not even realize that their state has protective legislation.

Here are some highlights from the laws of Minnesota and Virginia, respectively. I encourage you to write to any of the aforementioned states for a complete copy of their legislation.

Notable Quotables

Business has only two basic functions—marketing and innovation.

—Peter Drucker

Minnesota (Invention Services 325A.02):

1. Notwithstanding any contractual provision to the contrary, inventors have the unconditional right to cancel a contract for invention development services for any reason at any time before midnight of the third business day following the date the inventor gets a fully executed copy.

2. A contract for invention development services shall be set in no less than 10-point type.

3. An invention developer who is not a lawyer may not give you legal advice with respect to patents, copyrights, or trademarks.

4. The invention marketer must tell you …

   a. the total number of customers who have contracted with him up to the last thirty days; and

   b. the number of customers who have received, by virtue of the invention marketer's performance, an amount of money in excess of the amount of money paid by such customers to the invention marketer pursuant to a contract for invention development services.

5. The contract shall state the expected date of completion of invention marketing services.

6. Every invention marketer rendering invention development services must maintain a bond issued by a surety admitted to do business in the state, and equal to either 10 percent of the marketer's gross income from the invention development business during the preceding fiscal year, or $25,000, whichever is larger.

Fast Facts

George Washington signed the first patent bill on April 10, 1790, and for the first time in history, the intrinsic right of an inventor to profit from his invention was recognized by law.

Virginia, Chapter 18, 59.1–209:

1. No invention developer may acquire any interest, partial or whole, in the title to the inventor's invention or patent rights, unless the invention developer contracts to manufacture the invention and acquires such interest for this purpose at or about the time the contract for manufacture is executed.

2. The developer must tell you if they intend to spend more for their services than the cash fee you will have to pay.

3. The Attorney General has the mandate to enforce the provisions of this chapter and recover civil penalties.

Bright Ideas

The first Apple computer was born in Steve Jobs's parents' garage in 1976. He and college bud Steve Wozniak assembled computers for fellow students. Their first commercial order was for 50 computers. To raise the $1,300 needed to buy parts, Jobs sold his VW bus and Wozniak his Hewlett-Packard calculator. In 1977, Apple sales soared to $800,000, and within five years it became a Fortune 500 company.

How to Find an Honest Broker

Here are three methods I endorse that, while not guaranteed, put the odds more in your favor that you will find competent and honest help:

Inventor groups. Call an inventor organization, preferably a local one, whose members may be able to recommend an agent. I think you will get a more complete picture of the situation and gain more confidence in the agent if you sit down with a satisfied customer.

Industry referrals. Ask the company to whom you would like to license your invention to recommend an agent. While not all companies are comfortable recommending invention brokers, many will. Some companies will even send you a list of names. You must, of course, talk to the agents and strike your own level of confidence and a fair deal; nonetheless, you know up front that the door is open to them. Furthermore, anyone recommended by one company likely has excellent relationships with other manufacturers, too.

Invention consultants. Do not confuse invention marketing firms with legitimate consultants. I strongly believe in paying consultants whenever their expertise can contribute to the progress and success of a project.

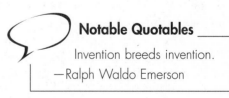

Notable Quotables

Invention breeds invention.
—Ralph Waldo Emerson

What is consulting? England's Institute of Management Consultants defines consulting as "the service provided by an independent and qualified person or persons in identifying and investigating problems concerned with policy, organization, procedures, and methods; recommending appropriate action and helping to implement these recommendations." There are as many types of consultants as there are problems to solve. These experts can bring new techniques and approaches to bear on an inventor's work. This contribution can range from helping to bridge a technological gap to the special knowledge and talent required to successfully license or market a particular innovation.

"I actually made my consultant a partner," says Richard Tweddell III, inventor of VegiForms, a device that press-molds vegetables, while still on the vine, into the likenesses of human faces. A former employee at Kenner Products, in Cincinnati, Ohio, Tweddell credits his consultant with moving his company from ground zero. "He showed me how to license the product, he reviews all our licensing agreements, and he found companies that were interested in taking the rights ...."

Advisers can provide impartial points of view by seeing challenges in a fresh light. They operate outside existing frameworks and free from existing beliefs, politics, problems, and procedures inherent in many organizations or situations.

Most consultants operate on the basis of an hourly rate plus expenses. You, however, as an inventor and by the nature of your work, may be able to make equity deals whereby in return for advice a consultant is given participation in any profits your invention might generate. Think long and hard before doing something like this, because it is often less expensive to risk the cash and hold all the points possible in-house.

Don't think that consultants have all the answers. They don't. Consulting is very hard work, and not everything can be solved as quickly as one would like. Don't look for miracle solutions.

Bright Ideas

While trying to create an extremely strong glue, Spencer Silver accidentally made an adhesive that was so weak it could barely hold two pieces of paper together. "If I had thought about it, I wouldn't have done the experiment. The literature was full of examples that said you can't do this," remarked Silver on the work that led to the adhesives for 3M Post-its.

Shop around. Get references on any consultant or research organization you're considering. Don't be impressed by a consultant's or organization's professional association alone (such as a university affiliation). Their success rate in fields related to yours is what matters. How much can they do with a single phone call? Results are what you want, not just paper reports.

The Least You Need to Know

◆ Invention marketing companies that advertise on late-night television and radio are mostly dishonest.

◆ If you are with an invention marketing company, get out while it's still a rescue. Don't wait until it becomes a body recovery.

◆ Empty barrels make the most noise. Verify everything you are told by an invention marketing company.

◆ Honest brokers and marketing services do exist—they are just harder to find.

◆ The FTC can provide air coverage. Don't hesitate to complain if you've had your pocket picked.

Chapter 3

Licensing Versus Venture Capital

In This Chapter

- ◆ Do you have something people will want to buy?
- ◆ Small businesses launch big ideas
- ◆ Licensing your invention—the advantages and disadvantages
- ◆ The pros and cons of Do-It-Yourself licensing

> I enjoy building businesses. New business development always begins with great innovation and fresh, new ideas. These ideas come from the independent thinker … the person who has no rules or limitations. We must always find ways to let revolutionary new thoughts harvest.
>
> —Tom Dusenberry, CEO, Dusenberry Entertainment

To get your invention to market, somebody has to sell it and somebody has to manufacture it. As your invention moves toward the marketplace, business skills become more critical than technical skills. You will require more interaction with people who have these skills, and, of course, your product will demand more money the closer it gets to commercialization.

If you opt to go the licensing route—always my choice—your invention becomes more important than you in the corporate decision-making process. The manufacturer, in fact, may not feel you are necessary once it has an understanding of your invention.

On the other hand, the inventor who seeks venture capital faces a maxim that says, better to take a chance on a first-rate manager with a second-rate product, than on a first-rate product in the hands of a second-rate manager.

In this chapter, we take a down-and-dirty look at your options when it comes to licensing and venture capital.

First Things First

Before you reveal your invention to anyone—potential licensees or investors—you must be able to answer "Yes" to all these questions:

- ◆ Do you have the right to your idea?

- ◆ Do you have a patent, a copyright, or some other form of legal protection?

- ◆ Do you have a working model or, better yet, an engineering prototype?

- ◆ Do you have credible data about the size of the market, including probable impact of selling price on quantity demanded?

- ◆ Do you know what it will cost to produce your invented product at various levels of output?

411

Some companies require employees to assign the entire right, title, and interest in for all inventions conceived while that person is employed by the company. Many universities and colleges have technology utilization offices and stake claim to ideas generated by their students and professors if institutional assets are used in the development of the concepts. In some hospitals, inventions conceived by doctors under contract must be assigned to the hospital.

With the "yes" answers to those questions in mind, let's get down to business.

Business Options

You can commercialize your invention in two ways. You can license someone else to develop, manufacture, and market it. Or you can do it yourself. Most other options are variations of these two possibilities.

When you license others to make and market your products, you don't have to raise venture capital and dedicate yourself to this enterprise. This limits your exposure to lawyers, bankers, and liabilities. Licensing also frees you to dream up other concepts, license, and work to make them happen. However, this does not mean licensing is the only option.

Some people thrive on building businesses, crunching numbers, and all that entails. Others are control freaks, people who do not like giving up dominion over their inventions. The do-it-yourself option allows you to be the boss. Licensing, the way I set up my business model, has none of these aforementioned demands or require-ments. It allows me to be free to create and develop concepts at my own pace and under conditions I control.

Of course, like everything in life, it's not perfect. But at least I captain my destiny to a greater degree than when I was working within an organization. And my worries do not involve the kinds of issues one must handle running a company.

Fast Facts

Science.gov searches over 38 databases and 1,950 selected websites, offering 200 million pages of authoritative U.S. government science information, includ-ing research and development results. The National Technical Information Service (NTIS; www.ntis.gov) serves as the largest central resource for government-funded scientific, technical, engineering, and business information available today, with approx-imately 3 million publications covering over 350 subject areas.

The Licensing Option

Licensing is tempting because the amounts of money, tasks, skills, and people required are considerably less than in running your own business. Of course, that does not necessarily mean it is the right alternative for you. Before I address the advantages and disadvantages of licensing, it's important that you understand the business climate within the licensing arena and what it will take to make things happen.

Universities Pass the Test

If you are a student or a professor at a university or college with a commercialization/technology transfer program, you may want to take advantage of the institutional assets and possible access to federal research and development (R&D) funding to get your invention going.

Universities once eschewed technology transfer. They wanted their faculty dedicated to teaching and research, not focusing on making money from their intellectual properties. Wow—it's amazing how things have changed.

Today institutions of higher learning covet revenue that comes from royalties and equity distributions and sales associated with intellectual property created on their campuses. Here are a few examples of products that generate income for their birth schools: Adenocard (Virginia), Allegra (Georgetown), Bose Corporation (MIT), Cisco Systems (Stanford University), Gatorade (Florida), Genentech (California–San Francisco), Google (Stanford University), and Lycos (Carnegie Mellon).

> **Fast Facts**
>
> The top five on the Patent Board's 2008 Universities Patent Scorecard in 2008 include the University of California (with 290 patents), the Massachusetts Institute of Technology (134 patents), the California Institute of Technology (119 patents), Stanford University (122 patents), and Rice University (44 patents).

"A strong technology transfer program enables universities to recruit top-tier faculty," Rod Casto, associate vice president, University of South Florida, told the *Tampa Tribune*. "That furthers local economic development and industry partnerships."

If you are a student or professor, or if you have a connection to a university with incubator programs and the like, I encourage you to investigate the opportunities. From what I see, the deals they offer to inventors are fair, given the institution's investment and risk.

Reinventing Inventors

Since we licensed our first product, Star Bird, to Milton Bradley on January 1, 1978, industry has changed, pushed by technology and economics in a restless, volatile atmosphere. A dramatic paradigm shift has taken place, and inventors who do not understand and adapt will be left behind like last year's Christmas toys. Just as businesses are reinventing themselves, inventors must do likewise or risk perishing.

The skill sets required to succeed today involve much more than technical talents. Manufacturers are no longer dependent upon the same kinds of products. Witness the explosion of new technologies; business models have changed. Marketing, not R&D, drives product decisions. There are uncertain executive hierarchies.

Fast Facts

A U.S. patent for an invention is the grant of a property right to the inventor(s), issued by the U.S. Patent and Trademark Office (USPTO). The right conferred by the patent grant is, in the language of the statute and of the grant itself, "the right to exclude others from making, using, offering for sale, or selling" the invention in the United States or importing the invention into the United States. To get a U.S. patent, an application must be filed in the USPTO.

While inventiveness remains a very critical element, I find myself depending more and more on business and marketing skills. You must be able to organize and inspire teams of creative people, provide leadership, navigate bureaucracy, analyze market opportunities, and narrow the focus while still seeing the big picture.

Manufacturers Seek Risk Reduction

Today companies favor developing extensions to established lines versus launching new products. *The Complete Idiot's Guide* is an example of brand extension. There are hundreds of titles in this line. I felt my work would fare better under a strong and successful brand like *The Complete Idiot's Guide* than as a one-off title battling for shelf space.

Brand licensing is estimated to generate around $187 billion worldwide. Many of my products have been based on marquee brands: *Men Are from Mars, Women Are from Venus:* The Game (Mattel); *Chicken Soup for the Soul:* The Game (Cardinal); Warner Brother's Trivial Pursuit (Hasbro); Duncan Yo-Yo key chains (Basic Fun); and the Easy Bake Decorating Sensation Frosting Pen (Hasbro), among others.

It is less risky for a manufacturer to launch a product within an existing brand than to dig out of a hole with something new. Try to adapt your invention to an existing line of products, to take advantage of brand equity.

Notable Quotables

Creativity comes from trust. Trust your instincts. And never hope more than you work.

—Rita Mae Brown, American writer

You Scratch My Back, I'll Scratch Yours

We independent inventors must work closely with our licensees. We have to invest ourselves in our products far beyond the invention stage. It is important to take an active role in whatever needs to be done—for example, finding engineering and design talent, sourcing components, conducting patent searches, pulling together research, writing and editing instruction manuals, creating package copy, and flying to R&D and marketing meetings, often in return for only expenses.

Your eye should be on the larger prize if you want to make money as an independent inventor. Position yourself as a *de facto* project manager; be the adhesive that holds things together and the oil that keeps things moving when problems arise and when people lose focus or, worse, confidence.

Know How + Know Who = Success

I taught our daughter, Bettie, an executive in the music industry, that in business up to age 24, it's about "know how." To advance a career from there, "know who" plays a huge role.

The company you are pitching must reach a level of comfort with you and have confidence in your capabilities. You must become a family member. Obviously, this relationship takes time to establish; just remember that you are always selling yourself first and your concept second. This way, if the idea is not accepted, you'll still be invited back.

Depth of involvement with the companies may mean fewer ideas generated and prototyped, but you will likely see a higher percentage of placements and new product introductions. This is because of the *value* your assistance adds to each project. It comes under the heading of taking care of your customers. If you do not take care of your customers, somebody else will.

Bright Ideas

In 1979, three young Canadians created a game called Trivial Pursuit and licensed it to Selchow and Righter for a reportedly astronomical royalty of 15.7 percent. (Industry average is 5 percent.) In 1991, Hasbro acquired it. More than 90 million Trivial Pursuit games have been sold worldwide in 18 languages and 32 countries. In 2008, Hasbro bought out the inventors for a reported $80 million, according to *Forbes*. There's nothing trivial about that.

The MBA Syndrome

To further complicate matters, we once created concepts for people with a nose for product, risk takers passionate and genuinely excited by innovation. Today we see more companies run by financial types and MBAs whose logic and overanalysis deftly immobilize and sterilize ideas. They spend less time with the inventing community and more time with the investment community. Their companies cannot grow evergreens because each year they cut down the forest and plant a new one. Alas, a very short-sighted, pump-and-dump, day-trader mentality pervades American industry.

Once I addressed a prestigious business school. In the audience were 130 graduate students and professors. I asked the future MBAs, "How many of you have an idea you'd like to see commercialized, something for which you have passion?" Not a single hand was raised.

A few weeks later, a friend to whom I told this story was talking to his son's fourth-grade class. He asked the 36 9- and 10-year-olds the same question. Every hand went up.

I may make what happens between elementary and business school the subject of another book, because this transition has changed the way industry does business.

> **Notable Quotables**
>
> It is curiosity, initiative, originality and the ruthless application of honesty that count in R&D.
>
> —Julian Huxley, British biologist

To help you make the decision on how best to commercialize your brainchild, here are some positives and negatives to consider about licensing versus do-it-yourself. This information was prepared, in part, by the Argonne National Laboratory.

The Advantages of Licensing

As you know by now, I favor licensing. Licensing multiplies resources to develop your invention. The licensee, if it is a dynamic firm—and you do not want to license any other kind—can put teams of professionals to work developing, producing, and marketing your idea. Insurmountable financial mountains to you may be petty cash molehills to them.

They see things you do not. Licensees often perceive uses—and, therefore, markets—for your invention that you didn't see. One licensee turned a salt-water taffy machine into a new and highly efficient type of concrete mixer. The more markets, the more potential income.

411

When you need to set up a conference call, try FreeConferenceCall.com and save the money you would pay AT&T. I use this service, and it has been of the highest quality and flawless. No reservations are required. The company claims to make more than 7.5 million connections a month and allows you to lash together as many as 96 different numbers in a single conference call. Each call can go for up to six hours, and there's no limit on how many calls you can make per month. This is a Public Switched telephone Network (PSTN) conferencing service that utilizes your regular telephone.

The licensee may pay you money up front, although probably not as much as you hope. In addition, they may agree to a minimum amount of guaranteed royalties for some period.

Licensing frees you up. If what you want to do is retire, or return to inventing, then giving up control may serve your interests rather than defeat them.

If you have a technology with a demonstrably strong potential, businesses may want your invention. Many large corporations regularly acquire new product, but smaller firms, though they may be less well known, offer possibilities as well. Many cannot afford expensive R&D departments but nonetheless need new product. Furthermore, smaller firms often operate much more dynamically than big ones, so do not write them off. I opted to pitch Furby to privately held Tiger Electronics and not to majors Mattel or Hasbro. Tiger sold more than 40 million Furbys—and sold itself to Hasbro.

The Disadvantages of Licensing

No situation is perfect, and licensing is about as imperfect and unstable as it gets. First of all, you'll lose control over your invention—usually total control, for a long time, maybe forever.

In addition, your involvement is reduced. In most cases, you will have no further direct involvement. You may stick around as a consultant, but usually for a limited time.

Finding a licensee isn't easy. The right one may make you rich, but the wrong one may bury your invention or butcher it. Even if you can eventually get it back, it may be too late.

Protecting your interests is crucial. But it is also extremely difficult. Negotiating with licensees means playing with the big boys. They confront you with the immense staff resources of a corporation: lawyers, market analysts, and production engineers—a tough team for you to take on by yourself. Licensing agreements, when properly done, result from negotiations between two parties. The other side has pros to represent it, so you'd better have one of your own. If you're an amateur at the licensing game, you need the help of a lawyer or business type with experience in ip licensing.

In spite of the disadvantages licensing poses, for the way I like to live, I find it the best way to get product to market.

Whoah! Not So Fast!

As I mentioned at the beginning of this chapter, unless you have adequate legal protection for your invention, a working model—or, better, an engineering prototype—market data, and cost estimates, get cracking at putting a package together. If you do not have these elements, how can you expect anyone to take you seriously?

Furthermore, if you do not know what your invention will be worth to your licensee, you do not know what money you can reasonably demand. Your licensee will work up its version of all these figures. If the company is reputable, it won't cheat you, but its estimates of sales and profits will be on the low end and costs on the high side. Count on it. You will struggle over the royalty, *advance*, and guarantee, if any.

def•i•ni•tion

An **advance** is a negotiated sum of money given to an inventor, usually against future royalties. It's typically nonrefundable.

In short, not only do you have to show technical feasibility, you also have to prepare a package of information about production and marketing that's close to a business plan. This document will help you decide whether you want to venture or license, and then execute that decision by supplying the data required to raise money for your own business—or to persuade a prospective licensee to talk you out of it.

At the very least, if you decide to license your invention, you will have to build a working model; reaching the engineering prototype stage greatly increases both your chances of finding a licensee and the amount of money you may convince him or her to pay. By contrast, if you want to start your own business or develop the technology within a business you already operate, you will have to do even more than this.

Doing It Yourself: The Venturing Strategy

Starting your own business to make and market your product, or *venturing*, as it is often called, requires more from you, but it has its own advantages and disadvantages to consider.

For a fun test I found on the Internet, check out the Entrepreneurial Readiness Survey by Venture Capital Tools at venturecapitaltools.com/surveys/entrepreneurialsurvey.aspx. I know nothing about Venture Capital Tools, and I in no way endorse the company or this test for efficacy. You just may find it amusing and self-enlightening.

The Advantages

Establishing your own enterprise has some advantages. Perhaps the most enticing is that running a company can be exciting. If you have the will and skill, you may enjoy it more than inventing. Some inventors are entrepreneurs by experience; some by instinct. The inventor/entrepreneur can achieve powerful things, as Edwin Land, inventor of the Polaroid 60-second camera, and Steven Jobs, inventor of the Apple operating system, have shown. But the combination occurs rarely.

Another big bonus: in the long run, you may make a lot more money. If your invention is a big success, your rewards could vastly exceed the royalties you could expect from any licensing agreement.

Even if it is your company, you may not have to run it. Building a successful business involves hiring all kinds of people. There are plenty of examples of inventors who retained a large or controlling interest in their companies but turned over the management of it to someone else.

Obviously, being in business for yourself can mean a lot of different things. You may decide you want to establish a company that offers the full monty, such as designing, manufacturing, and selling your product. More likely, you will focus on parts of the process while making arrangements with other firms to do the rest of it. After all, even car manufacturers buy a lot of parts from independent suppliers and let franchised dealers do the retailing.

As an inventor, you may already be in business. Even if you think you do not have a company in the legal sense, the day you commit yourself to making a financial success of your invention, you start a business enterprise in the eyes of the Internal Revenue Service—however small and informal that enterprise may seem to you. So if you haven't yet thought of the time and money you've invested getting this far in terms of a business proposition, start now, whether you think your business will stay small or grow.

If you haven't created a structure that provides you limited liability (that is, a structure that legally insulates your personal assets against losses you may incur in your business), you should see a lawyer—soon. Prospective investors will concern themselves with this issue even if you haven't. And you may be asked to indemnify a licensee on the intellectual property (ip) front.

If you develop a business around your invention, experience suggests that your company will have to grow, even if it is sometimes possible to get an invention into the marketplace without involving yourself in the complexities of building a large company. For example, if you've invented a specialized tool with a large profit per sale, you may be able to bootstrap your business by selling one, taking the proceeds and making two more, selling them and making four, and so on. Even in such rare cases, however, you will ultimately have to decide to stay small (running the risk that some larger firm, seeing your success, may invade the market with a competitive product) or expand.

If you run a growing business, you will eventually need capital from outside sources, which means you will need a formal business structure providing limited liability to investors—one in which tasks are subdivided functionally (manufacturing, marketing, etc.) and assigned to professionals. The two intertwine, because no rational investor will put up the kind of money you will need for a company of even modest size unless you have at least a plan for a formal structure.

Investors know, even if you won't admit it, that inventors generally prefer doing everything themselves. Moreover, they know that building a successful enterprise absolutely requires genuine delegation of authority, something most inventors find extremely difficult to do. If you hope to grow a business, you must accept the ironic proposition that, to keep overall control yourself, you will have to delegate a lot of specific authority to other people. You will have to learn to accept some reflected glory.

411

The USPTO needs you! If you are a scientist or engineer and want to become a patent examiner, call 1-800-786-9757 or visit jobsearch.usajobs.opm.gov/A9PTO.asp. The USPTO allows its examiners to work from home under a telework program that frees office space and attracts more talent. While examiners are required to work at the main office in Alexandria, Virginia, every pay period, they can avoid traffic and high housing costs in the national capital area by working from their homes.

Successful management requires launching, mastering, and controlling a dynamic process and dealing with continuous change caused by growth, new technologies, competitors, and so forth. A successful, growing, and dynamic business rests on a foundation of continuous planning, involving constant updating to reflect things like changing circumstances, goals, and human resources. A plan will keep you on track, and it is an invaluable tool with which to sell yourself and your business to prospective investors, customers, and suppliers—and to the people you want to recruit. The latter has crucial importance because you cannot grow without first-class help, and people worth hiring want to know what they're getting into, especially future opportunities.

The Disadvantages

Many new businesses fail. A new business built around a new product runs a double risk, especially since the list of reasons for new business failures reads like a catalog of many inventors' weaknesses. These include (among many, many others) …

Undercapitalization. Typically, start-up businesses do not have enough financing to go the distance or even do what needs to be done in the short haul. They base their business models on multiple stages of capital infusion. If things don't work in stage one, however, there is no future. Companies take public money in the form of grants for the first two rounds and then enter the Valley of Death, where products die after transitioning from public to private financing.

Lack of management skills. Do you know how to build and run a business that involves employees, lawyers, bankers, accountants, et. al? You don't need a Harvard MBA to start a business, but you do need certain skills and experiences—or you need to hire someone who has them.

Overestimation of the market. In your enthusiasm, it is easy to overestimate the market for your concept. As a lone inventor, you may not have any checks and balances—i.e., others who have more experience than you or, at the very least, another point of view.

> **Notable Quotables**
>
> When you do the common things in life in an uncommon way, you will command the attention of the world.
>
> —George Washington Carver, botanist and inventor

Inability to delegate responsibility. Are you able to lead by example and allow others to do their jobs? Or do you feel that only you know how to do things? If you do not understand "reflected glory," or if you are a one-man band, this can be dangerous to the health of a business.

Limited resources. A major risk you run is to have too few resources. There's a saying used in the Army:

Never bring up the artillery until you have the ammo in place. It's no different in business. Without the resources, you'll have no firepower.

Tendency to be spread increasingly thin. As the number of tasks and skills required multiplies—and it does, with a vengeance—you will spend more time either doing them or finding someone who can, and will. I call it the Law of Strawberry Jam. The wider something is spread, the thinner it gets.

Not much money made for quite a while. Building a business swallows cash, and a lot of it will be your cash. If you can found a company and finance it adequately, you may be able to pay yourself a wage, but it'll probably be modest—your backers will expect you to be frugal with their money.

Prerequisites Common to Licensing and Venturing

Despite the apparently great differences between licensing and venturing as commercialization strategies, they have a lot in common, including certain prerequisites. Either way, somebody has to spend money—a lot of money. Whatever you may have spent so far will pale in comparison to what's required henceforth. So whether you want to market it yourself or convince someone else to buy the rights to do it, you need a convincing package. This includes …

Proof that it works. This means a working model or, better yet, an engineering prototype. There's no substitute for showing investors or potential licensees something they can see, touch, and watch do its stuff. Without a looks-like, works-like model, you haven't much chance of interesting anyone beyond family and friends (see Chapter 4).

Market analysis. This is a serious breakdown of potential customers, how many of them exist, how much they will pay, what the competition is, and how you will beat it. You need to know exactly what the market channels are through which products like yours reach the market. You should be able to show significant points of difference between your product and the competition's. If you cannot, you've got a problem. You'd better be sure your invention has no fatal flaws.

Above all, you have to be able to show why people will buy your product through statements from prospective customers and focus group results, backed up with believable figures in dollars and cents. The surest way to turn off a prospect who asks about the market is to respond, "When they see it, they will love it." It ain't necessarily so. Your market analysis will determine whether it is worth going on with your invention, regardless of its technical elegance, and that analysis forms the basis for the next thing you need.

Commercialization plan. This is a detailed analysis showing how you will develop, market, and sell your invention; the cost; and who will do the work—with all this information translated into a year-by-year, dollars-and-cents format, projected five years out. Investors (other than friends and family) will absolutely demand a plan; prospective licensees may insist, too. Even if they do not, you should have one.

Other Thoughts on Choosing a Commercialization Strategy

In deciding to license or venture, accept that, either way, you will have to give up a measure of ownership and control. In a sense, therefore, you're not deciding whether to get out, but when, how completely, under what circumstances, and by what method. In other words, you're looking for an exit strategy at the same time you're looking for a commercialization strategy.

No matter which commercialization strategy you follow, you will increasingly have to involve yourself with people who wear suits. They have different imperatives, have different expectations, and speak different languages. Many care nothing about you or your technology except as possible money-spinners. Like it or not, you do need such people—and you will need more of them as you go through the process—so learn to deal with them pretty much on their terms. They're no more inclined to translate their professional language for you than Parisians are to speak English to American tourists.

If you decide you aren't cut out to be an entrepreneur or you do not want to be one, that does not mean you cannot create a business around your invention. It does mean you will have to get an entrepreneur on your team. They do not come easy, and you will have to work to turn up enough evidence to persuade one to cast his or her lot with you and your invention.

And entrepreneurs do not come cheap, either. He or she will want a piece of the action—probably a big piece. But it may be worth it: Chester Carlson was an inventor who couldn't balance his checkbook, much less run a company, but an entrepreneur named Joe Wilson made him a multimillionaire by building a company called Xerox.

Think About Costs, at All Costs

You'll face three kinds of costs: money, time, and personal. They are intertwined—and. to some extent. interchangeable. If you think you cannot afford to hire a model-maker, for example, you may decide to save money by building it yourself at a cost of your time, which, in turn, often involves a personal cost to your health, your marriage, and so on, not to mention the fact that you may produce a poor model.

Be guided by this reality: if you think a pro is expensive, hire an amateur.

If You're Still Not Sure

To help you further analyze which route to commercialization is best for you and your invention—and, for that matter, whether your invention is efficacious—federal, state, and private organizations can help you. Most of them can be found through the Small Business Administration (SBA) or a similar state agency. Call toll-free 1-800-827-5722 or visit www.sba.gov.

Fast Facts _____

The laws of nature, physical phenomena, and abstract ideas are not patentable subject matter. Nor can a patent be obtained upon a mere idea or suggestion. The patent is granted upon a new machine, manufacture, etc. and not upon the idea or suggestion of the new machine. A complete description of the actual machine or other subject matter for which a patent is sought is required.

From my experience, one of the most professional and effective places to go for help in assessing the marketability of your inventions is the Wisconsin Innovation Service Center (WISC), a cooperative effort between University of Wisconsin–Whitewater Small Business Development Center, UW-Extension, and the federal Small Business Administration. Run by a Ronald "Bud" Gayart, a true friend to the independent inventor, the fee-based service just might make the difference if you are on the fence. Plus, you will obtain, through studies, all kinds of information you may never have seen otherwise.

Since it opened its doors in 1980, WISC has evaluated thousands of new product ideas at the request of inventors and small businesses. It has many success stories to share with you.

For information, contact Wisconsin Innovation Service Center, 1200 Hyland Hall, University of Wisconsin–Whitewater, Whitewater, WI 53190; 262-472-3217; fax: 262-472-1600; ask-sbdc@uww.edu; wisc.uww.edu.

The Least You Need to Know

- However you commercialize your brainchild, protect it.

- If you choose to license, you'll vary your mental gymnastics, spread the risk, and, frankly, have a life.

- Things fail no matter how well researched and intentioned. Remember Ford's Edsel and "New" Coke.

- If you're not sure, seek the counsel of an organization that can provide you with an assessment of your invention vis-à-vis the marketplace.

- Whichever road to commercialization you take, if it doesn't get you there, take the other road. Don't be afraid to change direction. Never stop trying.

Part 2

How to Build 'Em and Make 'Em

No one buys ideas. Executives license and investors put money into *concepts* that have been proven. Just as mere shape determines whether iron floats or sinks, ideas must be well formed to survive. Before you take your idea out on the road, you should have a prototype. This prototype will go through many hands and creative—and not-so-creative—minds.

A new product is a fragile thing, and it doesn't take much to kill even a superior idea. It can be knocked out of contention by a yawn. It can be butchered by a quip. It can be nitpicked to death by someone who suffers from the Not Invented Here Syndrome. You need to put *magic* in front of your audience. And this starts with a looks-like, works-like prototype that delivers a strong first impression and withstands scrutiny. Part 2 covers various prototyping and model-making choices and discusses their characteristics. Here we take a look at a typical timeline for product development and manufacturing. I take you step by step through the process. This is followed by a set of guidelines for finding and managing a factory to produce your dream.

Pay particular attention to Part 2.

Chapter 4

Mock-Ups and Models

In This Chapter

◆ Prototypes—they're mandatory

◆ Exceptions to the rule

◆ Your prototyping options

◆ Finding people with golden hands

> It is better to have enough ideas for some of them to be wrong, than to be always right by having no ideas at all.
>
> —Edward De Bono, physician, inventor, and originator of the term *lateral thinking*

No one buys an idea. To have any chance of licensing your concept for a new product, you need to present some form of model or a PowerPoint presentation, at a minimum. It's show and tell. But if you don't have the time, money, skills, or commitment to follow through on this critical step, the odds of ever licensing your brainchild are reduced to practically zero.

Manufacturers react best to physical objects, not theories, so don't count on anyone being able to imagine what your idea will look like or how it will operate. Even if they were capable of doing so, executives don't usually have the time or interest to engage insuch exercises, nor the stomach to invest in dreams. When it comes to new ideas, licensees are all from Missouri, and you gotta show 'em.

The Necessity of Prototypes

Strangely enough, when you make application to the U.S. Patent Office for protection of an invention, a proving model is no longer required. Models were once part of the application, however, and the models became part of the record of the patent. They demonstrated to the examiner that your idea worked. This requirement disappeared after 1880.

But you still need a prototype for many reasons:

- A prototype can prove that you are the inventor if you are ever challenged by someone who claims otherwise. Put a photo of the prototype in your inventor's notes.

- A prototype can work out any kinks in the invention and demonstrate that the idea works. It provides a proof of function.

- A prototype can help ensure that your invention is the right design (dimension, shape, and form).

- A prototype is an invaluable tool when you present your idea to potential investors or licensees.

- A prototype brings your idea to life. It betters the odds that your invention will become a reality.

- A prototype makes people you meet along the way to commercialization take you more seriously.

"The factories I am dealing with in China told me that I was the very first customer to submit a working prototype for evaluation," says Window Wizard inventor Ken Thorne. "I can honestly say that my submitting a working prototype to the factory saved me months of R&D and engineering hours, not to [mention] money."

A prototype gets everyone on the same page and helps avoid misinterpretations. Building a prototype will prepare you to draft your patent specification and claims (see Part 5). It helps identify key features that should be included in your patent application. A prototype also makes it much easier for your patent draftsman to do accurate drawings. Finally, a prototype helps verify the best materials and processes for the manufacture of your invention.

Bright Ideas

Minneapolis-born Patsy O. Sherman and Samuel Smith received U.S. Patent No. 3,574,791 on April 13, 1971, for their invention of block and graft copolymers containing water-solvatable polar groups and fluoroaliphatic groups, otherwise known as Scotchgard®. Sherman and Smith were employees at 3M Company when they collaborated on what became the most famous and widely used stain repellent and soil removal product. What prompted this innovative product? An accidental spill of a fluorochemical rubber on a tennis shoe. The shoes showed resistance to water and oily liquids. This lab accident led to the Scotchgard® family of products. Sherman holds 13 patents with Smith in fluorochemical polymers and polymerization processes. The pair was inducted into the National Inventor's Hall of Fame in 2001.

"There was a time when drawings were an acceptable form of submission and companies were willing to invest in the breadboards and prototypes," says Michael Brown, marketing and development consultant for Duncan's WarStone™ trading card game and a former vice president of marketing and development at Moto-Concepts. "Today companies expect inventors to submit proven concepts. They no longer want to risk investing in blue-sky ideas."

Furthermore, people who are asked to commit money and resources to a product love to touch and feel prototypes—to kick the tires, so to speak. They typically won't buy something from a verbal pitch or off a piece of paper. I say "typically" because there are exceptions to every rule.

Exceptions to the Rule

I once sold an idea over the phone. But the situation was very unique, and it required no R&D and no financial investment. It happened during the Tickle Me Elmo craze.

As Tickle Me Elmo was taking the country by storm, a ubiquitous yellow plastic sign was a popular item on the rear windows of cars. It read "Baby on Board." My idea was to ride both product waves by printing an image of Elmo at the steering wheel, under which was the warning "Don't Tickle Driver." Cute, right?

Here's how things went: I got on the phone and shared the "Don't Tickle Elmo" idea with my partner, Richard Maddocks, a brilliant designer and engineer, who lived nearby. He made a sketch of the idea. Next I called a manufacturer of infant products in New York City and pitched the idea. I faxed the sketch. He loved it.

> ### Bright Ideas
>
> Undertaker Almon Strowger, from Penfield, New York, came up with the idea for the rotary-dial telephone in 1888. Necessity is the mother of invention. When he found that the town's telephone operator was intercepting and diverting people calling him to his competitor (the operator was married to the town's other undertaker), Strowger invented the first dial system. It permitted people to make their own calls. He reportedly made his first prototype from a round collar box and some straight pins. In 1891, he patented the first telephone exchange.

Within an hour, the manufacturer had called and faxed the sketch to a buyer at Toys R Us, who, upon seeing the drawing, promised an opening order of 25,000 units. We hadn't even made a prototype! In fact, we never did a prototype. We simply bought some Baby On Board signs and mocked them up with our design. The manufacturing specs would be the same.

This was possible only because the concept was so simple that a baby could understand it and trusted personal relationships were in play—mine with the manufacturer and his with the retailer.

Another time I came up with an idea to miniaturize a working yo-yo to the scale of a key chain fob. This took a bit longer to license than the Elmo novelty, but again, I didn't have to build a prototype. In this case, I called the presidents of Duncan and Basic Fun, respectively, shared the marketing concept, and affected the marriage. Duncan gave Basic Fun the rights to its trademark and some sample yo-yos. I worked with Basic Fun and its engineers to make it happen. Basic Fun went on to sell over 2 million units of Duncan Imperial and Butterfly yo-yo key chains.

The prototype of my best-selling board game Adver*teasing* cost no more than $25 to produce. I took some paper, markers, cards, and a scissors—voilà, I had a playable prototype. Adver*teasing*, still on the market, has sold over 1 million units, to date.

Once I made a seven-figure deal for a product that had no prototype, but that, as Kipling would say, is another story.

Clearly these examples are anomalies. They are also based on many years of trusted relationships. And you have to know when to play such cards. Normally I do use prototypes in presentations, even to my closest friends.

Models of a Different Fashion

Models and prototypes come in many different types and levels. They also have a slew of names, depending on your field of invention—alpha prototype, beta prototype, breadboard, developmental prototype, global prototype, high-fidelity prototype, horizontal prototype, industrial design prototype, looks-like prototype, low-fidelity prototype, proving model, rapid prototype (SLA/SLS), vertical prototype, works-like prototype, and so forth.

Physical model prototyping can be extremely complex. I'm not an engineer, and you might not be, either. So let's keep it simple. After all, this book is designed to make the process easy to understand. Knowing the five basic types of models and prototypes, you'll be good to go.

Breadboards

A breadboard, or proving model, is an experimental model of a concept. Breadboards are used for proof of concept and developmental testing. A breadboard does not address the look and feel of a product. If you need to show that a particular mechanism will work, you can show the company a breadboard of it.

Breadboards don't need to be painted. I prefer to show them in white. Why? If the prototype has moving parts, a paint job can cause interference. And why risk painting it in a color someone may not like? Believe it or not, I've seen it happen: just as a colleague of mine was about to start his pitch, a CEO said, "Why did you paint it green?" The presentation went downhill from there.

On the other hand, if a licensed property is involved, it could pay to spruce up the prototype in signature colors.

Looks-Like Models

An appearance, or looks-like, model can be made of inexpensive materials like styrene and cardboard. It is really a 3-D picture of your product.

Fast Facts _____

On April 10, 1790, President George Washington signed the bill that laid the foundation of the modern American patent system. This date marks the first time in American history the law gave inventors rights to their creations.

Looks-Like, Works-Like Prototypes

This is a unit at scale that sports the key promotable features. It's my preferred level of prototype for presentation to potential licensees. It can be used by the engineering team that needs to gauge the product's technical feasibility, the design team, and the marketing team.

Mark Hartelius, president of Hartdesign! in Chicago, gives his clients the following advice when they order looks-like, works-like prototypes: "First, write down your performance expectations. Too many times I hear about would'a, could'a, should'a. Identify your key elements. Second, remember cost. If you know what key elements will sell the item, spend money on those features. Third, realize that manufacturing is a science, not necessarily an art. Pretty pictures don't always translate into products that can be produced. Be flexible with your factory. They don't want to build something that they can't manufacture. Lastly, listen to your customers and make the necessary changes. If they are asking, that means that they will embrace those changes."

Rapid Prototypes

This is a software-driven process. Three-dimensional physical objects are automatically built by means of solid freeform fabrication (SFF), guided by Computer-Aided Design (CAD) data. A working model or prototype can be made quickly. Components are grown from a photo-sensitive polymer (epoxy resin) using an ultraviolet laser system. The devices are actually 3-D printers.

Miami-based inventor/designer Jose Longoria is very experienced in rapid prototyping. "Rapid prototyping can be extremely useful and quick. Once a file is created, all you have to do is e-mail it to the right shop and you can expect a sample on your doorstep the next morning via FedEx," he says.

"Every surface is defined in these documents, so designers can create any shape and texture imaginable!" But he cautions that when novices see the shimmering images of their dream product rotating on the PC screen, or they hold the 3-D prints, they assume success. However, in the factories, they have to bend metal, sew fabric, and inject thermoplastics to make products. Longoria's advice to the novice: "Be warned that many professionals that master 3-D modeling and most rapid prototyping shops don't understand manufacturing. You must work with engineers that understand how to design for mass production."

Many kinds of rapid prototyping systems exist. The two that will be most helpful to you are *stereolithography* (SLA) and *selective laser sintering* (SLS).

def•i•ni•tion

Stereolithography creates solid, plastic, 3-D objects from CAD drawings in a matter of hours. A stereolithography machine uses a computer-controlled laser to cure a photo-sensitive resin, layer by layer, to create the 3-D part. **Selective laser sintering** offers the key advantage of making functional parts in essentially final materials. The system is mechanically more complex than stereolithography.

While not inexpensive, rapid prototyping grows models that, when painted, look like the real deal.

Virtual Prototypes

CAD programs simulate an invention in 3-D. They can test that an invention works before you go ahead and invest in a physical prototype. The people who make virtual prototypes are capable of providing you with an animation or a video of your invention working.

When asked for advice on ordering virtual prototypes, veteran industrial designer Steve Chininis of Atlanta says:

"Often people you hire to do 3-D CAD work [so you can print models from the 3-D files] have a great deal of knowledge about how the process works but do not help you understand the process. If you do not understand the process, you can spend a lot of time and money and get nowhere. Try to find someone willing to advise you on the best way to proceed and who doesn't mind spending a minute to explain the process. A quickie $300 CAD job could cost 10 times that in the end, while an $800 job with someone you trust, or have found through a trusted referral, is a safer bet."

Do things in the proper order. "For instance, if you are designing a case for something, there is no need to spend extra time designing and modeling all the screw bosses and interior ribs if you don't even know that you have an acceptable exterior form of the case," he continues.

Steve recommends printing out parts during the process so you can evaluate them and see if you can learn anything before ordering final prototypes. "If you are rushing to finish for a meeting or a show, without allowing time for evaluation, you may end up with an amateur result, not worthy of presentation."

Last but not least, be sure the CAD program you're using produces files your factory or licensee can read. Steve often sends a test file at the start of the project to be sure no surprises pop up later. "You can lose a whole week if you have conversion problems," he cautions.

> **411**
>
> NASA needs ideas. The publishers of NASA *Tech Briefs* magazine run the Create the Future Design Contest to help stimulate and reward engineering innovation. In 2008, the annual event attracted more than 1,000 product entries from engineers, entrepreneurs, and students worldwide, and featured a grand prize of $20,000. For details, go to www.createthefuturecontest.com/index.html. Contest co-sponsors include COMSOL, Hewlett-Packard, and National Instruments.

Prototype Components, Cost Estimating, and Parts Sourcing

In my experience, nothing beats ThomasNet® (previously known as The Thomas Register) for one-stop shopping when you're looking for components for prototypes or manufacturers of a particular component. ThomasNet® offers information about where to find every conceivable industrial product or service. It lists more than 607,000 industrial companies in North America, indexed by 67,000 product and service categories.

> **Notable Quotables**
>
> Happiness is not in the mere possession of money; it lies in the joy of achievement, in the thrill of creative effort.
>
> —Franklin D. Roosevelt, thirty-second president of the United States

ThomasNet® is brought to you by Thomas Publishing Company, LLC. The company, connecting industrial buyers and suppliers for over 110 years, is headquartered at 5 Penn Plaza, New York, NY 10001; 212-695-0500. ThomasNet® has regional sales offices throughout the United States and Canada.

Know Your Audience

The better you get to know your audience, the easier it will be for you to know the level of model required for a particular concept. At the end of the day, your goal is to get your product under contract or to land investors. Once a company takes over, the item may begin to take different forms and functions. In the case of a licensee, if the company respects you, you will be part of this decision-making process. And when the planets line up, magic can happen.

Inventor Ken Thorne came up with Zephyr, a do-it-yourself converter that transforms a standard oven into a convection oven, thus saving time and money when cooking.

When Ken started to prototype Zephyr, his first stop was Grainger Industrial Supply to find a motor that closely resembled what he had in mind. A sheet metal guy made the fan blade, at minimal cost. Ken then approached a pottery artist to design a housing to enclose the motor and fan blade.

Ken knew his idea was feasible, but once the parts were assembled, and after some tweaking, he knew he was on the right track. "I contacted the San Francisco distributor for small GE motors. They sent a salesman to see me," Ken explained. "I showed him my prototype and suggested that a successful product could result in the sale of a million motors or more," he continued. "The guy saw the potential because a week later I had a call from GE and the following week I was off to Fort Wayne, Indiana, to see the top brass."

GE loved the idea and adopted Ken's modifications to their motor in lieu of his filing patents. They assigned the new motor a special part number and gave Ken 10 percent of the motor's wholesale price in perpetuity.

Building a Better Prototype

Before you call anyone, you need to decide how much functionality is required in your prototype to communicate the idea and get people to embrace it. A good rule of thumb is to take things as far as you can. The prototype needs to stimulate your target audience, a group that may see hundreds, if not thousands, of submissions. If you need to do more work, you will know after a few pitches.

I remember a product we submitted to PlayTime Toys called Grab-a-Bag. It was an innovative packaging concept for inexpensive toys and games. "You were number eighty on the table today," I was told by the VP of marketing. I cringed. Having been part of such exercises myself, I could see these decision-makers glazing over by the time they got to number 25.

411

The National Science Foundation (NSF) offers fellowships to students in their early stages of pursuing a research-based Master's or Ph.D. degree. The Graduate Research Fellowship Program (GRFP) offers our nation's future research leaders exceptional funding with three years of graduate support worth thousands of dollars. For more information, go to www.nsfgrfp.org.

When he told me we made the cut, I knew they understood the product and loved it. In this case, being number 80 was reassuring. It obviously stimulated them even after a grueling day.

Our prototype was a flexible snack bag my partner Richard Maddocks cobbled together. He did a brilliant job. Again, this is all about applying the right talent to the task.

> **Fast Facts** _____
>
> The father of modern rocket propulsion is American Dr. Robert Hutchings Goddard. Along with Konstantin Eduordovich Tsiolkovsky of Russia and Hermann Oberth of Germany, Goddard envisioned the exploration of space. A physicist of great insight, Goddard also had a unique genius for invention. By 1926, Goddard had constructed and tested successfully the first liquid fuel rocket. The flight of Goddard's rocket on March 16, 1926, at Auburn, Massachusetts, was a feat as epochal in history as that of Wilbur and Orville Wright off Kill Devil Hill, near Kitty Hawk, North Carolina.

Help Wanted

I've learned all kinds of shortcuts and tricks over the years when it comes to prototyping and making presentation models. For example, a great way to get parts—and save time and money—is to cannibalize commercial products. But there's no substitute for someone who has "golden hands."

If you don't know model makers or designers personally, it's not hard to find talent. Using an Internet or Yellow Pages search, look for "model makers" or "prototype makers." Depending on the requirements of your idea, you'll know if you need a mechanical engineer, electronic engineer, chemist, or industrial designer, or a combination of skill sets.

Look into local trade schools, universities, and colleges with technical schools or courses of study. You may be able to find student talent at a very affordable price. You also get the benefit of fresh thinking. I love to toss problems to youth. While younger people do not have the empirical experience of more seasoned pros, they are more in a groove, not stuck in the rut of habit. I absolutely love hearing young, can-do talent resolve issues. "What about …?" "What if we …?" This is music to my ears.

Artists are available under headings such as artist, graphic designer, industrial designer, and so forth. Many artists post their portfolios and rates online, together with contact information.

Hobby groups and inventor organizations are great places to network, and all inventors need good prototypes.

They Need to Take a Lickin' and Keep on Tickin'

Prototypes should be well made because they can take quite a beating as they're presented and represented and travel among a company's departments. Sometimes models are sent to remote locations. Don't be surprised to have your prototype returned broken. This can happen from mishandling or improper packing. It comes with the territory.

On a few occasions, companies have lost our prototypes, and we were paid the cost of replacement. Companies are insured for such instances. Submission agreements often include a line that says the company has no responsibility for the submission. Strike out this clause. Never agree to let a company off the hook in the case of breakage or loss. If the company has any interest in working with you, they'll delete that clause and repair or replace a damaged submission.

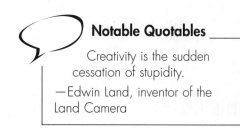

Notable Quotables

Creativity is the sudden cessation of stupidity.

—Edwin Land, inventor of the Land Camera

Paying for Prototypes

If you don't have the money to pay for a prototype and you need something complex, think about making the prototype maker a partner. You could strike all kinds of deals. Each project has to be considered on its own merits, but this could be a win-win option.

I have made many such deals. What I have never done is give an engineer a fee plus a royalty. I believe in shared risk and shared reward. There are no guarantees; there are only opportunities. If need be, I remind people that fruit is usually out on a limb.

Bright Ideas

In 1868, New England resident Margaret Knight, working in a shop that produced paper bags, invented a device that mechanically folded and glued paper to form square-bottomed paper bags. This improvement created a bag that would stand on its own. She was awarded U.S. Patent No. 116,842 on July 11, 1871. But she did not stop here. A prolific inventor, Margaret was one of the first women to be awarded a patent. Before she died in 1914, Margaret held as many as 26 patents in diverse categories. She also co-founded Eastern Paper Bag Company in Hartford, Connecticut.

Before You Hire a Prototype Maker

Before you share your idea with a prototype maker (or anyone, for that matter), have the person sign a nondisclosure agreement (NDA). I've provided an NDA template for your convenience in Appendix B.

Be sure the prototype maker you hire or partner with completely understands your invention. And don't hire someone until you understand the invention and have drawings, specifications, etc. to share with that person. Once you do start working together, be sure that you can communicate effectively and that your milestones can be met. Be sure the prototype maker has no conflicts of interest.

Set the fees, expenses, and deal points in advance, and put everything in writing. If the person is working for fees, have a work-for-hire agreement signed.

Finally, at some point, a licensee will begin the prototype process, in whole or part, all over again. It will have its own people or factories make models and prototypes as they re-spec, redesign, and re-evaluate your submission.

The Least You Need to Know

- Strong relationships enhance prototypes.
- See how much you can do, not how little you can do.
- Partner up, if you need to.
- High-tech works only with a high touch.
- Surprise people. Make your prototype sing.
- Just because a prototype looks good doesn't mean it will be considered. How many people do you know who are impeccably groomed, but … rather lackluster?

Chapter 5

Made to Order

In This Chapter

- From scratch to finish
- Foreign exchanges
- Person-to-person
- Quality control (QC)
- Safety first

> I have always found that if I move with seventy-five percent or more of the facts that I usually never regret it. It's the guys who wait to have everything perfect that drive you crazy.
>
> —Lee Iacocca, former chairman, Chrysler Corporation

Ideas are developed and then turned into products by factories. So let's take a look at what this involves. As you will soon realize, this is not for the faint of heart. You'll need real commitment to handle this leg of the journey.

Development and Production Cycles

Whether you're developing and manufacturing the product yourself or licensing it, you need to understand product cycles. As in every business, information is power. You want to know as much as possible about each phase of the business. Your involvement should not stop after the moment of invention. Even if you're not involved in each phase of development and production, you'll benefit from knowing what's going on. Omitting a critical stage or neglecting a detail decreases the possibility of success.

> **Notable Quotables**
>
> Creativity comes from looking for the unexpected and stepping outside your own experience.
>
> —Masaru Ibuka, co-founder, Sony Corp.

Individual companies have slight variations of a development and manufacturing process. The specific cycle depends on the complexity of the product or products to be developed and prepared for market, and the size of the company. The following schedule was generously provided by Hasbro, Inc. A form of it will come into play if you control manufacturing yourself (or use a subcontractor) or if you opt to license the ip rights to others.

November: The product concept is approved. Then comes market research. The marketing, design, and engineering teams join forces to assess consumer reaction to the new concept. Consumer input is invaluable in evaluating the potential for a new concept or in fine-tuning a product prior to its launch. Next up is preliminary costing, followed by the PTO (preliminary takeover) model from the shop.

December: First up, the preliminary takeover. The PTO conference is a critical stage in a product's transition from concept to reality. At this phase, a product passes from the hands of designers to engineers, with close scrutiny given to such issues as design, cost, reliability, packaging, and manufacturing plans. Next comes the marketing line review. Then the R&D model is finished. The R&D model shop constructs product prototypes early in the development process. Later, model makers may fine-tune mechanisms and build models for use during the ongoing product review process. If hand samples are required for trade shows, they're made now.

January: The PTO package is approved and the appropriation approval is requested. Also in January is the FTO (final takeover), followed by the marketing line review.

February: The final sculpture is up next. Product sculptors work in consultation with design engineers and marketing managers to transform the product idea into reality.

March: The preliminary drawing is released and the EDM review (engineering, design, and marketing) takes place.

April: The final drawing is released, as is the pattern. The cost is also verified.

May: Tooling starts.

June: The proving model is reviewed and the graphic model completed. Any final engineering changes are made.

July: July first brings MTO (manufacturing takeover) costing. Final packaging specifications are made and final product specifications are set.

August: First up, MTO. Next, marketing line review.

September: The package and art are released. Designing a product's packaging is an important part of the overall product-development and marketing process. Preliminary instructions are also drafted.

Fast Facts

On July 31, 1790, Samuel Hopkins of Philadelphia, Pennsylvania, received the first U.S. patent for an improvement in "the making of Pot ash and Pearl ash by a new Apparatus and Process." President George Washington signed the patent, as did Attorney General Edmund Randolph and Secretary of State Thomas Jefferson. The original document is still in existence in the collections of the Chicago Historical Society.

October: The art is released, and the first shots (samples of the molded parts) are made.

November: November brings the marketing line review. All the functions involved in the creation of a product, including R&D and engineering, come together. Features such as design, packaging, and advertising are evaluated, and the overall design and production schedule is monitored.

December: First up, VSP (vendor sample pilot). Some products are manufactured by outside vendors. If so, before full production is started, the vendor produces a sample product. Marketing, design, engineering, and R&D teams evaluate all aspects of the pilot product to determine whether it conforms to design and engineering specifications before authorizing the start of production. Final packaging is also decided upon and the final instructions are released. Finally, another marketing line review takes place.

January: January brings the FEP (final engineering pilot) and RTP (release to production).

February: The product is taken to trade shows and shown to buyers.

March: Production starts.

Bright Ideas

The first patent for the new millennium was issued on January 4, 2000, to Leonard Siprut from San Diego for a multiple component headgear system. U.S. Patent No. 6,009,555 is a sun visor/eye shield for surfers, kayakers, bikers, and athletes in other extreme sports. In contrast, the first patent issued in 1900 was to Louis Allard of Utah for an early version of the washing machine.

Offshoring Your Product

Obviously, you would prefer to manufacture your product in the good old U. S. of A. There's no need for me to list the benefits of manufacturing at home, especially as they relate to project command and control.

But if you have to work in part or whole overseas because of cost efficiencies, let's review some guidelines.

Does It Make Dollars and Sense?

Lower labor costs are clearly the reason you would consider taking your product overseas. But be careful. Run the numbers. Do the math. In addition to the cost of taxi fare, consider every aspect of the decision, from labor costs and labor skills to turnaround times, profit margins, shipping, taxes, and duties, to name just a few items on a long list of must-knows.

> **411**
>
> U.S. Customs and Border Protection will facilitate about $2 trillion in legitimate trade this year while enforcing U.S. trade laws that protect the economy and the health and safety of the American people. For information about U.S. trade laws, go to www.customs.gov/xp/cgov/trade/basic_trade.

Last, but far from least, is your order large enough to qualify for offshore production? Unless you have large volume, foreign manufacturers typically have no interest.

Be honest in your estimates. Do not promise large orders unless you have booked them. Factory owners and managers have heard all the stories. Just have a long-term plan and stick to it.

"Toto, I Have a Feeling We're Not in Kansas Anymore ..."

Things are different on foreign shores. You are no longer in the land of the free and the home of the brave. You are in a land of strangers. The red tape is different. The culture is different. The customs are different. The currency is different. The language may be different. Very little you encounter will be equivalent to the United States. As Kipling reminds us, "All the people like us are We, and everyone else is They." And They come at a price that may be too high for a small business to pay.

Do your homework. Hire a consultant to help you flesh out the pros and the cons of foreign manufacture, country selection, etc. Study up on any trade agreements between the United States and the countries under consideration. You need to light a candle of understanding. You are contemplating travel through uncharted waters into uncharted territory from your point of view.

Inventions Wanted

IBM, a pioneer in information technology, has established a formal channel for unsolicited inquiries. The company is interested in seeing proposals for marketing and development relationships; software and software technology proposals; equity, acquisition, and joint venture proposals; patents, including those issued and pending; and ideas relating to IBM products and services. All proposals need to be submitted electronically. To that end, go online to www-01.ibm.com/contact/submissions/extsub.nsf/BusinessProposal?OpenForm to find how to proceed.

Find a Local Lieutenant

Once you decide upon a country of manufacture, you are well advised to hire a foreign national based in-country, on your payroll, to represent your interests. It is too risky to depend 100 percent on the factory. This is like trusting the fox to watch the hen house. Set up a system of checks and balances that is under your control.

Get recommendations from three different people before you hire anyone, and for sure arrange a face-to-face meeting here or in the country of manufacture.

Many people are out of work today and looking for consulting assignments. I'm sure that if you go to a trade show and ask people for manufacturing contacts, they will be generous with their recommendations. Pros like to help other pros get work. One day you might be able to repay the favor.

Kick the Tires

Visit factories to evaluate them firsthand. Many people work with foreign makers through United States–based agents, often relatives of a factory owner based here for the purpose of drumming up business and serving as liaison between you and the factory.

If you opt not to go overseas and to work through a United States–based agent, odds are good that you will be put in the agent's factory of choice. You won't get the benefit of having makers compete for your business.

> **Fast Facts** _____
>
> U.S. Customs and Border Protection's (CBP) Office of International Trade has developed a new online trade violation reporting system called eAllegations. If you suspect trade violations, you can report them anonymously via https://apps.cbp.gov/eallegations. CBP has established this reporting system to make it easier for the public to notify CBP of possible trade violations. CBP will confidentially research concerns, determine the validity of the allegations, and take any actions required based on the subsequent review.

I cannot be more emphatic about factory visits. Nothing is more reassuring than meeting the owners and managers of your factory and building a personal relationship. Walk the floors. Get a feel for the workers and their environment. Be sure they understand your product. Independent inventor Ken Thorne, who is making his Window Wizard overseas, warns that with offshore companies your product could be as foreign to them as an artichoke is to an Eskimo.

A visit will pay major benefits when there are problems (and there will be problems) and you're trying to make sense of things from thousands of miles away, working with people who don't have a command of English.

On a personal note, when Mike Sanders at Alpha Books decided to offer me a contract to write the first edition of this book, my wife and I took a trip to Indianapolis for the sole purpose of meeting Mike and his team. We have since been back two more times.

A project several years ago had us working with an electronics engineer in San Jose, California. After a few months, I noticed some communication problems between us and this engineer. I asked the team if anyone had ever met the engineer face-to-face. No one had ever laid eyes on him. He was hired through references.

I picked up the phone and told the engineer I wanted to fly to San Jose from the East Coast and take him and his wife to dinner. "Pick your favorite restaurant,"

I said. I landed at Mineta San Jose International Airport, rented a car, and went to a Sheraton in a nearby suburb. That evening we had a wonderful dinner and talked on into the night. That dinner and the postprandial exchange cemented our relationship, and everything was smooth from there on.

Sometimes the travel works in reverse. When we were developing Furby, there was so much technical mechanism data to transfer to the Chinese engineers that I suggested a delegation from the factory travel to see us in the United States. Two days later, several engineers landed, and we had a seamless transfer of information. In this case, it made more sense for them to come our way.

I could not agree more with Ben Stein: "Personal relationships are the fertile soil from which all advancement, all success, all achievement in real life grows."

Making You Feel at Home

Foreign manufacturers are most hospitable when customers come to visit. They love to roll out the red carpet and lay on meals and entertainment in an effort to get to know you, make you feel comfortable, show off their capabilities and their country, and hopefully get your business.

We always take gifts when we go overseas on business. We like to take handicrafts or books of photographs from the USA, especially from the area where we live. When I had contacts at NASA, I would get satellite photographs of their country or, if possible, their city. People go wild for such mementos. If you would like to purchase prints, go to http://earth.jsc.nasa.gov/sseop/EFS/vendors2.htm.

In many Asian countries, there is something called "debt of the spirit." This means that for every gift you give, you'll get a gift in return. And in these cultures, it is important for them that they give the last gift. I recall once in Taiwan we found ourselves in the battle of gifts. At one point, we ran out of gifts and started to buy local curios and gewgaws in an effort to keep pace with the generosity of our hosts. It was quite a scene. After four or five rounds, we allowed them to win.

In summary, create linkages. Sound business is about relationships, not just commerce.

Diplomatic Missions

Contact a country's embassy in Washington, D.C., and have a word with people in its trade or economic mission. See if they can send you booklets about doing business in their country. The mandate of international trade missions is to encourage and facilitate trade and investment in their countries. Google and Bing are great ways to track down the web pages, phone numbers, and e-mails for these United States–based organizations.

Bright Ideas
Christopher Latham Sholes (1819–1880), Collector of Customs during the Lincoln Administration, and co-inventor Samuel Soule patented a numbering machine in 1866. Two years later, they joined forces with another inventor, Carlos Glidden, and patented their first typewriter. In 1873, Sholes developed the QWERTY keyboard, still the standard for keyboards, to help keep the keys from jamming.

Make it a point to learn about the local culture, its customs, and its business practices. Memorize some phrases in the local language to prepare for your visit.

Having lived in Spain, France, Italy, and Panama, and traveled worldwide, I know firsthand the value of language proficiency and how far simple words like *hello*, *good-bye*, *please*, and *thank you* go in establishing relationships.

Protect Your IP

In most foreign countries, intellectual property protection is not adequate. Especially in Asia, there are no secrets and very little enforcement of ip rights. It does not matter that nondisclosure agreements (NDAs) are signed. People leak, especially underpaid labor.

Some American companies take the added precaution to divide manufacturing contracts for a product's components among several factories. Only their most reliable suppliers perform the final assembly.

We were making a popular product in China. When other factories started to manufacture knock-offs, we showed the authorities our patent protection, and the government put a stop to the unauthorized products. Then in 1999 NATO put three Cruise missiles into the Chinese mission in Belgrade, and a diplomatic chasm was opened between NATO and Beijing. Suddenly those enforcement actions ceased. Here foreign diplomacy interfered with our business.

Put English on the Deal

My first job was working for the president of Paramount Pictures International at 1501 Broadway, New York City. I recall him telling me to be sure all contracts and other legal documents were in English whenever I went overseas for the company. I still follow this advice today, even if I am fluent in the foreign language.

I do all business in English. Linguistic construction is a minefield. Being polyglot, I know too well from firsthand experience the frequency of semantic rupture and its results.

Avoiding Problems

It's Murphy's Law. Whatever can go wrong will go wrong. Expect the unexpected. Skate ahead of the puck. You want to be proactive, not reactive. Work out the issues with your factory so problems do not recur.

"If there is one lesson I could pass on about dealing with offshore manufactures, it would be, have plenty of patience," counsels Window Wizard inventor Ken Thorne. "Don't be in a hurry to rush your idea to market. Sit back and review, retest, and review over again. Be certain it is ready for market; test it and test it again. It is much easier to launch a new product the first time than to have to recall it and launch it all over again."

Avoiding Packaging Problems

Don't forget to keep pace with the design of your packaging so it's ready when the product comes off the line.

Do the package design at home. Do not rely on foreign creativity for anything other than value engineering and production engineering.

Avoiding Logistical Nightmares

Do not leave transportation decisions to your factory.

Get a first-class freight forwarder who understands the fine points of cargo, e.g., negotiating the required paperwork, insurance, bonds, etc.

Avoiding Customs Conundrums

Import duty and import taxes are one of the most confusing subjects I have ever encountered.

Import duty is the tax you are obligated to pay to Uncle Sam for the privilege of bringing foreign-made products into the commerce of the United States. The U.S. Customs Service enforces duties.

Avoiding Quality and Safety Issues

"Safety and quality problems will put you out of business faster than lightning," cautions Mark Hartelius, president of Hartdesign!, a Chicago-based product development–to–manufacturer company.

Now that you've established what product you're going to make and the performance expectations for that product, you need to ensure it's done correctly.

411

If you want to research safety standards, a great place to start is Philadelphia, Pennsylvania's ASTM International, one of the largest voluntary standards development organizations in the world and a trusted source for technical standards for materials, products, systems, and services. Learn more at www.astm.org.

Before you start manufacturing, be sure you and your factory understand the safety standards in the country of origin, as well as here at home. Safety can be expensive. The foreign governments and your customers will have certain standards and specifications that must be met before a product will be approved for export. Quality control inspections and tests must be passed before any product is released. These services take time and come at a price.

As for quality, it is a function of performance. Establish high performance expectations, and build your quality around it. Hartelius gives this example: gears can be made out of many different materials—delrin, nylon, metal, brass, etc—each at a different price and a different performance. Your choice of material depends on performance parameters. A gear in a Spin Pop has different performance expectations than a gear in a kitchen blender. They both spin, but the expectations are not the same.

If you haven't figured this out yet, the cliché is true: you get what you pay for. Peanuts attract monkeys. While you want the best pricing from the factory, if you force someone to bid too low, you could be in trouble. I've seen situations where a factory bids low and then makes up the loss by using regrind instead of new plastic to mold products or slips in paint that is laced with lead (a heavy metal) in place of a less toxic, more expensive substitute.

At the end of the day you want price, quality, service, competence, and dedication.

The Least You Need to Know

- ◆ Know your product intimately so you can fully explain it to others who are in this with you.

- ◆ Meet your maker. It will improve the odds of success for both of you.

- ◆ Don't be an ugly American. Get to know the customs and habits of the country where your product is being produced.

- ◆ There are no easy answers; there are no easy ways.

Part 3

Getting High Marks

American business depends on innovation and creative thought. Free enterprise is always dissatisfied with the status quo. It wants the biggest, the best, and the newest. We are a "throwaway" society. And like the oyster that is irritated by a grain of sand, America frequently produces priceless pearls. This gives inventors a target-rich environment for capital and licensing opportunities.

In Part 3, I discuss the advantages and disadvantages between large and small companies, public versus private. I follow this with pointers on how to get critical background information on each of these business models. I also explain opportunities you may not have considered. For example, today's companies are risk-averse when it comes to new product introductions, but they feel warm and fuzzy extending their stable of evergreens. In such cases, brand equity trumps innovation.

Even with the best and most accurate information, there are no guarantees—just opportunities. In Part 3, you will learn how to take your best shots, make the pitch, and, if you strike a nerve, close the deal.

Chapter 6

Finding a Home for Your Brainchild

In This Chapter

- Finding companies with the right stuff
- Trading information at trade shows
- Making connections at conferences
- Companies, great and small, private and public
- May I see your license, please?

Independent inventors tend to make the most radical innovations in technology because they are not held back by corporate group-think.

—Paul Herbig, author, *The Innovation Matrix*

Well, have you decided yet whether you want to license your invention to a manufacturer or start your own company to develop, produce, and bring it to market?

If you want to raise venture capital, skip to the chapters on how to protect your intellectual property (see Parts 4 and 5). If you are new to divining for capital, find a nearby university or adult education center where you can take a class or two on how to raise venture capital. To learn about state and federal programs, call the Small Business Administration's toll-free information line at 1-800-827-5722.

On the other hand, if you want to license your product, read on.

Finding a Licensing Partner

Keep in mind that until you have made personal contact with company executives, paid a visit to their offices, gotten to know them, and most importantly, talked with others who have licensed products there, you will not have a full picture of the situation.

Consider some tips on how to find the right home for your invention:

◆ Put a lot of time into researching and selecting which potential licensees to approach. Do not rush the process. Match your inventions with company capabilities and profiles.

◆ Do not make the error of insufficient options. Expect rejections—lots of them—so line up as many candidates as possible.

◆ Find out if the company works with outside inventors. The best tests for this are: how many, if any, licensed products are in the company's line, and does the company have an inventor relations department or system for outside submissions? Study product. Get catalogues. Surf the web.

◆ You want to sell to a company that would be classified by the U.S. Navy as a "friendly port." The best way to find out is by meeting other inventors who have licensed to the company. I have found that although companies in the same industry do not talk to each other, inventors discuss contract terms, share impressions, and otherwise spill their guts to each other at the drop of a hat. After all, it is us against them.

Every September, a group of toy inventors and their spouses get together and spend a three-day working weekend at a beautiful country inn in Vermont. Some folks travel from as far away as California and England. What do they do while walking through the woods, biking, antiquing, and eating? They share experiences. "Mike is a terrific guy." "I was ripped off by so and so." "I got a $75,000 advance from David. What did you get?" "How did you have that clause removed?" And on and on it goes.

After the weekend, attendees' phones typically ring with executives wanting to know if their names came up in conversation, and if so, in what context. As for the executives, they reap what they sow.

In south Florida, there is another group of toy inventors called The Sunshine Santas. These elves share information on an almost daily basis, socializing throughout the year and even collaborating on projects.

A key question inventors ask each other is whether they have had an audit conducted of a specific company's books and if so, what the results were. The answer could tell volumes about the company.

See Chapter 23 for details on how to hook up with a group. There tends to be great camaraderie among inventors.

Attend Trade Shows

There are national, regional, and local trade shows for everything from hardware, consumer electronics, apparel, and aircraft to nuclear medicine, dental equipment, comic books, and musical instruments. If it is manufactured and sold, you can be sure it has been marketed at a trade show somewhere, sometime.

Bright Ideas

The first safety pins were used in Europe some 4,000 years ago. But people jabbed themselves with their sharp, open tips. It wasn't until 1849, in New York City, that Walter Hunt invented a pin that was, indeed, safe when he put a clasp over the dangerous tip. Actually, had he not been in debt, he might never have invented the safety pin. A guy he had tapped for $15 said he would forgive the debt and pay Hunt $400 if he could make something useful from a piece of wire. Hunt bent and twisted the wire for a few hours and came up with the safety pin design. His creditor made the fortune, however.

One-Stop Shopping

Trade shows are not the best venues to present inventions to potential *licensees*. But they are a must for getting the beat on a particular market and its dynamics. It is all there for you to peruse, at your leisure. Competitors line up side by side, allowing you to compare products and pricing and look for industry innovations and trends.

def•i•ni•tion

Licensee is a term used in licensing agreements to designate the party buying the rights to commercialize an invention. **Licensor** is a term used to designate the inventor, or the person selling the rights to an invention.

There is no better or more cost-effective way to acquire product literature than at a trade show. Manufacturers publish product sheets and info kits just for trade show distribution. And many come with a price list!

Although some shows have closed booths to control access to new product, that's not a problem for you. You're inventive, and to gain entry you may have to be particularly inventive. Companies pay to exhibit. Depending upon the show and city, costs can run from a few thousand dollars to the millions. The manufacturers' primary reason for being there is to ring up sales and get leads. They are not there to meet inventors. So you want to blend into the background, observing and picking up flyers, news releases, and so on.

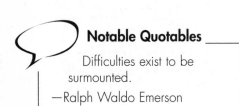

Notable Quotables

Difficulties exist to be surmounted.
—Ralph Waldo Emerson

The sales force does not review new concepts. Sales is responsible for selling, not developing product. It is a waste of time and dangerous to expose inventions to salespeople at trade shows—or anywhere, for that matter. However, sales types can be excellent sources of information about their companies and the industry, and normally love to chat about their products, the state of the market, and so on.

Meet 'n' Greet

Trade shows are also an excellent place to meet and network with executives to whom you otherwise would not have access. They rarely take their bodyguards to events; after all, they are there to meet new people. Executives make it easy to ID them by wearing name tags. I have made super contacts in hotel elevators, lobby lines, and bus rides, and shared taxi rides to and from the exhibition centers with some big names in the business.

The best kinds of shows at which to meet senior executives are national or international. The heavyweights typically don't frequent the smaller regional or local trade shows. Nonetheless, such shows provide a less hectic atmosphere and many of the same resource materials.

Worth the Price of Admission

For most trade shows, admission is free to the trade. All you usually need is a business card to enter the exhibition area.

Whenever possible, register in advance by mail, and you may not even have to present a card at the door. Advance registration forms are typically found in trade magazines and online a few months before the event. Allowing people to do this takes the pressure off the registration process at the event. The organizers and the trade want people to be inside buying, not in the lobby waiting for nametags.

Finding the Right Trade Show

You can use a few methods for discovering where and when trade shows for any particular industry will be taking place:

- Ask a manufacturer or distributor in your field of invention. The sales and marketing people will have such information at their fingertips.

- Contact the trade association that covers your field of invention. More than 3,600 trade associations operate on the national level in the United States. A great way to start is to peruse the *Encyclopedia of Associations*, available at most libraries.

- Look online for information on some of the 15,000 trade shows worldwide. Search "trade show" plus your field of invention.

Conferences and Meetings: Networking Meccas

The biggest difference between trade shows and conferences is that you almost always pay to attend conferences. The primary reasons for attending conferences include hearing experts speak, picking their brains, sharing your ideas, and networking—and that costs money.

Conferences are excellent places to get to know the people behind the products. Socializing is encouraged, and the atmosphere is calmer than at trade shows. There is no pressure to buy. There is no pressure to sell. The object is to make friends, brainstorm, and exchange ideas. Participants can increase their *know how* and *know who* at the same time.

Many conferences offer simultaneous resource fairs. Many trade fairs have conferences or seminars scheduled.

Several methods are available for finding conferences:

- Ask a manufacturer or distributor in your field of invention. Many larger manufacturers have training departments that can provide helpful information.

♦ Contact the trade association that covers your field of invention. Go online and search for the *Encyclopedia of Associations.* It covers more than 159,000 nonprofit membership organizations. Or search on Google or Bing.

♦ Ask department heads and professors at nearby universities where your field of interest is taught. Universities, particularly those teaching engineering and kindred technical fields, will have a current schedule of conferences on hand.

Big Companies vs. Small Companies

The reality is that 80 percent of any business is done by 20 percent of the companies in a particular market. And given a choice, you want to be with the larger company.

Unfortunately, you usually don't have a choice. So often it is any port in a storm.

Large Companies

Let's look first at large companies and the opportunities they offer.

Large companies need so much to fill their pipeline that a failure could still make you more money than a hit with a small company. Hasbro and Mattel, for example, would not publish a game that did not launch with at least 250,000 copies and then have the possibility of increasing in year 2 and so forth. A smaller publisher might be content with 10,000 copies the first year, and see 50,000 copies as having hit the mother lode.

Hasbro and Mattel would not license a toy that could not do at least $15 million to $20 million in year 1 and then expand into a line. Their overheads do not allow them to license single items, no matter how clever the item is. A smaller company might launch a toy that sells a few thousand units per year.

Large companies can give you a huge advance/guarantee package. Smaller companies are normally lower in the advance and are reticent to guarantee anything, but are willing to give a higher royalty and more flexible terms.

Large companies typically have advertising and promotion budgets and departments to spend these dollars on your product. They may have outside agencies, too. Smaller companies sometimes barely get out a press release—unless the president writes and mails it—and have no budget for making noise.

> **Notable Quotables**
>
> The secret of genius is to carry the spirit of the child into old age, which means never losing your enthusiasm.
>
> —Aldous Huxley

Large companies have clout. I recall years ago asking a senior executive at Mattel how confident he was about securing shelf space for a new, edgy product of mine it had licensed. "If they like that pink aisle, they will give us a shot," he quipped. Of course, he was referring to Barbie. Smaller companies often have trouble getting a buyer on the phone to set up a meeting and show your product, let alone get an order.

Large companies could pay you millions of dollars in royalties and not bat an eyelash. The smaller company might pain over signing a royalty check for $1,000.

411

Do you have an energy-saving invention you need money to perfect? If so, the Department of Energy, Office of Industrial Technologies' Inventions and Innovation (I&I) Program funds up to $200,000 to promising projects demonstrating both energy-saving innovation and future commercial market potential. The I&I Program emphasizes funding projects that will have significant energy savings on a national level within the agriculture, aluminum, chemical, forest product, glass, metal-casting, mining, petroleum, and steel industries. Visit www.oit.doe.gov for details.

Large companies can afford to invest in product. The smaller companies are usually undercapitalized or otherwise unwilling to gamble on large runs without a guarantee in hand.

Large companies can license your product without first showing it to trade buyers for their approval. This is what you want. Do not permit anyone to show your product before it is ready for prime time. Smaller companies may lack the confidence to license new products without a prior vote of confidence from a trade buyer(s). They want to know that someone will buy it before they make an investment.

Large companies are typically multinational and get global distribution for your product, and quickly. Small companies usually do not have sales and distribution offices overseas and usually make their foreign deals through agents after the product has proven itself in America.

Large companies have strong front lines and benches deep in talent: engineers, programmers, model makers, sculptors, quality control experts, designers, copywriters, packaging people, and more.

Notable Quotables

Embrace rejection. Sometimes it's the only thing you have going for you.

—Barbara Slate, creator of Angel Love and other comic characters

Smaller companies farm out most work to freelancers, which can be problematic when the crunch is on.

Large companies benefit from economies of scale. Small companies are not able to hammer vendors for lower prices because their minimum order quantity (MOQ) is less.

Large companies typically carry higher product liability insurance than small companies and usually add inventors to it if so requested. Small companies frequently balk at adding licensors to a policy or increasing their insurance.

Perhaps the best way to sum it up: large companies can power product in ways small companies cannot.

Small Companies

On the other hand, smaller companies do have positive attributes. For example, we were awarded a U.S. patent for a dramatic departure in baby bottle design. Inspired by the spiral pattern on the Nerf Turbo football, our design featured a spiral grip. Most companies saw it as being too "far out." No one wanted to license it.

Then one day the phone rang. It was my old friend Harvey Lepselter calling to tell me he had landed a job as senior vice president for R&D/marketing at a start-up Long Island company Babies 'n Things.

"What do you have for infants?" he asked. I thought for a moment, mentioned a couple items, and sent them up for review. They did not pass muster. After explaining why the submissions were not appropriate, he asked if there was anything else. "No," I responded. Not one to take no for an answer, Harvey asked me to look around in my prototype closet again. Because he's such a close friend, I took the time. Then I remembered the baby bottle.

> **Bright Ideas**
>
> James Fergason holds over 100 U.S. patents, among them a series that is the foundation of the multibillion-dollar LCD industry. The Wakenda, Missouri, native invented the first practical uses of liquid crystals. A former associate director of the Liquid Crystal Institute at Kent State University in Ohio, today he is an independent inventor.

A year after his call, we were in production overseas, samples of the bottle had been shown to the trade, and purchase orders were landing. Amazingly, we went on to sell over 2 million bottles before the company ran out of gas. Harvey expanded the line into spiral-grip juice bottles, spill-proof cups, fork and spoon sets, comb and brush sets, and so forth. This is what happens when a great product concept meets a great product champion and marketer like Harvey.

Here was a product that had no home. Then a small company made us some money with it. Unfortunately, the company was undercapitalized and unable to take the bottle all the way. I recall that some retailers asked to see the bottle in a certain type of packaging, and the company did not have the money to comp up the packages, the product's success notwithstanding. But we were always paid, if not on time, then soon after the contract called for payment. And a product that might never have seen the light of day made us some money and gave us the satisfaction all inventors get when they see their products on the market.

Here are some of the most salient issues to consider when you look at a small company:

Small companies may give your baby tender loving care because it is likely more important there than at the large company. Large companies eat like elephants and, to put it politely, evacuate like sparrows. They always have back-up product in development, and if one product hits a snag, rather than solve the problem, someone may kill your item and pick up a new one that is easier to develop.

Small companies frequently need the inventor and tend to embrace his or her assistance. Large companies sometimes look at the inventor like a hitchhiker with pets. I have lost track of how many times I have put together the development team for a particular product. In some cases, I have even found the manufacturer for my licensee.

Small companies with aggressive leadership are decisive. There's less molasses of process and *administrivia* and other paperwork. I have seen smaller companies move like a raven on road kill while the large company misses the meal. After all, at the larger companies, process often comes before product, more so today than in years past.

Small companies mold opinion while larger companies are busy measuring it. You may be familiar with what is called the paralysis of analysis.

411

The Inventor Assistance Program (IAP; formerly Office of Independent Inventor Programs) reports directly to the Commissioner, and provides invaluable assistance and a direct channel to the highest levels of the USPTO. IAP is managed by John Calvert (571-272-4983). He is supported by Cathie Kirik (571-272-8040). They are consummate pros and inventor advocates. IAP organizes online chats between inventors and senior USPTO officials. To see if a chat is coming up or see if there is an event of interest to you, check out www.uspto.gov. In 2009, IAP hosted more than 50 web-based teleconferences. If you are a member of an inventor group or university and would like to take part in such a teleconference, contact John or Cathie, or check out www.uspto.gov/web/offices/com/iip/index.htm.

So What's the Answer?

When all is said and done, there is no one correct answer. Even when a company does everything right and the planets align, products fail. Therefore, what I look for in companies—whatever their size—is that they apply their best efforts to develop, market, and sell my product, in commercial quantities, and under terms and conditions that are fair and equitable to both sides.

Both large and small companies can be, as they say in Texas, all hat, no cattle. Both types of companies have disappointed me, just as I've been surprised and delighted by them, too.

Public Companies vs. Private Companies

When it comes to public versus private, I have no preference. Your decision should be based on what is best for your product and the integrity of the company's management. Maintain the frame of mind that you are evaluating the company, not that you're in the inferior position and the company is considering you and your product.

Once I tore up a proposed license agreement and returned a check in the sum of $10,000 because I had no faith in the integrity of the company's CEO. My instincts are pretty good in this regard. And if someone slips through my defenses, I know my wife, Sheryl, will sound an alarm. Her instincts are awesome.

> **411**
>
> Athena, the Greek goddess of warfare, wisdom, and arts and crafts, was skilled at weaving, embroidery, and spinning. The Ancient Greeks credited her with the invention of the earthenware pot, plough, flute, rake, chariot, ship, ox-yoke, bridle, and trumpet. The aim of Inventive Women is to feature female inventors who embody the spirit of Athena by offering inspirational stories about Canadian women inventors. Check it out at www.inventivewomen.com.

Finding Information on Public Companies

The best place to obtain deep, detailed information on a publicly traded company is the Securities and Exchange Commission (SEC). The independent, bipartisan, quasi-judicial federal agency was created on July 2, 1934, by an act of Congress. It requires a public disclosure of financial and other data about companies whose securities are offered for public sale.

The SEC requires all public companies (except foreign companies and companies with less than $10 million in assets and 500 shareholders) to file registration statements, periodic reports, and other forms electronically. Anyone can access and download this information for free. Go to www.sec.gov to find links to and instructions for searching the EDGAR database. A stock broker can also pull it for you.

You can learn a lot about publicly held companies by perusing a copy of their annual reports. Corporate annual reports are on file with the SEC or can be obtained directly from the company. There is no charge for annual reports that are ordered from a company; if you get annual reports from the SEC, it requires copying, which costs money. Contact the executive in charge of Investor Relations or the senior VP and CFO at the particular company you are researching.

Form 10-K, the most useful of all reports filed with the SEC, reveals the following important tidbits in addition to the registrant's state of business:

- When the company was organized and incorporated

- What the company produces and percentages of sales any one item may be

- How the company markets: via independent sales reps or its own regional staff offices

- Whether it pays royalties, and how much per year

- How much money is spent to advertise and promote its products

- Details on design and development

- Significant background on production capabilities

- Whether the company is involved in any legal proceedings

- An accurate picture of the competition

> **Notable Quotables**
>
> Good companies respond quickly to change; great companies create change.
>
> —Robert Kriegel and David Brandt, co-authors, *Sacred Cows Make the Best Burgers*

And that's just the tip of the iceberg!

Part 1 of the 10-K reveals, among other things …

How long the company has been in business. What you would expect from an established company may vary from what you would tolerate at a start-up firm.

What the company produces, percentages of sales any one item constitutes, seasonal/nonseasonal, and so on. It is critical to have a complete picture of the company's products, its strengths and markets, and any seasonality or other restrictions.

How the company markets, such as via independent representatives or regional staff offices. It is important to know how a company gets something on the market and where the sales staff loyalty is. For example, company employees typically have more loyalty than independent sales reps who handle more than one company's line.

Whether it pays royalties and how much per year. You can often see how much work is done with outside developers and whether it licenses anything. An example of such wording is this from a 10-K: "We review several thousand ideas from professionals outside the Company each year." Another reads, "The Company is actively planning to expand its business base as a licenser of its products." Such statements show that doors are open!

How much the company spends to advertise and promote product. If yours will require heavy promotion and the company does not promote, you may be at the wrong place. It is counterproductive to take promotional products to companies that do not promote.

Details on design and development. You should know before approaching a company whether an internal design and development group exists and what its strength is. I found one 10-K in which a company stated, "Management believes that expansion of its R&D department will reduce expenses associated with the use of independent designers and engineers and enable the Company to exert greater control over the design and quality of its products." It could not be more obvious that outside inventors were not wanted.

Fast Facts

Fiscal year 2008 saw a record number of federal trademark applications filed at the USPTO: approximately 268,000 applications comprising 390,000 classes. This represents a record rate of filing; 96.9 percent of all applications were filed electronically.

Significant background on production capabilities. It is valuable to know in advance the company's in-house production capabilities and what its outsourcing experiences are in your field of invention. It is no use taking a technology to a company that does not have experience making it.

Whether the company is involved in any lawsuits. You may not want to go with a manufacturer that is being sued. Maybe it has just risen from a bankruptcy. All this kind of information is an excellent indicator of corporate health.

The ownership of certain beneficial owners and management. This gives you the pecking order and power structure. You will see who owns how much stock (including family members), and what percentage this represents. Age and years with the company are also shown.

Competition. This will give you a frank assessment of the company's competition and its ability to compete. One 10-K I read admitted, "The Company competes with many larger, better-capitalized companies in design and development …." It is unlawful to paint a rosy picture when it doesn't exist. The 10-K is one of the few places you can get an accurate picture of the company's competitiveness. Consider whether you would want to license a product to a company that states, for example, "Most of the Company competitors have financial resources, manufacturing capability, volume, and marketing expertise which the Company does not have." This signals that you should check out the competition.

Bright Ideas

Check out these mothers of invention: Mary Anderson patented windshield wipers in 1903. Melita Bentz invented the Melita Automatic Drip Coffee Maker in 1908. Josephine Cochrane patented a dishwasher in 1914. Hattie Alexander found the cure for meningitis in the 1930s. Lise Meitner discovered and named nuclear fission in 1939. Marion Donovan patented the first disposable diaper in 1951. Helen G. Gonet invented an electronic Bible in 1984.

I think the 10-K is the most useful of all SEC filings. This form is filed within 90 days after the end of the company's fiscal year and remains on file at the SEC for 10 years.

Private Companies

No regulations require private companies to fill out the kinds of revealing reports public companies do. You will not have details about private companies at your fingertips like you do with public ones. But by digging, you can come up with some useful stuff. Here are some questions I try to get answers to before talking to a private company:

Is the company a corporation, partnership, or sole proprietorship? This can have legal ramifications from the standpoint of liabilities the licensee assumes. A lawyer can advise you on the pluses and minuses of each situation.

When was it organized or incorporated? If a corporation, in which state is it registered? When a company was organized will give you some idea of its experience. The more years in business, the more tracks in the sand. The state in which it is registered will tell you where you may have to go to sue it.

> ### Bright Ideas
>
> The telescope was accidentally discovered in 1698 when Dutch eyeglass maker Hans Lippershey held one lens in front another and realized that the image was magnified.

Who are the owners, partners, and officers? Always know with whom you are going into business. In the end, companies are people—not just faceless institutions.

What are the bank and credit references? How a company pays its bills is important, for obvious reasons, and its capital base is worth assessing.

Is the manufacturer the source for raw material? Does it fabricate? This helps estimate a company's capabilities for bringing your invention to the marketplace.

How many plants does the company own (lease) and total square footage? Warehouses? This kind of information will help complete the corporate picture.

What products are currently manufactured or distributed? Do not waste time pitching companies that do not manufacture your type of invention. Maybe a company you thought to be a manufacturer is really only a distributor.

How does the company distribute? Find out about the direct sales force. Make inquiries concerning outside sales reps and jobbers (wholesalers). Does the company use mail order, house-to-house, mass marketing, or another form of distribution? This will quickly reveal how a company delivers product and whether its system is appropriate for your concept. With a mass-market item, it would be foolish to approach a door-to-door marketer, regardless of its success.

Answers may come from a combination of sources, ranging from state incorporation records to interviews with competition, suppliers, stores (as appropriate), Internet sources, and the owners themselves. Finding the answers requires digging, but this background information may be critical to your long-term success.

Where to Find Product and Corporate Profiles

You can get background information on a company and its product in many ways. Here are some of them:

Online data banks. ThomasNet® not only rocks for tracking down components for a prototype or a particular manufacturing source, but it is one of the best and most comprehensive sources for corporate profiles. Visit www.thomasnet.com to get *free* industrial market trends and news about product introductions.

Hoover's. A D&B (Dunn & Bradstreet) company, Hoover's (www.hoovers.com) offers profiles and data on 32,000 companies and 37,000 people.

Standard & Poor's. If your focus is on the financial condition of a public company, you can gain access to a range of information on thousands of companies through S&P's website (www.standardandpoors.com). These snapshots provide a great deal of information, including names of top corporate officers. Standard & Poor's is a division of the McGraw-Hill Companies.

Also online, try Dow Jones (www.dowjones.com), OneSource (www.onesource.com), and ZoomInfo (www.zoominfo.com) for corporate lowdown.

The abbreviation *Inc.* after a company name is not significant. Nice offices, a few secretaries, a fax machine, a copier, and computers do not a successful company make.

411

Check out these websites, which are among the best about inventors and inventions for children: www.historyworld.net/wrldhis/PlainTextHistories. asp?historyid=ab23, www.designboom.com/history/useless.html, www.cbc4kids.ca/general/the-lab/history-of-invention/default.html, web.mit.edu/invent, www.kidinfo.com/American_History/Inventors_Inventions.html, www.ti.com/corp/docs/company/history/tihistory.shtml, www.inventornet.com, www.uspto.gov/go/kids, and www.invention.smithsonian.org/home.

After you have read all the literature and investigated the company inside and out, you must ask yourself these questions: Can the company deliver? And will you be comfortable working with its people?

Brand Licensing: Another Way to Say "Opportunity"

Licensing is not only the act of granting or leasing rights to a piece of legally protected *intellectual property*, e.g., an invention, design, image, or trademark.

def•i•ni•tion

Intellectual property is anything that can be patented, trademarked, or copyrighted—any idea.

It also signifies the imprinting of a brand, character, logo, signature, design, personality, or highly recognizable entertainment property on a product for the purpose of heightening its awareness or sales.

The Brandwashing of America

Over the past 30 years, brand licensing has exploded. I recall attending the first licensing show in 1980. It was held in a couple rooms at the New York Hilton. In 2010, this show, now called the Licensing International Expo, was held at the Mandalay Bay Convention Center in Las Vegas, Nevada, where consumer product manufacturers, retailers, brand and property owners, licensing agents, business development executives, marketing executives, and promotional strategists from more than 80 countries attended. It has grown into the largest show for licensing in the world. More than 500 exhibitors touted 7,000 brands and properties in a wide range of categories. For the most current show dates, check out www.licensingexpo.com.

The total worldwide retail sales of licensed merchandise surpass $190 billion, according to a report compiled by the editors of *License! Global* magazine.

So What Does This Mean to You?

In the current risk-averse business environment, companies are staying close to home and opting to sell products under recognizable licenses, or extend their own well-known house brands internally and through outlicensing. "Licensing is the god now," says inventor Jim McCafferty, president of JMP Creative. "We have to figure out how to make the gods happy."

To survive in an atmosphere of economic despondency and a fragmented retail marketplace, think about inventing specifically for a brand and be prepared to take a smaller piece of the pie.

If your new product or enhancement of an existing product is wed to an existing licensed brand, a licensee will reduce your royalty because there is a maximum royalty load any product can support. If a 5 percent royalty is being paid on an item or a line, for example, and you bring in a new product or an enhancement to an existing product, the company will probably ask you to take less to accommodate your royalty. In many cases, such eventualities are already covered by a license agreement. If a company is already paying an intellectual property (ip) owner 5 percent, it is very doubtful that another 5 percent would ever be added for you. But take heart: 1 percent can be a lot of money on certain products.

If a product is paying no inventor royalty but is well known, a company may give you less than a standard royalty. For example, in the toy business, a standard inventor royalty is 5 percent of net wholesale, but not on an existing brand unless what you bring to the party is guaranteed to boost sales. If you bring in a promotable feature that Hasbro wants for Transformers, it might offer 2 percent. But it might give Lucas 25 percent or more for the *Star Wars* license. Everything is negotiable.

You can make a good living inventing for existing brands, but it will take a different approach to the business. You will need to study the marketplace and see if any of your ideas can be applied in whole or part to an already successful brand.

Going to the Source; Inventing to the Source

One way to approach this opportunity is for you, as the product inventor, to go directly to the brand and make a deal to tie the brand into your concept. Then take the package to a potential licensee.

In 1998, I tracked down and telephoned *Men Are from Mars, Women Are from Venus* author John Gray and struck a deal for us to create a board game and license it. I saw this as a sleeping giant of an opportunity. No game publisher had yet approached Dr. Gray. Had a publisher first gone to him, there would have been no room for an inventor royalty. The game company would have done the game in-house or on a work-for-hire basis with a freelance talent. But I pitched the idea prepackaged to Hasbro and Mattel, and Mattel made us an offer we could not refuse. The game sold more than 1 million units.

I put together similar win-win-win deals creating products such as Duncan yo-yo key chains and board games based on Uncle Milton's Ant Farm, Martin Luther King Jr., *Jeopardy!* winner Ken Jennings, and Magnetic Poetry, to name a few.

Prolific Chicago inventor Jeff Breslow once saw an opportunity to compete with Monopoly, published by Parker Brothers. He went to real estate tycoon Donald Trump and secured his interest in a Trump real estate game. Jeff licensed the game to Parker's rival, Milton Bradley. He also did a Planet Hollywood game, among others, using this business model.

A couple years ago, working with a team of associates, we developed and patented a front-loading, battery-operated extruder for cake frosting. We positioned it as an alternative to the popular pastry decorating bag. Rather than attempt to license it as a stand-alone product, we approached Hasbro, manufacturer of the Easy Bake Oven, and pitched it as a brand extension. Hasbro licensed the concept and named it the Easy Bake Decorating Sensation Frosting Pen.

In 2010, a version of this concept for moms and professional bakers was introduced by Kuhn Rikon, a Swiss company known for high-quality kitchen tools.

Opportunities Abound

On its website, HP indicates it is actively looking for partners with products that can benefit from its brand. The notice reads, in part: "HP's Brand Licensing Program invites companies with innovative and exciting solutions to share in the power, prestige, and pull of the HP brand. We are looking for unique, customized, and specialty opportunities to enhance the HP customer experience."

Over at IBM, there is also an interest in such opportunities. On its website, a notice reads, in part: "IBM has an active brand licensing program. IBM is willing to consider licensing an IBM trademark for use with suitable complementary products in exchange for appropriate compensation."

Some companies use outside agencies to sort through and manage licensing opportunities. The Beanstalk Group, as one example, represents a wide range of marks such as L.L. Bean, Proctor & Gamble, Purina, Samsonite, Volvo, The Stanley Works, the U.S. Army, and Harley-Davidson, Inc., to name a few.

So as you come up with ideas, pay attention to which existing brands your ideas may compliment, and go after the intellectual property owners. If the brand owner does not want to license your idea itself, the company may put you in touch with a licensee that would consider your product.

Licensing is here to stay. Embrace it. Give yourself an added edge.

The Least You Need to Know

- Just because a company gives a successful image doesn't mean there is steak under the sizzle.

- Get business references, especially from inventors who have licensed products to your prospects.

- Attend trade shows and conferences to better understand your industry, its products, and technologies, and meet potential licensees.

- Be sure the companies you approach are really worth the effort.

- Default to the company with which you are most comfortable working.

- Dress your invention for success. See how it looks in a license.

Chapter 7

Knock. Knock. Buy My Invention, Please!

In This Chapter

♦ Getting your foot in the door

♦ Only fools rush in

♦ Pick your targets

♦ A look at the corporate culture

> For every entrepreneur-inventor like Aaron Lapin and his Reddi-Wip, there are hundreds of thousands of engineers working away daily at institutionalized inventing, and countless pauper-inventors twisting pieces of wire into shapes that will never see a merchant's shelf …. But the free-enterprise system holds out the opportunity for those who wish to take it.
>
> —Henry Petroski for *The Wall Street Journal*

Have you decided yet whether you want to go with my *modus operandi* and license your concepts to a manufacturer or start your own company to develop, produce, and bring them to market? If you want to raise venture capital (a.k.a. vulture capital), skip now to Parts 4 and 5 on how to protect your intellectual property. Then, if you need training, find a nearby university or adult education center where you can learn how to raise venture capital.

To learn about state and federal programs, call the Small Business Administration's toll-free National Answer Desk at 1-800-827-5722, or visit www.sba.gov to read "A Venture Capital Primer for Small Business," by LaRue Tone Hosmer, a professor at the University of Michigan's Graduate School of Business Administration.

On the other hand, if you want to license product, stay where you are and read on. This chapter focuses on the process of licensing inventions that can throw off royalty income. Licensing offers a target-rich environment and, in my opinion, a far less-stressful business model. In the end, I have found that licensing has given my family and me a wonderful lifestyle.

But know going in that, whichever path you take, it won't be easy. The road to success is always under construction.

First Impressions

You cannot present your invention until you get through the door. And this action, by its high visibility, becomes an integral part of your presentation.

If you have never dealt with a company, you're a stranger and, as such, untested. You will stand out. So do it right, and you will always be welcome. Mess it up, and it could haunt you into the future. First impressions are lasting impressions.

Fast Facts

Here are the top 10 companies awarded U.S. patents in 2008: International Business Machines (4,186 patents—and the first organization to break the 4,000 patent barrier), Samsung (3,515 patents), Canon (2,114), Microsoft (2,030), Intel (1,776), Matsushita (1,745), Toshiba (1,609), Fujitsu (1,494), Sony (1,485), and Hewlett-Packard (1,424). All told, that's 21,378 patents awarded to the 10 companies. Impressive.

While your mission is, of course, to sell your invention, you are always selling yourself first. Don't ever lose sight of this fact. Your credibility is more critical than any invention because few people will put their career on the line for a person whom they do not trust or whom they feel is capable of delivering the goods. Loose cannons can cause unpredictable and indiscriminate damage to livelihoods.

Your first concern must be how you will be perceived. Even if you are capable of dreaming up innovative product, without a delivery system, nothing will happen. If you cannot command respect from corporate management (or investors), your inventions will never be taken seriously—if at all. You cannot put a dollar value on your ability to make an encore presentation. *Stop! Look! Listen!* Give considerable thought and attention to how you're going to get yourself through the door. Do not take it lightly, because this initial stage sets the tone for future discussion. Images will be engraved into psyches. This undertaking requires imagination, experience, and the ability to think out the ramifications of future moves before making them. Like a game of chess, the process resembles war, in that it consists of attack and defense—and your ultimate object is to make the king surrender.

Anyone can get a company's attention if he or she is willing to pay the price. If it is not done in the right way, the price can be steep. It takes a very talented person with a unique concept to gain access and then be invited for lunch, dinner, and, if you are really good, an overnight stay, so to speak. Getting inside is one thing, but the amount of time you hold this position separates the amateurs from the pros.

> **Notable Quotables**
>
> The fact is that one new idea leads to another, that to a third, and so on through a course of time until someone, with whom no one of these ideas was original, combines all together, and produces what is justly called a new invention.
>
> —Thomas Jefferson, director of the first U.S. Patent Board

By the time you finish reading this book, it is my hope that you'll possess the knowledge required to not only be invited inside to show your product, but also become part of the corporate family and a trusted creative resource.

The N.I.H. Syndrome

Not every company welcomes outside submissions. Many companies do not want to see anything from independent inventors. The *Not Invented Here* (*N.I.H.*) *Syndrome* is very much alive and well in American industry. It is an established management pathology.

Consider Apple, for instance. The company makes no bones about not wanting to see outside submissions. On its website it warns, in part:

> Please do not submit any unsolicited ideas, original creative artwork, suggestions or other works in any form to Apple or any of its employees. The sole purpose of this policy is to avoid potential misunderstandings or disputes when Apple's products or marketing strategies might seem similar to ideas submitted to Apple. If, despite our request that you not send us your ideas, you still submit them, then regardless of what your letter says, the following terms shall apply to your submissions.

Terms of Idea Submission

You agree that: (1) your submissions and their contents will automatically become the property of Apple, without any compensation to you; (2) Apple may use or redistribute the submissions and their contents for any purpose and in any way; (3) there is no obligation for Apple to review the submission; and (4) there is no obligation to keep any submissions confidential.

This notice notwithstanding, I know people who have had audiences to show product to Apple's senior management. Clearly this harsh warning is to wave off the great unwashed. If you have the "know who," you will be seen. And obviously, this policy does not refer to iPhone apps, which Apple encourages.

Companies have many reasons for this situation. A lot of the resistance comes from selfish self-interests. "If you have a 100-person R&D department spending millions of dollars a year and a lone inventor comes along with a better idea, it makes it harder to justify your department to your boss," Michael Odza, publisher of *Technology Access Report*, told *The Wall Street Journal*. Woody Freelander, a former director of marketing and licensing at Union Carbide Corporation, has another take on the problem. He feels that if a corporation reviews and then rejects a submission, it opens itself for potential lawsuits if the company ever does something akin to the submission, even if what it does is not influenced by the submission. He adds that being so careful "may insulate corporations from lawsuits, but it also insulates them from great ideas."

Some companies are N.I.H. only in select areas and are open to ideas in others. On its website, IBM states particular areas it does not want inventors to address. IBM will not consider the following submission types because they are impractical to evaluate:

- Advertising, slogans, sales promotions, or public relations

- Algorithms, mathematical formulas, or theories

- Marketing and other business methods

- Applications and procedures for using IBM products

- Broad concepts still to be developed

- Type styles, type elements, and keyboard arrangements

- Features or functions available on other products

- Manuscripts, books, manuals, research papers, theses, and other similar documents

- Ideas for computer programs

- Suggested changes to computer programs

- Niche markets—low-volume, higher-cost products aimed at very specific markets

Nonetheless, in my experience, if you have a trusted relationship with a power in senior management, companies are always open to hearing about opportunities to make more money. "Do Not Enter" signs are really to protect the company from uninvited submissions.

For many years, *World Book* paid no attention to my proposals for a line of educational learning aides under its trademark. Then one of my closest friends became publisher of the encyclopedia. I resurfaced the idea, and he said, "Go do it."

When I come into an N.I.H. environment and I have no powerful advocate inside, I find a connection or I go elsewhere. It is the company's loss. There are too many potential licensees for me to waste time on people or companies that don't want to see me or appreciate the potential of the business opportunities in my bag.

Choosing Your Target and Making Your Mark

Once you have decided which companies to approach, pick out a target and a point of entry. Depending on how the company is organized, entry could be via senior management, legal, research and development, marketing, an outside consultant, or anywhere in between. Every company is different. Hit the wrong target, and it could result in wasted time, review and comment by the wrong people, rejection, or worse.

Common to all situations is that you have to approach a company as if planning a first-time military operation.

To sell an idea is to engage in warfare (me again with my military metaphors). It is a battle of wits and nerves to convince a stranger to open a door and invite you inside. It is a battle to get the stranger to listen, invite colleagues to listen, and then ask you back for a reprise. It is a battle to get anyone—friend or stranger—to take on the challenge of a new and untested invention; make a financial commitment; work like the devil to overcome growing pains inherent in any development cycle; and then manufacture, test, market, and sell your item.

Corporate jobs are at stake. Careers are on the line. The harder the challenge, the more commitment is required. The natural tendency of people is to take the easy way out, which may mean to deep-six your product before it can be called a failure. No one likes to fail, but that's especially true for executives if their company has no tolerance for failure and they will not be rewarded for success. Unless the executive has something to gain, such as a bonus, raise, or other benefit, why rock the boat? Those experienced in corporate culture know that 1 *gotcha* cancels out 100 *attaboys*.

There are three basic approaches to warfare: direct attack, compromise, and retreat. Anything less than direct attack isn't worth the energy. No one has ever won a battle who was willing to compromise before a shot was fired.

Try to deal with people who have responsibility and decision-making power over product acquisition. You won't know who this is within any particular company until you do your intelligence gathering. Finding people who are authorized to say "no" is easy. You need to reach people who have the power to say "yes."

"Never be afraid to talk to the right people, regardless of how big and unreachable they may appear," says independent inventor Ken Thorne, creator of the Zephyr cooking system. These people may not be the company's president or CEO, and usually are not. Great leaders allow their people to do their jobs. This is why they were hired. If the idea survives the internal review process, sooner or later it will reach the front office.

Now, once you have built relationships, if you feel a decision has been made that's wrong, you may consider taking it to a higher authority. I have frequently done this. Sometimes I am successful; more often I am not able to turn a negative decision around. But I am appealing to friends and do it in a very professional manner. I begin every pitch with something like, "In matters controversial, my position's well defined; I always see both points of view, the one that's wrong and mine."

Experience does dictate, however, that you should not put too much faith in people who just ferry product submissions back and forth between points in a building. These folks, while perhaps very nice people—some may even have vice presidential stripes— are tossed into the fray by their bosses as cannon fodder. They are typically so far removed from the main theater of operation that they need a road map to find the president's office. And even if they can find it, they do not have his or her ear.

Be polite, respectful, and friendly to the supporting cast. But you need to know upon whom to spend your personal capital and energies. Screen actors learn not to waste their energy on wide shots, but to conserve their most emotional performances for close-ups, especially extreme close-ups. It's no different when you are presenting product.

> **411**
>
> USA.gov is an awesome website where you can access all corners of the federal government. At this cutting-edge site, you can browse a wealth of information—everything from researching intellectual property (ip) at the Library of Congress to tracking R&D at national laboratories.

The Corporate Culture

The people most successful at getting through the door and building relationships are those with previous corporate experience, because they can relate to and empathize with executives. The corporate culture is quite different from anything most independent inventors have ever experienced. It is rife with dynamic inaction and optimization of the status quo. As author James Boren put it, people in bureaucracies can devitalize ideas with deft thrusts of *yesbuttism*s and forthright *avoidism*s.

If an executive does not return your calls, don't take it personally. He or she is probably on overload. Your time will come. Many amateur inventors take this personally. If someone who has become a close friend tries to hammer you in a deal, don't take it to heart. This person is just following orders. Time and time again, those with whom I am closest are sent in to do battle.

People who have not worked in executive management usually do not have a clue what corporate types have to deal with on a daily basis. It isn't easy, and the last thing they want is some inventor who thinks there is a troll under every bridge.

Lookin' to Hook 'Em

You need a hook, one beyond the appropriateness of the invention you are hawking. I like to look at an executive's background for some connection to me—where he or she grew up, went to school, or spent summer holidays, along with common interests, and so on. If I can find this out before our first meeting, all the better. It just might help me get the meeting.

I have lost count of how many times I have been able to break the ice through some connection. At one company, I actually found a distant cousin through marriage. I use a variety of sources:

Fast Facts

National Science Foundation studies consistently show that small companies introduce, on average, 2½ times as many innovations per employee as large companies.

Internet search engines. Three of my favorites are Google.com, Bing.com, and Dogpile.com.

Who's Who. There are many versions of this directory, including *Marquis Who's Who in America, Who's Who in Manufacturing, Who's Who in Entertainment, Who's Who in the East*, and so on. In addition to detailed biographical and career information such as schools, birthplace, names of spouses and children, government service, awards, and so forth, I have even found home addresses.

Annual reports/websites. Public companies frequently run bio sketches of senior management. These can be found on company websites; via stockbrokers; through the SEC (www.sec.gov), Hoover's (www.hoovers.com), ZoomInfo (www.zoominfo.com), OneSource (www.onesource.com), or Dow Jones (www.dowjones.com); and so on.

Industry associations. If the executive is an officer of an industry group, the organization will likely have his or her background information.

Media archives. I love to run names through Lexus/Nexus or another full-text news information service.

Trade publications. Often magazines specific to an industry interview or otherwise profile a person. While these articles are not heavy with personal information, I can get great insights into a person from a good interview.

You need the company, or you would not be there. So while it's important that you show yourself as independently creative, take the *we* approach, not the *I* approach. There is no *i* in the word *team*, and companies function through teamwork. The faster the invention goes from *my concept* to *our concept*, the better.

Sign on the Dotted Line

Many companies will ask that a submission agreement (or nondisclosure agreement, or NDA) be signed before they will review outside ideas. This may surface when you first approach the company or on the day you make the formal presentation. I rarely have had a problem with such requests. I always know with whom I am dealing and feel confident in the relationship. If I did not, I wouldn't be there in the first place.

I recall my presentation of Star Bird, our electronic toy spaceship, at Milton Bradley in 1978. I was asked to sign a nonconfidentiality form and replied, "Okay. I'll do it because you're too big a company to rip us off, and we are too little to worry about it." We went on to build a relationship that still exists today with current management 32 years later.

The best way to handle this eventuality is to have the document faxed or e-mailed to you in advance. This way you can at least verify what you are being asked to sign and can suggest modifications, if required. If you are uncertain about the language, consult an intellectual property attorney.

Even if you sign such a document, it does not give the company *carte blanche* to steal your idea. In some states, the law of torts affords limited protection to the owner of a *trade secret* (see Chapter 19) for the misappropriation of his or her ideas. Not all ideas are trade secrets. In fact, most of what you may be sharing in your meeting would be covered by the submission agreement.

Some inventors go for a *quid pro quo*, i.e., if they sign the company's NDA, they expect the company to sign their agreement. Do what makes you comfortable. Many companies have no problem reciprocating in this way.

def•i•ni•tion

A **trade secret** is a plan or process, tool, mechanism, or compound known only to its owner and people to whom it is necessary to confide it.

A suspicious attitude may seriously inhibit your progress. Put your time and energies into creating concepts versus overprotecting them. Become paranoid over this, beyond what is reasonable caution, and no one will ever see your ideas.

Inventions Wanted

Kellogg's is looking for *Gr-r-reat* Ideas (and innovations). The company describes a *Big Idea* as a new product idea, recipe, or suggestion for improving the food or packaging performance of a current Kellogg product. A *Great Innovation* may be a new product that's partially or fully developed and could be ready to launch quickly; a proposed business collaboration; or a patented food, packaging, or processing technology that may have application for Kellogg. Go to www2.kelloggs.com/greatideas for the details.

The Least You Need to Know

- First impressions are lasting impressions.

- Plan your approach and entrance very carefully.

- If you don't understand the corporate culture, team with someone who has the experience. Rookie moves can get you thrown out at first.

- Look out for number 1, but don't step in number 2.

- Don't freak out over signing nondisclosure agreements.

- Life's a pitch!

Chapter 8

Turning a Proposal into a Marriage

In This Chapter

- Flaunt the truth
- Now presenting … you—and your ideas
- Putting together a great proposal
- Shotgunning proposals to various companies
- Start strong, end stronger

> The truth isn't the truth until people believe you, and they can't believe you if they don't know what you're saying, and they can't know what you're saying if they don't listen to you, and they won't listen to you if you're not interesting, and you won't be interesting unless you say things imaginatively, originally, freshly.
>
> —Bill Bernbach, legendary advertising executive

Life's a pitch! And nowhere does a pitch need more energy than when it comes to new product concepts. The pitch not only has to be powerful and efficacious, but it needs post-pitch propulsion (PPP)—the ability to survive long after you have departed. And above all, it must be honest.

Honesty Is the *Only* Policy

A little B.S. is okay. After all, it takes some fertilizer to make beautiful flowers. And it is part of the entertainment factor. Seasoned execs have B.S. meters and will let you know if you start to pin their needles or redline. But this is a business, and a lot is riding on decisions, so make it the truth, the whole truth, and nothing but the truth, please.

When you were a child, you were taught that honesty is the best policy. I'd make these words by Cervantes stronger: honesty is the *only* policy. It does not pay to be less than totally up front. If you think that by hiding or fudging a flaw or fact about an invention's origin, ownership, technology, and so forth, you are avoiding a problem that might break the deal, you are so wrong. If you are not honest up front, you are asking for trouble down the line.

Full and honest disclosure makes for smoother sailing. No one likes surprises, especially licensees after they have made an investment. On the other hand, no one expects your product to be perfect. Every rose has a thorn.

I cannot guarantee that your candor will be met by the same level of honesty from the other side, but in the end, your reputation will be all the stronger for it. Your reputation, by the way, will have more to do with your success than your concepts. You can take this fact to the bank.

You Should Hear a Pin Drop

When you are pitching, and doing it well, you should have the rapt attention of everyone within your cry and gaze. If you do, telephones will not be answered, incoming Blackberry messages will not distract, and eyes will not glaze over with ennui. You will have them in the proverbial palm of your hand. How do you accomplish that? Let's review some pointers.

Get a face-to-face appointment to show your idea. Never send in a model or prototype unless there is no other way to do it. Products are best demonstrated by their inventors, and questions can quickly be answered.

Get as high up the corporate product review food chain as possible. Lots of people can say "no." Only a few can say "yes," and you want them at the pitch.

Unless the reviewer knows you well, begin the meeting briefing on your most significant accomplishments and any other personal choice morsels that might help set the scene and make the audience more receptive.

While inventors are passionate about their brainchild, offer up some objective information about the concept. This might include the results of focus group testing, patent searches, competitive product data, etc.

Make the presentation professional. If you want to operate in today's marketplace, you need to exhibit to your audience that you are in step with it.

Bright Ideas
"Be it known that I, Harry Houdini, a citizen of the United States, and a resident of New York City, borough of Brooklyn, in the county of Kings, in the State of New York, have invented a new and improved diver's suit ...." So began the specification of Patent No. 1,370,316 issued on March 1, 1921, to the famous magician and escape artist.

If you hit a snag, think fast. Many times a manufacturer will say to me, just as I am getting into a presentation, that the product is not right for the company. This is when you need to be even more inventive and see if, through some modification, you can make the item fit.

If the potential licensee is on the fence after you have completed your dog-and-pony show, offer to continue to work on speculation. This can keep the product alive and get the manufacturer invested. It increases the likelihood of the product getting a curtain call.

Finally, always have a call to action when you wrap up the meeting. Everyone needs to know what happens next and who does what. Chances for a sale at the pitch session are rare (although not impossible). Typically, manufacturers like to bring back good ideas for different people within the company to opine. As you will learn, if you do not know it already, falling in love and getting to the altar are quite different experiences.

Bright Ideas
In 1989, Tomima Edmark, a 36-year-old marketing rep for IBM, saw a woman in a movie theater sporting a French twist hair-do. She turned to her mom and wondered aloud if it was possible to turn a ponytail inside out. Soon after that epiphany, Edmark made a prototype from circular knitting needles and started testing it with friends. The results were beyond positive. Women loved it. Topsy Tail, one of the most successful hairstyling products, was born and ultimately brought in over $80 million in global sales.

Covering Every Base When You Pitch

Once you are no longer in the spotlight and everyone has returned to their desks, all kinds of disparate forces come into play. The idea you presented may not even be remembered shortly thereafter, prototypes and videos notwithstanding. When it is time to show your submission to a wider audience—a day, five days, or even a few weeks hence—to people who did not get to see your original presentation and feel your passion, watch out. This is when products frequently start circling the drain—or worse, get sucked down it. This is where the product needs PPP (post-pitch propulsion)!

Charlie Brower, an inductee to the Advertising Hall of Fame, explains the fragility of a new idea. "A new idea is delicate," he says. "It can be killed by a sneer or a yawn; it can be stabbed to death by a quip and worried to death by a frown on the right man's brow."

I was the new product acquisition consultant to a public company a few years ago. My assignment was to sweep across the country, accompanied by the vice president for R&D, meet with inventors, and bring back appropriate product for the company's marketing department to consider. I recall how, on more than one occasion, when it came time to present a particular product, we would look at each other in hopes that the other guy remembered how to operate it. If the inventor had provided a *background binder* or video, we were off to the races. But when we had nothing to refresh our collective memory, we took the product off the table. We would reschedule to give the inventor time to supply us with a video and instructional information, but it was never as advantageous the second time around. When you make that first pitch, be sure you cover every base.

Background Binders

If you don't have computer skills, present written material about your product in three-ring binders or folders, the kind that have cover and spine pockets. These notebooks become one-stop information sources for you and the executives. Binders are available at any office supply store in a large selection of colors and sizes.

Design a cover page, and use tabs to separate sections. Be sure every product submission is accompanied by its own background package. This can take many forms, but typically I favor a written proposal (more on this coming right up) plus marker renderings, if appropriate, and a video.

Presentation Software

My preferred method is dynamic and great-looking presentations using leading presentation software applications such as Microsoft PowerPoint, Adobe Persuasion, Harvard Graphics, and Lotus Freelance. Companies are more accepting of these kinds of presentations, given the impactful nature of the technology. Software-based elements do not necessarily take the place of written material, but they can make a killer enhancement to a background binder and prototype. These presentations can also be printed and distributed as hard copies.

We built a PowerPoint pitch for a line of travel games. We took a digital video of our prototype, the centerpiece of which is a unique randomizer, and embedded a video link to it in a panel. It was visually very exciting. I remember when we used marker renderings on white paper mounted to Bristol board. That seems like such a long time ago. At Richard C. Levy & Associates, we've traded in our markers and pencils for bits and bytes, and what we can do in Photoshop is amazing. Art moves forward, and I am eager to see what radical new breeds of technology are coming our way.

Skype

Skype is a software application that lets you make inexpensive domestic and overseas voice calls and free video conferencing over the Internet. We use Skype to show prototypes to each other, to companies, to factories in China, and so forth. If your computer does not have a camera component, you can get one for under $50 and download the software for free.

Just be careful that with all this technology, you present an honest portrayal of your product. Do not oversell the concept in a way that can come back to bite you later. An overly complex or elaborate PowerPoint presentation can overwhelm people. You want your presentation to be slick but not slippery.

Depending on your time and computer skills, you can either learn PowerPoint and Photoshop or hire a computer artist to render the subject matter for you. I have an associate handle the technical side of building the presentations while I produce and create the text. Language is, after all, a critical part of any presentation. To quote Faith Popcorn, a respected forecaster of

Notable Quotables

Don't blame manufacturers for not wanting your invention. They have their own needs; learn what they are.

—Israel Gamzo, inventor

consumer trends: "We wear it [language], show it off and discard it when it's no longer stylish or no longer fits. For that reason the interaction of language and fashion is a particularly fertile growing medium."

The Executive Summary

Every proposal (paper or electronic) I write begins with an executive summary, a paragraph that allows executives to get a quick read on the product and do a gut check. This is a simple paragraph—nothing elaborate—that paints an image of the invention and your objectives.

Here are some examples of an executive summary:

Oops & Downs: The Firehouse Full of Fun plays like a 3-D Chutes & Ladders. The multilevel board game is designed around a toyetic environment that features playing piece figures with internal reeds or other air-activated sound-making devices. The levels are interconnected by vertical or near-vertical tubes of various lengths (depending on the levels connected). Each playing piece figure has a different sound signature when dropped down a tube. Alternatively, the reed/sound-making device may be located in the base of the tube, or connected to the tube in such a way that the air drives not only sound, but also elements, such as a randomizer. The playing pieces can be used as whistles. U.S. patented.

Insecta GigANTica is an anthropomorphic ant habitat designed inside a three-dimensional, injection-molded, plastic representation of a prehistoric beast or other creature.

Switchblade is a pair of training skates that transforms from four-wheel quad (standard configuration) into four-wheel in-line. It is based upon a variable geometry chassis, i.e., a collapsing parallelogram. U.S. patented.

Fast Facts _____

The first North American patent was awarded in 1641. The Massachusetts General Court granted it to Samuel Winslow, a colonist, for a method to extract salt. Many North American patents that issued prior to independence and the formation of the United States were concerned with the manufacture of salt because it was so important in the preservation of foodstuffs.

Categories for Success

Now let's go over the categories (as appropriate) I like to include in a presentation:

Operating instructions. Take nothing for granted. *Nothing!* The worst thing that can happen is an executive's inability to use and/or explain a product after you depart. Do not let the simplicity of your item draw you into a false sense of security. If I were to submit something as simple as a ballpoint pen, I would prepare written, illustrated, and video instructions. No item is fail-safe when you are not there to demo it. It is hard enough to guarantee successful operation when you *are* there.

Marketing plan. Highlight and detail your item's unique features and advantages over existing products. Define its appeal and target audience. Suggest follow-ups, including second-generation product and line extensions, if appropriate. Manufacturers like products that have a future, especially if they are looking at beaucoup start-up dollars in the development and launch phases. You do not need a graduate degree in marketing to work up this kind of information. The more you can do to define the market and positioning of your concept, the better.

Trademarks and slogans. Offer possible trademarks and taglines. I like to suggest everything from word marks to logotypes. If you have conducted a trademark search, include its results or the status of any applications you may have in play. The right mark or slogan can go a long way toward securing a sale. For information on trademark searches, see Chapter 17.

Patents. Before you submit any concept to a manufacturer (or to an investor), conduct a patent search. Include the results of any search, USPTO actions, and so on. If a patent has been issued to you already, submit a copy. For information on patent searches, see Chapter 12.

def•i•ni•tion

A **logotype** is an identifying symbol (as in advertising), sometimes called a logo.

Advertising/publicity. Suggest advertising and publicity hooks. This information, like a good trademark, helps make presentations more persuasive and polished. These hooks are also available to the manufacturer for focus groups.

Video. If a still picture is worth a thousand words, moving images are worth a million words. We do not let anything that features motion out of our studio without a demo video. Playback machines, DVD players, and multimedia framework capable of handling various formats of digital video, media clips, sound, text, animation, music, and interactive panoramic images are on most PCs and laptops. If you cannot be there in person, nothing beats moving pictures.

If the video file is too big to send as an attachment, take advantage of the free service offered by www.mailbigfile.com. You simply upload the file, the recipient receives an e-mail with a link to download your video, and the recipient downloads the file. It is simple.

Some companies do not allow video attachments. In this case, ask the executive if he or she has a personal account you can use. Many people use Google or Yahoo! accounts to receive larger files stopped by their companies. If you know the executive well, you may be invited to send the video material to a personal account.

If security is an issue, send the company the presentation on a DVD and do not transmit it via the Internet.

Don't worry if the camerawork is a bit rough. This can work to your benefit. There is a warm and sincere feel and tone to home-brewed video. If a video is too slick, the viewers may think you are covering up something. Put it all out there, and let the product do its stuff.

In addition to using video as a medium for instructions, we use it to do technical briefings and to show people testing prototypes. Nothing beats showing satisfied consumers. If we have a technical briefing and ideas for a focus group, we might consider submitting two separate shows so two departments do not have to share one tape.

Your worst nightmare is a breakdown in communications. Full-motion audiovisual components added to a presentation help avoid problems.

Technical. In writing and on video media, you should address everything from design, engineering, and manufacturing issues to component sourcing and costing. Include exploded views, part lists, and anything else that will help a corporate research and development designer understand your item's technical and manufacturing profile.

Personal resumé. If you are unknown to the company, provide a background sheet on your capabilities. Depending on the nature of the submission, a green light may hinge on a manufacturer's confidence in your ability to make the product happen, albeit under the company's guidance.

> **Notable Quotables**
>
> There's no such thing as a crackpot inventor. Edison might have been the crackpot of the century ... but his stuff clicked.
>
> —U.S. Patent Commissioner Conway Peyton Coe (1940)

Inventions Wanted

Kraco Enterprises, Inc., specializes in items for the automotive aftermarket, as well as related home, workshop, and garage products for development, license, and retail distribution. Your submissions must have at least a provisional patent application working to be considered. Go to kraco.com/ideas.htm for details.

Getting Technical

When possible, include with your proposal (in the "Technical" section) …

◆ A list of all components with respective prices from various sources. Pricing from three different sources is a good start. Do not forget to include the volume the quotes are based on, plus vendor contacts.

◆ Note the type of material(s) desirable—for example, polyethylene, wood, board, and so on. Provide substitutions and options for consideration.

◆ When you calculate the cost, do not forget to consider the price of assembly (if any). The quoting vendors will be helpful here.

◆ If your item requires retail packaging, add an extra 15 to 30 percent.

◆ Add an extra 20 percent for modifications and losses. At this point, you have the item's hard cost.

◆ To arrive at the manufacturer's selling price, add in your royalty, an amount of money for promotion (if appropriate), and a gross profit margin for the manu-facturer (65 percent would get their attention). You might want to estimate the mark-up at the retail end (if appropriate). A good estimate is the hard cost multi-plied by three or four, or five for a TV-promoted item.

411

Don't cost components and quote work-for-hire fees based on the size of a com-pany. Once I was working on a new game and puzzle line, and an artwork pro-vider put an outrageous fee on reproduction rights. When I tried to get the price down for my licensee, the agent for the artwork said that he was holding firm because the licensee "could afford it." Notwithstanding the fact that our licensee was a multibillion-dollar, multinational company, each product it manufacturers has its own budget, price point, and so on, and must stand on its own. So make your decisions according to the specific product—even then, sometimes it pays in the long run to give a bit. It's worth repeating: pigs get fat; hogs get slaughtered.

Pitching Isn't Enough: Pitch In, Too.

Approach every product submission in such a way that, if you were contracted by the manufacturer, you could take the item outside and do it for them. More manufacturers are relying on inventors to take products to tooling. This was not the case years ago, but with personnel cutbacks and increased workloads, often the only way a product gets done is through the inventor's being able to manage a development program.

And don't expect to be paid for everything you do in this regard. Frequently, other than out-of-pocket expenses, I don't ask for payment. This is always a judgment call.

After we licensed our WarStone™ trading card game to Duncan Toys, I built the outside team to develop and manufacture the product. I found and affected the hire of freelance developers, copy editors, back story writers, an experienced project manager, and even the agent to find us a manufacturer for the components in China. Having been a TV producer in a previous life, I am very comfortable putting together talented teams of pros and helping manage them.

Fast Facts

To patent or not to patent, that is the question. A patent can be a double-edged sword. While it allows the inventor the right to exclude others—for 20 years from the date the application was first filed—from making, using, and selling an innovation, it also makes it public for everyone to see. To get a patent, one must reveal invention. That's why not every inventor seeks patent protection. For example, the Coca-Cola Company prefers to keep its formula secret, receiving some protection under trade secret laws instead of patents.

Multiple Submissions

If you have more than one prototype, and the situation is appropriate, you might want to consider making submissions to more than one potential licensee at the same time. I have no set rule about this. I take it case by case, guided by experience. The decision is made easier for me if I have patent or trademark protection.

If a company asks you to hold off further presentations until it has an opportunity to review the item at greater length, set guidelines. In all fairness, some products require a reasonable number of days to be properly considered. However, if you feel the company is asking for an unreasonable period of time, seek some earnest money to hold the product out of circulation. The amount of time and money is negotiable. Also insist that the product not be shown to anyone outside the company, such as trade buyers.

def•i•ni•tion

A **multiple submission** is a submission by an inventor of the same concept simultaneously to several potential licensees.

The value of the *multiple submission* goes beyond having your idea reviewed by more companies at a faster pace: it may also set up a bidding war. I have done this from time to time, and it is an understood tactic of negotiation. Do not be timid about suggesting it, but do know when and where to do it—and only for special products.

Unfavorable Odds

The odds you are up against are staggering. For example, Mike Hirtle, vice president for product acquisition and inventor relations at Hasbro, says his company sees 3,200 external concepts per year. Of these, on average …

800 are brought in-house.

400 are presented to marketing.

60 to 80 are optioned or licensed.

25 to 35 are taken to market.

6 to 10 are successes.

2 or 3 are *big* successes.

And those numbers don't include the products the company comes up with itself internally and pitches to management.

Other industries are not that heavily bombarded. Once we designed a neat water faucet and found no competition to distract those to whom I pitched, save for the in-house development department. In such instances, companies tend to be all the more conservative. Because their market is steady and loyal, they do not want to do anything that could upset their market share.

Your Champion

For your product to sustain itself through the review and development process, it needs a champion, a white knight. Typically this standard-bearer will come from among those attending your first meeting. This is the person who will be representing your product as it passes from review to review. This is a process that can resemble a flight through the Danzig Corridor at night being tracked by enemy radar and dodging triple-A fire.

It will be the responsibility of this executive to keep you up-to-date on the progress of review. Try to get a schedule. No manufacturer should be allowed an open-ended time frame. Parameters need to be set before you leave the meeting.

Fast Facts

The world's first patent was granted to architect Filippo Brunelleschi in Florence, Italy. The year was 1421. The patent was for a barge crane to transport marble.

Schedules slip, however, and things may not fire off on time. Each case is different, of course, so use your best judgment to determine when it is time to pull the plug if things start dragging. I am typically guided by how the product is moving along through the internal system. If I get a sense that it is sitting in a closet, I'll ask for it. One thing you can be assured is that no manufacturer will send something back that it is sold on. If your product comes back, it means there is no constituency for it.

The Least You Need to Know

♦ Nothing is as powerful as truth—be honest when it comes to your invention and your business.

♦ Don't play the Big Room like a lounge act—if you get an executive's attention, strive for the heights of quality and professionalism.

♦ Speed doesn't kill—stopping fast kills. People appreciate presentations that move apace, but abrupt stops can spook your audience.

♦ Scratch the place that itches—if there is a problem, fix it before things get out of hand. Be proactive, not reactive.

♦ If you're not gonna kiss 'em, don't make 'em stand on their tip toes. In other words, do not tease people with concepts you cannot deliver.

♦ Invention reviews, like trains, run on a schedule. Unlike trains, they are frequently late—you be on time even if the company is not.

Chapter 9

Negotiating Your Deal

In This Chapter

♦ When to use lawyers and when to negotiate yourself

♦ Disclosure forms—signing on the dotted line

♦ Everything has its price, including winning

♦ Agreeing to agree is the best first step in negotiation

♦ 10 Commandments of Contract Negotiation

My father said: "You must never try to make all the money that's in a deal. Let the other fellow make some money too, because if you have a reputation for always making all the money, you won't have many deals."

—J. Paul Getty

Negotiating contracts is a skill that can be learned. People tend to make it complex. It ain't. But sooner or later in the process, you may come face to face with lawyers—those on the side of your opposition and your own. So let's discuss the lawyers first.

On Lawyering

Lawyering, once a respected profession, has evolved into just another business, one involving self-promotion, boredom, greed, and billable hours.

"I call it the *Twilight Zone* factor," said a lawyer interviewed by *Philadelphia* magazine. "Nothing we do as lawyers is rooted in reality. The fees we charge have no economic basis in the work actually done. It's whatever the market will bear. The issues we dispute are increasingly not real world issues, but artificial conflicts that we created and that we prolong. And the worst part is that the expectations we have of ourselves all call for Superman in a three-piece suit. What I hate about being a lawyer is always reaching out to touch something—but it's never there."

> **Notable Quotables**
>
> I don't mean to criticize lawyers, just the need for so many lawyers. Lawyers don't dig ditches or build buildings. When a society requires such a large number of its best minds to conduct the unproductive enterprise of the law, something is wrong with the legal system.
>
> —Associate Justice Antonin Scalia, U.S. Supreme Court

There are many very good lawyers. However, while a lawyer may know more than you do about the fine points of law, few practicing attorneys have proven themselves to be sharp in business, especially when it comes to making tough decisions that make deals sing. Law school is, after all, just a trade school. Nothing beats empirical business experience. And many lawyers with marketplace experience no longer practice law, but join the ranks of management and entrepreneurism.

Should You Use a Lawyer to Approach the Company?

Absolutely not! This sends the wrong message. It may set off all types of bells and whistles at the company and likely trigger a response from the legal department, fighting fire with fire. This is not what you want. There's more than enough time for legal advice during the ritual dance of license negotiations. Go in alone, or with partners, and always confident. Lawyers intimidate most people. If you let them, they'll confound situations with facts, blind people with Latin, and plague everyone with precedents. Attorneys love ambiguity, complexity, and advancement of only their side of the issues. The last thing they want is candor, clarity, or compromise. Frequently business executives have to rein them in and apply sound business principles.

If at all possible, you want to go one-on-one with a senior executive or several representatives from marketing or research and development, depending on which department drives product selection.

> **Notable Quotables**
>
> Every new invention, every triumph of engineering skill, is the embodiment of some scientific idea; and experience has proven that discoveries in science, however remote from the interests of everyday life they may at first appear, ultimately confer unforeseen and incalculable benefits on mankind.
> —Robert Routledge, editor

Of course, if you are asked to sign a product disclosure form and you feel uncomfortable with the language it contains, then by all means run it by counsel. But do not take a lawyer to your pitch meeting or subsequent technical reviews. You need to be perceived as an athlete, not a spectator.

Do You Need a Lawyer for Contracts?

Perhaps. This decision depends on your own experience in the art of negotiation and crafting intellectual property deals. I used a law firm for my first licensing agreement, got the feel for it, and then went it alone for the most part.

This first experience was invaluable also for what it taught me about how lawyers bill. I now know how to direct my lawyers and avoid all kinds of unnecessary expenses. (Frankly, this could be the topic of a *Complete Idiot's Guide* because that is what I felt like after getting that first bill, a complete idiot.) Take advantage of me once, shame on you; do it again, shame on me.

Nonetheless, even today, after having done hundreds of deals for my own intellectual property (ip) and helping friends negotiate their packages, I call in a business lawyer from time to time if I'm faced with an extremely complex deal with a major licensee, especially if it involves important third-party partners. See Chapter 22 for attorney Howard R. Fine's advice about license agreements. Howard is a seasoned pro who specializes in ip negotiations.

The most efficacious way to find yourself a business attorney skilled in your field of enterprise is to seek personal recommendations. In my case, I considered all the chief legal officers at the toy companies with whom I had negotiated over the years. I looked for the one who had been most fair to me, who took my side if it

Bright Ideas
Four days after the United States detonated an atomic bomb on Bikini Atoll, French designer Louis Reard presented his new design for a bathing suit for the first time. He called it the bikini.

was right, and who did not stonewall for his company just to grandstand and look like a hero to his or her bosses. Then the day this person resigned to open a private practice, I was the second inventor to sign up.

Do You Need a Lawyer for Patents?

Yes! Yes! Yes! See Chapter 13 for in-depth information on this topic.

> **Fast Facts** _____
>
> On August 25, 1814, the British burned Washington. Dr. William Thornton, superintendent of patents, saved the Patent Office from destruction by pleading with the British commander not to "burn what would be useful to all mankind." The Patent Office was saved. Then on December 15, 1836, the Patent Office was completely destroyed by fire. The loss is estimated at 7,000 models, 9,000 drawings, and 230 books. More serious is the loss of all records of patent applications and grants.

Conducting Business

The most basic rule is to conduct your business in your style. Set the pace. Do not get caught up in your prospective licensee's timetables and priorities. Things tend to get worse under pressure during a negotiation.

Before you negotiate a contract, put these pearls of wisdom into your head:

- Stop. Look. And listen.
- Say no; then negotiate.
- Trust everybody, but cut the cards.
- Don't wish for luck; *prepare* for luck.
- If it looks like a duck and it quacks like a duck, expect a duck.
- Don't get mad; don't get even; get ahead.
- Never murder a person who is committing suicide.
- Bite the bullet only if you can stand the taste of gunpowder.

Winning at What Cost?

Getting what you want does not always have to be at another person's expense. It is possible to get what you want and still let your opponent have something. After all, you are entering into what you both hope will be a long and mutually beneficial relationship. As our political process demonstrates, societies thrive best not on triumph in domestic debates, but on reconciliation. Nothing would ever be accomplished if every technical disagreement turned into a civil war.

A good deal is one in which all sides meet their needs. Need can be reconciled. Compromise is okay. Unfortunately, not every person you meet at the bargaining table believes in this theory. Some people will give off signals that they are not trustworthy from the start. Then there are the slick ones who never appear to be the killers they are.

Terms aside, I have my own rule of thumb: unless I am totally comfortable with the executives and the company, I don't even sit down to deal. I have always been guided by the feeling that a bad deal isn't worth it under any circumstances.

Agreeing to Agree

Prior to discussing the nuts and bolts of a specific licensing contract, I want to know three things up front:

Does the company license from outside inventors? If it does, I want to know which products and from whom they were licensed. I will definitely call the inventors if I have no experience with the company. If they tell me that there is no inventor product in their line, then I need to find out why. I have seen some companies that welcome inventors just to get a look at what's being shown. They never license anything.

Is the company willing to pay me a fair royalty on the net sales of each unit sold? Executives should have no problem telling you which products have inventor royalty loads. If they don't want to share that information, you're outta there.

Is the company willing to pay me an advance against future royalties and possibly a guarantee? No strings attached. There should be no problem telling you the levels of advances and guarantees the company pays. Some companies do not pay guarantees.

Once I establish a basis for negotiation, contractual terms typically do not stand in the way. And they should not, as long as I want to sell and the manufacturer is serious about licensing. Everything usually shakes out.

Many inventors suffer from a disease I call "sellitus." These folks license their inventions to anyone who shows interest and for just about anything, under any terms. Their feeling is that if they can get an advance, they should take it. Some money is better than nothing. Not true! No amount of scratch or level of royalty/guarantee is worth a bad deal. No amount of money or level of royalty/guarantee is worth taking unless you are 100 percent confident in the company and its honesty, stability, and ability to deliver on the specific performance required by the contract. Contracts are only as good as the people who sign them.

I have experienced situations when I could not get companies to honor their contracts on a product that bombed. I have experienced situations when I could not get companies to honor their contracts on so-so products. I have experienced situations when I could not get companies to honor their contracts on hit products. Nothing is worse than a revenue-generating product, at any level of performance, that is not filling your coffers with royalties when due and payable. This is an inventor's worst nightmare. You must *always* be strong enough to walk away from an uncomfortable situation.

Advances

The advance is important because it can help you recoup a portion of your outlay for research and development, and it serves as a barometer for gauging the amount of interest at the company. It is not always possible to earn an advance that will cover all your expenses.

A good way to calculate an advance is to base it on a quarter or a third of the royalties the manufacturer estimates you'll earn during the first year based on projected sales.

For example, if the company tells you it estimates 100,000 units in year 1, and that it will sell at an average net wholesale price of $10, your royalty, if 5 percent, would amount to $50,000. Twenty-five percent of $50,000 is $12,500. At a third, the number works out to an advance of $16,667.

This advance could be paid as a lump sum upon signing or in stages during the first year of the agreement. This is all open to negotiation, but the more you can get up front, the better.

But do not be locked into these percentages. I have received advances that go from a few thousand dollars to the low seven figures.

Fast Facts

I normally ask the company what it typically pays and justification for the figure. Whatever it offers, try for more. At the same time, double-check with others who may have licensed products to the manufacturer. Inventors tend to share information with each other quite freely.

Royalties

Most industries that license concepts from outside inventors have royalty structures worked out. In publishing, a sliding scale climbs from 10 percent to 12.5 percent and, after a certain number of copies sold, levels off at 15 percent of the cover price. In character licensing and toy invention, the royalty rate ranges from 4 to 15 percent, although *E.T.* in its heyday captured 20 percent and *Star Wars* is said to be at 25 percent and more. Most character and toy invention licenses hit somewhere between 5 and 8 percent. But there are exceptions to every rule, and I have seen more exceptions than there is space in these pages to enumerate. Best advice: if you don't ask, you don't get.

An honest company will tell you what is fair and equitable within its industry. There is nothing to be gained in the long run by lying because, sooner or later, you'll know whether you have been treated fairly.

Guarantees

Guaranteed minimum royalties can also be negotiated. In this case, the licensee of your item would guarantee you no less than a certain amount of money within a predetermined time frame. Again, this amount would be based on what the licensee projects your item will earn on an annual basis. But again, there are always exceptions. Go for it, right?

Many agreements have clauses for both earned royalties and minimum guaranteed royalties.

The Option Agreement

Sometimes a manufacturer is not quite ready to do a licensing agreement but wants exclusive rights to study or research your invention for a limited period of time. In this case, an option agreement is appropriate.

The amount of money a manufacturer is willing to pay for an option is open to negotiation. I have received options as high as $20,000 for a 30-day hold. The money is usually against future royalties if a deal materializes. If no deal is struck, you keep the money. If you can get the money and not have it repayable against future royalties, all the better. This would be like a signing bonus.

I do not know a formula for negotiating option money. The fact that a manufacturer is willing to pay an option shows a certain level of interest and commitment. From there, it follows that the greater the interest and commitment, the greater the amount of money the manufacturer is willing to risk.

I have received options and then seen products sit in a closet until the option period expired.

> **Bright Ideas**
>
> Atlanta pharmacist John Pemberton was trying to mix a remedy for headaches when he discovered what would become Coca-Cola.

Options are not always desired. You may not want to do an option if it will throw off your timing in terms of opportunities to present the same product to other potential licensees. Furthermore, you must be sure the option is not offered as a ploy to take your invention out of play for a period of time.

I put a sample option agreement in Appendix B. You might want to use it as drafted or as the basis for something you are stylizing.

Levy's 10 Commandments of Contract Negotiation

I have developed this list of guidelines over nearly a quarter-century on the front lines of contract negotiation:

1. *Negotiate yourself.* In choppy seas, the captain should be on the deck. No one will do it better than you. No one has more to gain or lose. If you need a lawyer, play good guy–bad guy.

2. *Thou shalt not committee.* Any simple problem can be made insoluble if enough people discuss it.

3. *Try to avoid corporate lawyers.* It is always best to negotiate with an executive who is in a decision-making position. Lawyers are paid not to make executive decisions, but to set rules for others to follow. They see themselves as protectors, saving the executives from themselves. Yet I have found that the most successful executives break rules all the time.

4. *Never respond to people chewing at your toenails.* Don't roll over just because someone says that without X, Y, or Z the project will not be approved. The company wants to do the deal, or you would not be in negotiation. Executives—not lawyers—are responsible for profits. If your invention can boost revenues, executives will shine. You'll know when you've hit an immovable object.

5. *Two plus two is never four.* Exceptions always outnumber rules. Established exceptions have their exceptions. By the time one learns the exceptions, no one remembers the rules to which they correspond.

6. *If it ain't on the page, it ain't on the stage.* Written words live. Spoken words die. Confirm every conversation with a memorandum to eliminate any misunderstanding about who agreed to what. Save every e-mail exchange.

7. *When in doubt, ask.* Asking dumb questions is far easier than correcting dumb mistakes.

8. *Keep it short and to the point.* The length of a business contract is inversely proportional to the amount of business.

9. *Do not accept standard contracts.* In any so-called standard contract, boilerplate terms should be treated as variables. Not until a contract has been in force for six months will its most harmful terms be discovered. Nothing is as temporary as that which is called permanent.

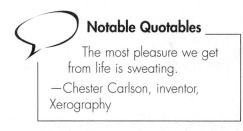

Notable Quotables

The most pleasure we get from life is sweating.

—Chester Carlson, inventor, Xerography

10. *Have fun!* The moment I stop enjoying a negotiation, I pick up my marbles and go home. An agreement is a form of marriage, and both parties must be compatible for it to succeed. But falling in love and reaching the altar are two different things.

Terms of Endearment

If you get to the point that a company wants to cut a licensing deal, you'll find the licensing agreements in Appendix B invaluable. These sample agreements are worth many thousands of dollars in terms of the time, experience, and effort put into crafting them. You or your lawyer may want to use them as the basis for your agreements, or you may want go through them, cherry-picking clauses and terms that you find appropriate to your situation.

It is my hope that these agreements alert you and your legal counsel to many points that either have been omitted entirely from a manufacturer boilerplate contract or are written entirely from the manufacturer perspective. Some manufacturers have standard licensing agreements they prefer to use. Others will ask you to submit your own. In either case, most issues usually are negotiable.

Fast Facts

Secretary of State James Madison gave the Patent Office the status of a distinct unit or division within the Department of States in 1802 by appointing Dr. William Thornton, at a salary of $1,400 per year, "to have charge of issuing patents." The salary was later increased to $1,500.

My dad taught me that contracts are only as good as the people who sign them. Remember this. Do not make a deal with people you don't trust, no matter how much you feel the agreement is in your favor.

He also instructed me that every deal has its own spirit and that I should always be clear about the spirit of any agreement I execute. Often I will articulate such an understanding and put it on record through e-mails to my prospective licensee. Even if not part of a formal agreement, should push ever come to shove in a court of law, a judge and jury would probably not disregard the e-mails.

Patents. Trademarks. Who Pays?

Some inventors believe in allowing the licensee to finance or control their applications. I say that it all depends. In some cases I have the licensee pay, especially if the licensee is going to have people on the patent with us as co-inventors. Yes, there are cases when a corporate engineer, for example, makes critical contributions to the invention. In such cases, the engineer merits his or her name on the patent.

In other cases, we pay. Why? Should there ever be a meltdown between you and your licensee, you may not want the licensee to be able to claim having contributed to the patent, and thereby seek a claim of partial ownership. I try to get enough money in the advance to cover the patent work. Even if I have to use the entire amount of the advance, I will, if appropriate.

This also allows me to control the patent from the standpoint of how it's sliced up. For example, if I control it, then I may be able to license the same technology, in a slightly different form, to various companies whose products are in dissimilar categories. You'll need to handle these decisions on a case-by-case basis.

I also try to own the trademarks for similar reasons. It's all about control of the ip, after all.

The Least You Need to Know

- Negotiate for yourself. Don't let others characterize your positions unless you like to play that game. It just makes lawyers wealthy.

- Never fear to negotiate. Never negotiate out of fear.

- Negotiation assumes parties are more anxious to agree than to disagree.

- Thou shalt not committee.

- Try not to deal only with lawyers.

- Written words live; spoken words die.

- When in doubt, ask.

- Keep it short and to the point.

Chapter 10

Key Deal Points

In This Chapter

◆ Understanding corporate boilerplate

◆ Relationships versus transactions

◆ Fairness and flexibility

◆ Management by objectives

◆ What you want in an agreement

> Nobody eats until someone sells something. And you can't sell something until it's been created. The independent creator and the marketer must behave as if they thoroughly depend on one another, because they do. That means that as tensions in the creative process emerge, as conflicts between making and selling arise, everything is on the table except the relationship itself. The relationship must survive. True partners in the creative process must focus on meeting the needs of the relationship as well as the terms of an agreement.
>
> —Michael Ross, senior VP/GM, Britannica

If you get to the point that a company wants to negotiate a license for your invention, congratulations! This is a major accomplishment and a credit to you and your invention. But your work is far from over. In a sense, it is just beginning. Now you need to forge a licensing agreement. This will take experience, patience, thick skin, stamina, common sense, a diplomat's ear, and a good sense of humor. And frequently you may have to be able to jump into troubled waters without making a splash, to borrow an appropriate metaphor from Art Linkletter.

In Chapter 9, I discussed how to negotiate. In this chapter, I comment on, in broad strokes, select issues from the sample licensing agreement in Appendix B. By the way, if you are not ready to negotiate a license, I have provided a sample option agreement, also found in Appendix B.

I Do Not Have All the Answers

I could never possibly address all the issues you may face and how they relate to your invention and industry. Every case is different. Contracts are crafted by the winds of change and the waters of time. No contract is 100 percent bulletproof. But there are common denominators to agreements, and I have attempted to break out a few of them for you in these pages. If I am missing something, hopefully you'll find it addressed in the sample agreement in Appendix B. If I missed an issue, please drop me a line care of my publisher. I am always open to suggestions and new ways to approach licensing.

> **Notable Quotables**
>
> If a contract is good, it gathers dust on the shelf. If you need to keep looking at it, you're in trouble.
>
> —Jason Smolen, Esq., Smolen and Plevy, P.C.

I have never seen a perfect contract from either the licensor's or licensee's point of view. The smartest and most experienced businesspeople and lawyers let things slip. Contracts are ultimately only as good as the people who sign them. Some people see a contract negotiation as a fight. I prefer to view it as a ritual dance. And I am most happy when my dance card is full. (Wow! That metaphor certainly dates me.)

You Show Me Yours, and I'll Show You Mine

Many manufacturers have standard license agreements they prefer to use. This assures them that everything they want is included. It's like a landlord's lease, and their lawyers can easily follow this agreement. It is more time-consuming for lawyers to work with an unfamiliar document and figure out whether all their issues are covered. On the other hand, smaller companies that do not have legal departments or do not want to spend money on outside counsel may ask you to submit a proposed agreement.

In either case, you will find that most issues are negotiable, if the manufacturer is serious about wanting to license your invention and work with you—and, conversely, if you want a deal. The more the company wants your ip, the greater its willingness to be fair and flexible.

I like to see what a company uses for its standard agreement, even if I plan on suggesting my language as the basis for the deal. This allows me to see the negotiation from the opposition's point of view. It is to your advantage to take a moment and consider your licensee's position. You will see what the future may hold for you, such as the licensee's exit strategy, ways to avoid payments to you, and so on. And frequently, I find in a corporate contract terms that play to my benefit and were not in my agreement. This is a real Eureka moment. So if you can see the company's proposed agreement, by all means, do it—in fact, ask for it. Inspecting the corporate agreement shows you quickly how fair a company is with inventors. Companies send a message through their boilerplate.

A few years ago, I was hired as a product acquisition consultant to a public company. Part of my charge was to negotiate license agreements on its behalf. I looked at the company's standard license agreement and found numerous issues missing. When I asked the CEO if he would agree to include them he said, of course, he would but only if someone asked.

I recommended we take a proactive stance and put the clauses in before I started negotiating. I wanted to send a comforting message to the inventors. I wanted to propose an agreement I would sign with certain modifications. Furthermore, I was being paid by the hour, and it was not worth my time to hassle over issues that were givens. The CEO, an enlightened fellow, wanted to reach out to the inventing community and send the right message, so he agreed to my recommendation. I must have negotiated over 20 licenses for the company, and all went through without a hitch.

Fairness and Flexibility Rule

Two important attributes of a win-win deal are fairness and flexibility as they relate to both the market and the license agreement. It is critical, of course, to have a written agreement that clearly spells out the terms of the deal. "But once that contract has been signed, the licensor and licensee must focus on meeting the needs of their relationship rather than the terms of the agreement," says Michael Ross, senior VP/GM Britannica. "It's the relationship that will sustain the partnership, not the contract.

"If as things move along the original terms of the agreement no longer make sense, if the signed contract puts either party at a disadvantage or threatens their business

411

Try not to conduct negotiations before 9 A.M. or after 4 P.M. Before 9 A.M., you appear too anxious, and after 4 P.M., corporate attorneys may have their minds on cashing in their chips at the end of the day, and not on the agreement.

model, then both parties must be willing to modify the agreement," Ross adds. "I have seen many partnerships fail because of an agreement that started out fine for both parties but, due to changes in the market, became unsustainable for one of the parties.

"You have to decide what you want more: a strong, long-term relationship or strict, principled adherence to a contract," Ross continues. "This is fundamental to a win-win partnership. Many people say they want a relationship, but they behave as if they want a transaction."

A few years ago, I noticed that, quarter after quarter, I was not making any money from a licensed product, even though sales were strong. So I looked carefully at the royalty statement. Then I saw the problem—a 3 percent royalty. Ouch! It should have been 6 percent. I called the vice president of marketing and asked why I was receiving half of what I deserved. "Because that's what you agreed to in the contract," he replied. (This man was not at the company when I made the deal.) I checked, and he was correct. I had made a serious error. I must have been asleep when I cut the deal. I asked him what he could do to cure my dilemma, and he said, "It's easy. We'll just change it to 6 percent." He even went back a couple quarters and made up the loss to me. This executive knew how to maintain a relationship. To this day, we still work together, and I'll never forget his gesture.

I have been blessed to have had the opportunity to do business with many wonderful people who have not sought to take unfair advantage. I have also been exposed to executives to whom the only win-win is when they win twice. They are uncomfortable when they don't have the advantage. These guys handle nickels like manhole covers. They are Loophole Louies who cannot be trusted no matter what they agree to on paper. They are the portent and epitome of moral and spiritual disorder. "Some rob you with a six gun, and some with a fountain pen," wrote Woody Guthrie. Be alert. Lerts survive.

Contracts are a two-way street. I have had companies request that I change an agreement long after it has been in force or that I take an unreasonably low advance or royalty. If I feel it is a fair request, I'll do my best to make it work. There is nothing greater for both sides or more enviable than a deal in which the inventor and the manufacturer feel victorious and share in the rewards.

I would much rather negotiate with an executive who is well rewarded, someone who has something to gain by my success. These are the kind of people who negotiate the fairest deals. The problems arise when companies do not give their people a strong incentive package.

Management by Objectives

Recently I was chatting about licensing agreements with Bob Jones, partner in the accounting firm Harriton, Mancuso, and Jones, P.C., North Bethesda, Maryland, and an indispensable member of our team at Richard C. Levy & Associates. I was wondering aloud why certain companies play hardball with an inventor when the win seems insignificant vis-à-vis the potential loss to a company's relationship with the goose that lays the golden eggs, the inventor. He called it "management by objectives":

> The basic concept of Management by Objectives is to 1) set goals for employees; 2) measure their progress in achieving their goals; and 3) compensate them based on their achievements. The problem is that the most important goals of the company (things like customer satisfaction and inventor relations) are the most difficult to measure. So management sets goals that can be quantified rather than goals that are important. Typically, the goals focus on short-term profit rather than long-term success. Thus, the employees focus their efforts in the wrong place, and frequently, such effort is counterproductive.

Notable Quotables

An independent inventor rarely has a product that merits multiple licensees in the same geographical and product areas—though it does happen. Exclusivity is generally the expected thing, and it is better for you.
—Calvin D. MacCracken, inventor, holder of more than 300 U.S. and foreign patents

The Spirit of Agreement

The licensing agreement provided in Appendix B, as written or as a form thereof, can be an extremely important document to you as an inventor faced with the opportunity to license an invention. In terms of the time and effort that was put into crafting it, the document is worth many thousands of dollars in legal fees.

Thirty-some years ago, when I cut my first deal, an executive and I might have handled many points informally verbally and on a handshake. But because of the way executives play musical chairs these days, jumping from job to job, company to company, it's best not to depend on informality, but to memorialize as much as possible in writing.

Every agreement has its own spirit. Therefore, you should always be clear about the spirit of every contract you sign. Corporate lawyers like things vague. It works to their favor, should push come to shove, because lack of specificity and haziness leads to more than one interpretation. The corporate lawyer can use this situation to muddy the waters. This puts you in a defensive position that likely forces you to spend money on legal counsel and the court for interpretation.

Sometimes I cannot get the spirit and specificity into an agreement. Then I articulate my understanding and put it on record through letters and e-mails to the manufacturer. Although it's not part of the formal agreement, if I ever get into a court of law, a judge and jury may take these into account. Save your e-mail!

Disclaimer: I am not an attorney-at-law. I am not giving legal advice. The agreements in this book are composites of many I have negotiated. They are provided as a quick-access reference only. Each deal you make, as in each industry, will have its own esoteric requirements. Seek legal advice from a lawyer.

Setting the Scene and the Mind

Yea, though you may walk through the alley of the shadow of debt, show no hunger. You need to think like a person who can walk away from a deal. Prepare yourself to postpone immediate gratification for long-term goals. Too many amateur negotiators suffer from "sellitus," an affliction that forces them to make a deal at any cost.

Avoid the temptation to overwhelm. You must not be perceived as either an egomaniac or a victim. The image you want to portray is that of a person who is modest, honest, generous, hospitable, and maybe a bit eccentric. Show yourself as a down-home person with a penthouse personality.

Let's look at some points I feel deserve explanation. These are in no order of priority once you get past the section on *indemnifications*. I put this first because it needs to be uppermost in your mind, even ahead of advances and royalties.

Indemnification of Licensee

In my opinion, this is the most important part of any agreement from the inventor's standpoint, because it can be a minefield in terms of personal risk. The last thing you want is to have to reimburse a company for losses and expenses.

In some agreements, mere *claims* of wrongdoing can trigger all kinds of nightmares for inventors. I have seen agreements that allow a licensee to hold up inventor royalties if someone simply *claims*, through a letter to the licensee, that a licensed invention infringes someone's patent. I have seen where a claim in a foreign country stops royalty payments generated in the United States. How unfair is that? Adding insult to injury, this agreement did not even require the licensee to pay interest to the inventor on held funds. Nor did it have a time limit on how long funds could be held. By the way, nothing stopped the licensee from continuing to manufacture and market the guy's invention.

Licensees have insurance, for product liability, errors and omissions, and so on, to protect themselves against all kinds of problems. Inventors typically do not self-insure. This is such a critical part of any license agreement that I highly recommend you have competent legal counsel review requests for indemnification you are asked to sign. The last thing you want to do is lose personal assets, such as savings or worse, because you get entangled in a liability fight.

You cannot indemnify against future damage from submarine patents (read more about submarine patents in Chapter 11). No one can do this. You can search prior art until the cows come home and never gain access to as-yet-unpublished patents. The good news is that until and unless another patent appears that reads on your invention, you would not owe that inventor or patent holder any money for past royalties. If a patent issued that conflicted with your patent or product, you'd have to deal with it from that point forward.

Indemnification of Licensor

Your licensee should not balk at covering you under an appropriate insurance policy. Usually this merely involves a letter from a licensee to its insurance company. It's as easy as adding another driver to a car policy. It should not increase the cost of the policy(s) to the licensee, nor require any expense.

Bright Ideas

The first scientific lie detector was reportedly invented around 1895 by Italian criminologist Cesare Lombroso. He modified a small water-filled container called a hydrosphygmograph. A person shoved his or her hand through a rubber seal into the water. Changes in the suspect's pulse or blood pressure would make the water level rise, causing a drum to turn when air was pushed through a tube by the pressure. Lombroso modified this instrument to record physical changes in pulse and blood pressure.

Description of Invention

You'll want to describe your invention as broadly as possible. Start extreme. Cut it large and kick it into place. You'll be able to edit the definition and work it to everyone's satisfaction.

If you open with too narrow a definition, it becomes difficult to introduce new ideas at a later time.

Claim Limited Knowledge

If you cannot make an unqualified statement to certain warrants and representations, insert the words "to the best of my knowledge, information and belief" as in this example:

> WHEREAS, LICENSOR hereby warrants and represents that, **to the best of its knowledge, information and belief,** it is the sole and exclusive owner of all rights in the ITEM, that it has the sole and exclusive right to grant the license herein ….

Exclusivity

Only license to a company that is capable of exploiting the rights covered it is willing to break out and pay for on an individual basis. Don't allow the company to cast a wide net. Part of every agreement should be the following stipulation:

> All rights and licenses not herein specifically granted to LICENSEE are reserved by LICENSOR and, as between the parties, are the sole and exclusive property of LICENSOR and may be used or exercised solely by LICENSOR.

In On the Take-Off, In On the Landing

You want the agreement to continue for as long as the product upon which royalties are payable to you, under provisions of the agreement, shall continue to be manufactured or sold by the licensee.

Many companies may try to tie your royalty term to the life of your patent. This is nuts. Why should you suddenly be cut out of the action just because a patent expires? This is easy to handle if the license is not dependent upon your being issued a patent. If it is, the manufacturer will claim that, without patent protection, competition will cut into its profits. This is a sound argument.

As a compromise, agree that—after the patent turns into a pumpkin—if there is solid evidence of market erosion from competitive product, you will take a reduced royalty based on a sound mathematical formula.

> **Notable Quotables**
>
> … we said "What is it that makes the United States such a great nation?" And we investigated and found that it was patents, and we will have patents.
>
> —Korekiyo Takahashi, later to be first Japanese Commissioner of Patents, 1886

Advance

The size of the advance is usually in direct proportion to the kind of support the company will give your product. For example, if you are paid $1,000, it is much easier for a licensee to deep-six your project (say, in the face of a manufacturing problem) than if it had paid $100,000. The greater the financial commitment, the more reason the company has to make the product go.

Frequently, advances are based on a third or a quarter of the first-year sales. This is a starting point, but there are always exceptions.

Advances should always be nonrefundable. In other words, if you deliver an acceptable prototype, you keep the money no matter what happens downstream.

Royalty

Every industry has its own royalty scale. Whatever that number is, the key to your agreement is how sales upon which the royalty is based are defined. Never sign an agreement that does not define in detail exactly how your royalty is to be calculated.

To make a sweeping generality like "net sales" and not define it is unacceptable. This can easily become a minefield.

Do not be timid about suggesting a sliding royalty scale. For example, if the industry standard is 5 percent, ask for an increased royalty if the product performs past a certain level. Find a magic number that can trigger a higher royalty.

By the way, in some industries, product that is manufactured and delivered to a buyer overseas earns a higher royalty for the inventor. Why? Because the licensee does not incur costs such as shipping product across from Asia and warehousing it. For example, many large retailers buy product in Hong Kong and have it consolidated and shipped across at their own expense, as a way of getting a better price from the manufacturer.

411

Camp Invention inspires creativity and inventiveness through engaging, relevant, and meaningful activities that allow child-size imaginations to run wild. Held in 47 major metropolitan areas, this weeklong summer day camp for children in grades 2 through 6 incorporates science, math, history, art, invention, creativity, and problem-solving. With 19 different curriculum modules that have been piloted and tested by certified educators, campers are guaranteed to have a new experience every year. There is a staff-to-student ratio of 1 to 8. For information, call the National Inventor's Hall of Fame at 330-762-4463, or visit campinvention.org.

Guarantees

The guarantee is negotiable and should be based upon what the company forecasts in sales over the term of your pact.

Best Efforts

You need to be sure your agreement requires the licensee to use its best efforts. I recall once when a lawyer tried to change the language in a contract of mine from "Licensee's best efforts" to "Licensee's reasonable efforts." I responded by asking how he would feel if a surgeon promised to use his or her reasonable efforts when operating on him instead of his or her best efforts. I won the point, but even so, not without a struggle. Obviously, there is a significant difference in the legal meanings of these terms.

Specific Performance

There needs to be milestones. Every right you license requires its own performance parameters. In this way, if the licensees fail to perform some function, you have an escape route.

Every agreement you sign needs a way out in case a licensor isn't getting the job done. Licensees can fail to meet product introduction dates, miss payment and/or reporting deadlines, and so forth.

Foreign Rights

If you are asked for foreign rights, make each country a separate deal in terms of specific performance and, if possible, advances and guarantees. In this way, the licensee will not take anything for granted. The company will know that it needs to pay attention to your product everywhere, not just at home.

IP Searches

Demand that your licensee conduct its own patent, copyright, and trademark searches and satisfy itself that your invention does not infringe anything in any of these fields. Make a part of your agreement the fact that the licensee did its own search.

Right to Audit

Always require the right to audit your licensee's books of account. Never sign an agreement without this clause.

I do not recall how many times I have opted to audit licensees, but except for once, we have always found money owed. In these cases, it was either human error; if done intentionally—for example, to show increased income for a certain quarter—no one tried to hide anything. As my auditor likes to say, "They don't hide their omissions— they just don't give me a road map to find them."

Once I was negotiating with a corporate lawyer who did not want to allow me to audit. After I explained why I had to have the right, he agreed. When I asked why

> **Notable Quotables**
>
> Business has only two basic functions—marketing and innovation.
>
> —Peter F. Drucker, author/expert on management and organization

the company didn't simply add the audit clause to its boilerplate, he answered, "Then everyone might want to audit and we don't have the time to deal with it." What a stupid answer, and how shortsighted. In the end, I did not sign with this company. That was a bad sign.

Take Interest on Late Payments

Insist that interest plus extra points be applied to late royalty payments. Here's why. Some corporate financial types like to play games with royalties. They hold them up to get the benefit of some extra float from your money. If the licensee has no obligation to pay interest on late payments, there is no incentive to pay on time. And if all the licensee has to pay is interest, you are essentially giving the company a free loan, and without the hassle of making application to a lender.

But if the licensee has to pay you interest plus a couple points over prime, for example, this will cost the company money, and it'll be more likely to pay you on time.

Three Strikes and You're Out

Whenever possible, I like to write my agreements in such a way that if I put the licensee on notice for the same problem three times, I can break the agreement. This is only fair.

Furthermore, if there are conditions beyond the licensee's control, I'll allow a certain amount of time for the cure and then it's over.

The Least You Need to Know

- Every deal has two sides—yours and theirs. Don't be selfish and over-reaching in your demands.

- Set the tone and volume for easy listening. The atmosphere needs to be friendly and nonconfrontational.

- Necessity has no law.

- It's all about relationships, not transactions. Your deal should contain the kinds of terms that make both parties desire a long-term relationship.

Part 4

Goin' for the Gold

On April 10, 1790, President George Washington signed the bill that laid the foundation of the modern patent system. In the 220 years since the ink on that bill dried, the patent system has encouraged and nurtured the genius of countless inventors.

Part 4 covers how we benefit from patents, trademarks, trade secrets, and copyrights, also known as intellectual property (ip). This content is not meant to take the place of advice from competent patent counsel, but to familiarize you with ways to protect your ip. It will also hopefully save you headaches and money.

After reading Part 4 you will be better equipped to defend yourself when discussing your ideas with prospective licensees and/or investors, and dazzle them a bit, too, with esoteric trivia, facts, and convincing repartee. Last, but far from least, Part 4 seeks to impress upon you the importance of patent attorneys. And if you can't tell a good patent counsel from a bad one, I provide some guidance.

Pay the tolls to protect your ip, and follow professional advice. It will bring down your cost per mile and lessen the wear and tear on you.

Chapter 11

All About Patents and the USPTO

In This Chapter

- ◆ Uncle Sam offers protection for your ideas
- ◆ If it ain't on the page, it may not be on the stage
- ◆ The USPTO works for you
- ◆ Disclosure documents—a bargain at $10

The patent system is the bedrock of innovation. … The sheer volume of patent applications not only reflects the vibrant, innovative spirit that has made America a worldwide leader in science, engineering and technology, but also reflects countless new jobs waiting to be unleashed. When patents are developed commercially, they create jobs for the companies marketing products, and for their suppliers, distributors and retailers. One such patent has positive stimulatory effects across almost all sectors of our economy.

—U.S. Senator Orrin Hatch (R-UT)

The U.S. government gives you several ways to protect your ideas, including patents, trademarks, and copyrights. If your ideas have physical form, it's the patent you want as your first line of defense.

Most companies will not license an invention unless it has been or can be patented. The stronger the patent, the better the deal you can negotiate. The stronger the patent, the better the chances are for keeping competition away for a limited time.

Important: The chapters in this book on the protection of your intellectual property (ip) are provided only as a general reference primer about ip and the operations of the United States Patent and Trademark Office (USPTO). They attempt to answer many of the questions inventors commonly ask but are not intended as a comprehensive textbook on ip law and complex issues. Intellectual property laws, regulations, filing fees, and so forth are in a constant state of change, pushed and pulled by technologies, marketplaces, and special interests. These chapters are not designed to take the place of competent legal counsel, which I encourage you to seek.

Also, in these chapters, whenever I refer to "you," the assumption is that you, the reader, are the inventor or a co-inventor of record.

The Big Three in IP

Here is a short introduction to the basic types of patent protection available to you:

- Utility patents

- Plant patents

- Design patents

Utility patents are granted to the inventor or discoverer of any new and useful process, machine, manufacture, composition of matter, or any new and useful improvement thereof. Here are some examples of inventions protected by utility patents:

Fast Facts _____

Patent applications are received at the rate of over 450,000 per year. The USPTO receives more than 5 million pieces of mail each year.

- The Wright brothers' airplane, U.S. Patent No. 821,393

- Thomas Edison's electric lamp, U.S. Patent No. 223,898

- Nintendo's GameBoy, U.S. Patent No. 5,184,830

Plant patents are granted on any distinct and new variety of asexually reproduced plants (see Chapter 15 for more on plant patents). Examples of inventions protected by plant patents include these:

- Bosenberg's climbing or trailing rose, U.S. Plant Patent 1
- Method of Growing Plants in Soil, U.S. Plant Patent 4,067,712
- Kalanchoe plant named Veracruz, U.S. Plant Patent 5,927

Design patents are granted on any new, original, and ornamental design for an article of manufacture (see Chapter 16 for more on design patents). Examples of inventions protected by design patents include the following:

- The Statue of Liberty, U.S. Design Patent No. 11,023
- A Dispensing Container for Tablets, U.S. Design Patent No. 200,000
- The Spirals baby bottle, U.S. Design Patent No. 340,771

Utility and plant patents are granted for a term that begins on the date of the grant and ends 20 years from the date the patent application was first filed, subject to the payment of maintenance fees. Design patents are granted for a term of 14 years from the date of grant. There are no maintenance fees.

Patents may be extended only by special act of Congress, except for some pharmaceutical patents whose terms may be extended to make up for lost time due to government-required testing.

> **Notable Quotables**
>
> A country without a patent office and good patent laws is just a crab, and can't travel any way but sideways and backways.
>
> —Mark Twain, humorist

Keepin' a List and Checkin' It Twice

This book is not about the process of invention, *per se*; however, it is, in part, about the *protection* of inventions. And in that regard, it is very important that you keep records throughout each project in an inventor's notebook. There are six important dates you need to memorialize in writing. Co-inventors, colleagues, or friends who have a grasp of your invention should witness each entry. Be sure to store your inventor's notebook in a safe place!

Now, here are those dates:

- ◆ The date you conceived the invention

- ◆ The date you reduced the invention to practice

- ◆ The date you first showed your invention to others

- ◆ The date your invention was first published

- ◆ The date you first offered the invention for sale

- ◆ The date you licensed the invention

Why are these dates important? For several reasons. If you and one or more inventors file for a patent on the same invention, at the same time, dates of *conception* and *reduction to practice* can give you the edge.

def•i•ni•tion

Conception is the moment you first thought of your invention. Document it with a notebook entry, for example, showing the time and date you had the brainstorm. A simple sketch makes the entry even more efficacious. Sign and date the sketch, too. The **reduction to practice** is the date when you built a breadboard or prototype or filed a patent application.

The law states that you must file a patent application within one year of the date you first use the invention for commercial purposes or put it up for sale or licensing at, let's say, an inventor expo. If you show it to others who are under a confidentiality agreement, this is not deemed to have been placed in "public use." A notebook entry of such activity can establish your position should the need arise.

If you are challenged, this date can be critical. You lose the right to apply for a patent within one year after you offer an invention for sale. So knowing this date may provide invaluable proof that you fall within the limit.

And "sold" does not mean that money changes hands. You could do a trade, for example. Whichever it is, should you ever need proof of this date, you will have it in the notebook.

Bright Ideas

Dutch inventor Cornelius Van Drebbel is credited with constructing the first compound microscope. During the early 1620s, he designed and built his most famous invention, the submarine. Greased leather stretched over a wooden frame, the U-boat was propelled by oars projecting through the sides and sealed with leather flaps, and it was capable of traveling 12 to 15 feet below the surface. Tubes running to the surface supplied fresh air.

Drebbel also invented the first thermostat, which used a column of mercury and a system of floats and levers to hold a steady temperature within a furnace. He later invented an incubator for hatching eggs that used his principle for temperature regulation.

What Is a Patent, Exactly?

A patent for an invention is the grant of a property right to the inventor, issued by the Patent and Trademark Office. The term of a new patent is 20 years from the date on which the application for the patent was filed in the United States or, in special cases, from the date an earlier related application was filed, subject to the payment of maintenance fees. U.S. patent grants are effective only within the United States, U.S. territories, and U.S. possessions.

The right conferred by the patent grant is, in the language of the statute and of the grant itself, "the right to exclude others from making, using, offering for sale, or selling" the invention in the United States or "importing" the invention into the United States. What is granted is not the right to make, use, offer for sale, sell, or import, but the right to exclude others from making, using, offering for sale, selling, or importing the invention.

The Patent Law

The patent law specifies the subject matter for which a patent may be obtained and conditions for patentability. The law establishes the USPTO to administer the law relating to the granting of patents and contains various other provisions relating to patents.

The American Inventors Protection Act was enacted November 29, 1999, as Public Law 106-113. To read the full text of the act, visit the USPTO website at www.uspto. gov, or request a copy of the act by calling the USPTO Information Line at 1-800-USPTO-9199 (1-800-878-7691) or 703-308-4357.

411

Keep these phone numbers handy: General Trademark Information: 1-800-786-9199, Automated Line/Status of Trademark Applications: 571-272-9250, Trademark Assistance Center: 571-272-9250, Correcting Mistakes on Registrations: 571-272-9500, Trademark Trial and Appeal Board: 571-272-8500, and Commissioner for Trademarks: 571-272-8900.

What Is Patentable?

For an invention to be patentable, it must be new as defined in the patent law, which provides that an invention cannot be patented if: "(a)the invention was known or used by others in this country, or patented or described in a printed publication in this or a foreign country, before the invention thereof by the applicant for patent," or "(b)the invention was patented or described in a printed publication in this or a foreign country or in public use or on sale in this country more than one year prior to the application for patent in the United States."

If your invention has been described in a printed publication anywhere, has been posted on the Internet, or has been in public use or on sale in this country more than one year before the date your patent applications is filed in this country, a patent cannot be obtained. In this instance, it is immaterial when the invention was made or whether the printed publication or public use was by you or by someone else. If you describe the invention in a printed publication, use the invention publicly, or place it on sale, you must apply for a patent before one year has gone by; otherwise, you lose any right to a patent.

Notable Quotables

Inventing is easy! Doing hardware and software is easy; building models ... a snap, if you know how. Selling the damn stuff ... that's the hard part! ... And by the way, when you've finally got a licensee, get smart, get legal help with the Agreement because they'll try to screw you every time!

—Ralph H. Baer, creator of the home video game industry

Even if the subject matter sought to be patented is not exactly shown by the prior art and involves one or more differences over the most nearly similar thing already known, a patent may still be refused if the differences would have been obvious. The subject matter sought to be patented must be sufficiently different from what has been used or described before that it may be said to be obscured to a person having ordinary skill in the area of technology related to the invention. For example, the substitution of one material for another, e.g., ABS (a type of plastic) for tin, or changes in size, are typically not patentable.

The Examiners (Say *Ahhh!*)

The work of examining applications for patents is divided among a number of examining groups, each group having jurisdiction over assigned fields of technology. Each group is headed by a group director and staffed by examiners. The examiners review applications and determine whether patents can be granted. Appeals can be made to the Board of Patent Appeals and Interferences from decisions refusing to grant a patent, and a review by the Commissioner of Patents and Trademarks may be requested by petition. The examiners also identify applications that claim the same invention and start proceedings, known as interferences, to determine who is the first inventor.

In addition to the examining groups, other offices perform various services:

- Receiving and distributing mail

- Receiving new applications

- Handling sales of printed copies of patents

- Making copies of records

- Inspecting drawings

- Recording assignments

411

The USPTO now accepts patent applications electronically. If you prefer to conduct your business with the USPTO via postal mail, address all correspondence relating to patent matters to Commissioner for Patents, PO Box 1450, Alexandria, VA 22313. Be sure to include your full return address, including zip code. Your presence there isn't necessary.

Established by Law, Built by Innovation—the USPTO

Congress established the USPTO to issue patents on behalf of the government. The office as a distinct bureau is thought to date from 1802, when a separate official in the Department of State who became known as the Superintendent of Patents was placed in charge of patents. The revision of patent laws in 1836 reorganized the USPTO and designated the official in charge as Commissioner of Patent and Trademarks. The USPTO remained in the Department of State until 1849, when it was transferred to the Department of Interior. In 1925, it was transferred to the Department of Commerce, where it remains today. The head of the USPTO is designated the Under Secretary of Commerce for Intellectual Property and Director of the USPTO.

The USPTO has about 7,000 employees, of whom about half are examiners and others with technical and legal training. These 7,000 folks process the more than 450,000 patent applications received per year.

Through the issuance of patents, providing incentives to invent, invest in, and disclose new technology worldwide encourages technological advancement. Under this system of protection, American industry has flourished. New products have been invented, new uses for old ones discovered, and employment opportunities created for millions of Americans.

Bright Ideas

African Americans have contributed greatly to the inventions pool: Dr. Patricia E. Bath invented a procedure for eye surgery. Otis Boykin, electronic controllers for guided missiles. George Washington Carver, peanut butter and 400 plant patents. Lonnie G. Johnson, SuperSoaker squirt gun. Lewis Latimer, carbon filament for lightbulbs. Jan Ernst Matzeliger, shoemaking machine. Elijah McCoy, oil-dripping container for trains. Garrett Morgan, gas mask and first traffic signal. Madam C. J. Walker, hair-growing lotion. Granville T. Woods, communications system between trains and stations.

You must write a separate letter (but not necessarily in separate envelopes) for each distinct subject of inquiry, such as assignments, payments, orders for printed copies of patents, orders for copies of records, and requests for other services. Do not include inquiries with letters responding to office actions in applications.

If your letter concerns a patent application, be sure to include the application number, filing date, and Group Art Unit number. If your letter concerns a patent, it must include your full name, the title of the invention, the patent number, and the date of issue.

An order for a copy of an assignment must give the book and page, or reel and frame, of the record, as well as the inventor's name; otherwise, the USPTO will hit you with an additional charge for the time consumed in making the search for the assignment.

Patent applications are not open to the public, and no information concerning them is released except on written authority from you, a co-applicant, your assignee, your attorney, or, when necessary, to the conduct of the business of the USPTO.

However, with certain exceptions, utility and plant applications filed on or after November 29, 2000, including international applications filed under 35 USC 363 on or after November 29, 2000, and those in compliance with 35 USC 371, shall be published promptly after the expiration of a period of 18 months from the earliest domestic or foreign filing date of the application. Publication of utility and plant applications is required by the American Inventors Protection Act of 1999, Public Law 106-113.

It is noted that an application shall not be published if an applicant makes a request *upon filing*, certifying that the invention disclosed in the application has not and will not be the subject of an application filed in another country, or under a multilateral international agreement, that requires 18-month publication. An applicant who has made a nonpublication request but who subsequently files an application directed to the invention disclosed in the application filed in the office in a foreign country must notify the USPTO of such filing within 45 days after the date of such foreign filing. An applicant's failure to timely provide such a notice will result in the abandonment of the application (subject to revival if it is shown that the delay in submitting the notice was unintentional).

Patents and related records, including records of any decisions, the records of assignments other than those relating to assignments of patent applications, books, and other records and papers in the office, are open to the public. They may be inspected in the USPTO Search Room, or copies may be ordered.

The USPTO cannot respond to queries concerning the novelty and patentability of an invention before you file your application; give advice on possible infringement; advise on the propriety of filing an application; respond to queries regarding whether, or to whom, any alleged invention has been patented; or act as an adviser on patent law or as your counselor, except in deciding questions arising before it in regularly filed cases. Examiners will gladly furnish information of a general nature either directly or by supplying or calling your attention to an appropriate publication.

411

You do not need an attorney to file for a trademark, but you are responsible for observing and complying with all substantive and procedural issues and requirements. The USPTO cannot select an attorney for you. Find names of attorneys who specialize in trademark law in the Yellow Pages, online, or by contacting your local bar association.

Only Inventors Need Apply

According to the law, only the inventor may apply for a patent, with certain exceptions:

- If a person who is not the inventor applies for a patent, the patent would be invalid, if obtained. The person applying in such a case who falsely states that he or she is the inventor would also be subject to criminal penalties.

- If the inventor has died, the application may be made by legal representatives— that is, the administrator or executor of the estate.

- If the inventor is mentally unstable, the application for the patent may be made by a guardian.

♦ If an inventor refuses to apply for a patent or cannot be found, a joint inventor or a person who has a proprietary interest in the invention may apply on behalf of the nonsigning inventor.

♦ If two or more people make an invention jointly, they apply for a patent as joint inventors. A person who makes a financial contribution is not a joint inventor and cannot be joined in the application as an inventor.

It is possible to correct an innocent mistake in erroneously omitting an inventor or in erroneously naming a person as an inventor.

Officers and employees of the USPTO are prohibited by law from applying for a patent or acquiring, directly or indirectly—except by inheritance or bequest—any patent or any right or interest in any patent.

Copy Documents, Not Ideas

Printed copies of any patent, identified by its patent number, may be purchased from the USPTO. Get the current fee schedule by calling 1-800-786-9199 or 571-272-1000, or visiting www.uspto.gov.

The USPTO website enables you to search and print copies of patents for free. Numerous nongovernment patent search engines on the Internet also are useful. I prefer not to recommend them by name because I do not know anything about them, and they may not be there by the time you take a look.

Speaking of documents, the USPTO no longer has a Disclosure Document program. It stopped February 1, 2007.

Fast Facts _____

The first inventions have been traced to the Paleolithic Period, which ran from about 2½ million years ago to 8000 B.C.E. Old Stone Age people created axes, chisels, and other hand tools by chipping bone, flint, horn, and ivory into myriad shapes. The bow and arrow and the spear were invented to hunt. People also discovered during this period that striking flint on metal ore could cause fire.

Submarine Patents—Periscope Up!

In the United States, patents remain secret until they are granted or 18 months after filing (unless you request nonpublication at the time of filing). In other words, once you file your application, no one other than select USPTO officials, such as examiners, know what you have invented. The process to get a patent can be a drawn-out affair, so it is possible for competitors to unknowingly develop and market a technology or mechanism, for example, for which others have already filed patents.

The term *submarine patent* applies to the situation in which a company or inventor surfaces with a patent to an invention that a competitor has been using for some time and asks for royalties. Furthermore, the inventor who has the submarine patent may never have proven the invention, as it is no longer required that inventors build proving models of their ideas.

The most celebrated of such cases involved Jerome H. Lemelson, America's most prolific contemporary inventor, who held more than 550 patents, including some on the bar code scanner. According to *Fortune* (May 14, 2001), Lemelson's theoretical patents earned him $1.5 billion in licensing fees.

Between 1992 and 1995, Lemelson licensed his bar-code scanning technology used in electronics and automobile manufacturing to more than 70 companies, including Sony, Apple Computer, and Daimler-Benz, but not before having to engage in huge legal battles.

> **Notable Quotables**
>
> Great spirits have always encountered violent opposition from mediocre minds.
> —Albert Einstein

In the April 9, 1997, edition of *The Wall Street Journal*, staff reporter Bernard Wysocki Jr. explained it like this: "It was as if the 1954 and 1956 filings were roots of a vast tree. One branch 'surfaced' in 1963, another in 1969, and more in the late 1970s, the mid 1980s, and the early 1990s. All direct descendants of the mid 1950s filings, they have up-to-date claims covering more recent technology, such as that for bar-code scanning."

One of Lemelson's former attorneys, Arthur Lieberman, told *Fortune*, "In many cases he didn't patent inventions. He invented patents. ... He would look at the magazines and determine the direction of industry." Lieberman said that Lemelson would use his knowledge, get to the Patent Office first, and thus lay the foundation for future claims, should there be breakthroughs by inventors in a particular field.

While Lemelson technically played by the rules to amass a $500 million fortune, recently the loopholes that allowed this were closed through the lobbying efforts of big industry. (By the way, Lemelson's contingency attorney is reported to have earned more than $150 million in fees!)

Bright Ideas

Men have been shaving off their beards with sharp implements since ancient times. Cave paintings show shells, sharks' teeth, and sharpened flint used as razors. But one American inventor changed the face of mankind by revolutionizing shaving habits. King Camp Gillette invented the first disposable blade in 1901. He created a thin, double-edged blade that was fastened to a special guarded holder and could be thrown away when it got dull. An entire generation was converted to the safety razor when the U.S. government issued Gillette razors to its troops during World War I.

The Inventors Assistance Program

In November 1999, Congress passed the American Inventors Protection Act. This act, among other things, laid the foundation for the establishment of the Inventors Assistance Program (IAP).

The principal mission of this office is to ensure USPTO-based support and encouragement of independent inventors and small business concerns. Through innovative educational outreach programs and a nationwide network of contacts, IAP offers a variety of resources to assist inventors with patent and trademark application processes. In addition, the office has taken aggressive measures to protect inventors from the growing menace of fraudulent invention-marketing firms.

USPTO independent inventors make up a substantial segment of the USPTO's customer base. IAP has established a variety of outreach efforts to provide educational services designed for the independent inventor. Outreach teams travel across the country holding inventor workshops on intellectual property. A list of upcoming workshops is available on the Independent Inventors Resource page at www.uspto.gov. The topics covered at these workshops include …

- Basic facts about patents and trademarks and the types of intellectual property protection.

- Advice on avoiding scam promotion and marketing firms, and what to look out for when getting advice.

- Tips on preparing patent and trademark applications.

- Help for writing patent claims—the do's and don'ts of claim construction.

- Updates on new rule changes affecting independent inventors.

♦ Hands-on computer search training so you can check to see if a patent or trademark already exists on a discovery.

♦ Hot technology discussions on Internet business methods, software, and biotechnology patents.

These specialized services are designed to help you with questions relating to your invention on a specific and personal level.

IAP also works closely with the nationwide network of Patent and Trademark Depository Libraries (PTDLs). PTDLs are public, state, and academic libraries that, like OIIP, disseminate patent and trademark information and support the diverse intellectual property needs of the public. PTDLs are a good place to find out if someone else has already patented your invention or obtained a federal registration for a trademark on goods or services similar to what you are seeking to use.

> **Notable Quotables**
>
> Just keep working hard, test models well … [and] keep in contact with potential customers to find out what types of products they want.
>
> —Ray Lohr, inventor, the Big Wheel

Here are some more of IAP's ongoing nationwide outreach programs:

♦ Annual Independent Inventor Conferences that provide comprehensive programs dedicated to serving and educating the independent inventor

♦ On-campus workshops held at universities throughout the country

♦ Workshops run in partnership with PTDL across the nation

♦ Participation in conferences run by professional organizations groups such as the American Society for Engineering Education

♦ Outreach team meetings with regional inventor and entrepreneurial organizations, such as the National Collegiate Inventors and Innovators Alliance

Best of all, many of the resources available through the Office of Independent Inventor Programs and PTDLs are free of charge. For information on any of these initiatives, consult the USPTO website or call 1-866-767-3848. IAP is managed by John Calvert (571-272-4983). He is supported by Cathie Kirik (571-272-8040).

Fast Facts _____

In 1994, one of America's most prolific inventors, the late Jerome H. Lemelson, and his wife, Dorothy, established the Lemelson–MIT Program at the Massachusetts Institute of Technology. Administered solely by MIT and based at the Sloan School of Management, the program is chaired by internationally recognized economist Professor Lester C. Thurow. The mission of the program is to inspire new generations of American scientists, engineers, and entrepreneurs by celebrating, through awards and educational activities, living role models in these fields. The national Lemelson–MIT Awards consist of the world's largest single prize for invention and innovation, the annual half-million-dollar Lemelson–MIT Prize, as well as the annual Lemelson–MIT Lifetime Achievement Award.

The Least You Need to Know

◆ Uncle Sam provides ways to protect your inventions.

◆ Consult a competent patent lawyer.

◆ Write your ideas down in a notebook, and have them witnessed.

◆ Patents and trademarks can be money in the bank.

Chapter 12

It All Begins with a Patent Search

In This Chapter

◆ You get the Mother of All Ideas—what to do next?

◆ Three ways to search (patents)

◆ Steps to the manual search (patents)

◆ How to search trademarks *for free*

◆ How to make money as a bounty hunter

There you sit, eating dinner, when, without warning, the Mother of All Ideas flashes through your mind at the speed of light. You leap up and write it down. Visions follow. A larger home. A sports car— perhaps two. Vacations. Private jet travel. Expensive watches. Jewelry. American Express Platinum. Fashion. Then, just as you reapproach Alpha Level, you ask yourself the sobering question that always follows the Mother of All Ideas: *has someone else already done this?*

—Richard C. Levy

You're not alone. Every inventor, gadgeteer, tinkerer, and daydreamer asks him- or herself this very same question after feeling the kind of exhilaration that only the Mother of All Ideas can cause.

Looking for a Green Light

Someone might have already had the same idea, or maybe you're the first. The only way to know for sure is through a patent search. The search will tell you if your idea has been patented already and, if so, whether the patent is still in force.

The USPTO's patent-cataloging system is pretty complex, and the amount of *prior art* you may need to look through can be staggering. The office has issued more than 7.5 million patents to date, and the number grows daily. At its Public Search Facility in Alexandria, Virginia, 30 million references are on file, according to the Public Search Facility. The Scientific Library has a collection of more than 120,000 volumes and provides access to commercial databases. The USPTO Public Search Facility has over 200 terminals offering access to more than 120 million documents electronically.

def•i•ni•tion

Prior art refers to previously issued patents that are discovered through a patent search.

You can't avoid doing a search if you want to know whether your idea is original. And you need the results of a search if you want to protect your idea with a patent.

When you apply for a patent, an examiner will do a search, and if your application is rejected based on prior art, you'll lose the application fee, not to mention significant time and energy. But even if none of the earlier patents show all the details of your idea, they may point out important features or better ways of doing the invention.

411

Want to learn how to search from the pros? The USPTO offers monthly training for its EAST, WEST, and X-Search systems. Monthly scheduled training for the automated systems is free and can be scheduled by calling 571-272-3275. Off-schedule, three-hour personal training sessions are available for $120. Classes take place at the USPTO Public Training Facility in Alexandria, Virginia, with hands-on workstation access.

In the event nothing is found to prevent or delay your application, the information gathered by a search will prove helpful, acquainting you with the details of patents related to your invention.

By the way, not all inventions are patented, so it's also a good idea to research your particular market for evidence of your idea. You might do this through a combination of library research, web surfing, and one-on-one interviews with experts in your field of invention or trade. (See Part 5 for information on how to search trademarks.)

How to Conduct a Patent Search

You may approach a search in three ways:

1. Hire a patent attorney.

2. Hire a patent searcher.

3. Do it yourself.

Let's look at all these options.

Patent Attorney–Directed Search

Going through a lawyer to search patents will cost the least amount of time and the most money. Attorneys don't conduct their own searches; they don't have the time, or skills, in most cases. They are too busy drafting claims, prosecuting patents, going to court, and fulfilling other duties. This is no different from dentists who no longer find it cost-effective to clean teeth, or physicians who don't give vaccinations because their time is better spent on services that can generate greater income.

Patent attorneys employ professional researchers. You hire the attorney, and the attorney gets someone to conduct the search. Then the attorney adds a mark-up to the search bill, sometimes as much as several hundred percent. Many lawyers cloak this in the term *handling fee*. To save this extra expense, some inventors hire their own researcher or do the search themselves.

Most patent attorneys don't render an opinion based on a search conducted by anyone other than their own searcher. I've always told my lawyers that if they wouldn't accept the work of my search firm, or searches done by myself, I would go elsewhere where such work would be acceptable. I figure I'm paying the bills, and if I'm willing to take the risk, the lawyer shouldn't have a problem. My lawyer agrees to this system.

I don't go through a patent attorney because I see no reason to pay for a legal opinion. If the search results show no prior art in my field of invention, I don't need an attorney to tell me the coast is clear. Conversely, if a search reveals prior art that's spot on my invention, I don't need an attorney to tell me my idea has been done before.

I might, on the other hand, hire an attorney to help me end-run an existing patent through the use of language in the application.

If you hire a lawyer, get a quote in advance. The fee will be based on how all-encompassing you want the search to be.

> **Notable Quotables**
>
> Step #1—Create
> Step #2—Develop
> Step #3—Pitch
> Step #4—Go back to Step #1
> Fail very fast and don't look back at the ones that didn't happen. Look forward to your next successful opportunity.
> —Jim McCafferty, co-inventor, Tekno, the Robotic Puppy

Direct-Hire Professional Search

If you want to save lawyer fees and mark-ups, consider going directly to a patent search firm. Searchers are best found through inventor grapevines, inventor associations, or university intellectual property departments. In larger cities, you can also check the Yellow Pages under "patent searchers." But be careful not to fall into a trap set by some disreputable invention marketing organizations. They list themselves in the phone book under "patent searchers" with a toll-free number. This is another way they hook unsuspecting inventors into service contracts. Get all the facts up front. See Chapter 2 for how to identify disreputable organizations and avoid being ripped off.

Some reputable searchers ask for money up front if they don't know you. This is understandable. Just be sure you get the cost of the search beforehand, and get—and check—references.

Ask for a rate sheet and then get on the phone and discuss the exact services you need. Costs vary depending on the complexity of the search. Electronic, chemical, biological, botanical, and medical searches are often more expensive than a mechanical search. In most cases, there will be incidental charges for copies, phone and fax, online fees, and shipping and handling of your materials. This is all standard.

Most important, ask if the searcher is experienced in your field of invention. If you're searching a chemical patent, don't hire someone skilled in mechanical devices.

Unless you have a history with a search firm, ask for a letter of nondisclosure before you sign on.

The cost to search a utility patent in the Washington, D.C., area runs between $500 and $1,000. It is roughly $100 per hour for a compentent search. Once the search has been completed, if you want to obtain an opinion on the patentability of your invention, add the cost of your lawyer. If you need to show a prospective licensee that your invention has a good shot at a patent or that it's unlikely to infringe on an existing product, a letter from competent patent counsel may do the trick.

We use Greentree Information Services (GIS), a patent search boutique, located in Bethesda, Maryland. George Harvill, founder of GIS (301-469-0902; g.greentreeinform@verizon.net), has been doing our work for over 15 years. You might want to contact GIS as part of your comparative shopping. There's no one more skilled or honest in the business than Greentree.

Bright Ideas

In the 1920s, Francis W. Davis was the chief engineer at the truck division of the Pierce Arrow Motor Car Company. Seeing how hard it was to steer heavy vehicles, Davis quit his job, rented a small engineering shop in Waltham, Massachusetts, and began experimenting to find a solution. He developed a hydraulic power steering system that led to power steering. Power steering was commercially available by 1951.

The Do-It-Yourself Patent Search

If you decide to do the patent search yourself, you have several search methods available:

The USPTO Public Search Facility. The USPTO operates a Patent Public Search Facility located in Alexandria, Virginia. Here every U.S. patent granted since 1790 may be searched and examined. Many inventors like to make at least one pilgrimage to the Patent Public Search Facility. It's located fewer than 15 minutes from National Airport by taxi; Metro Rail serves it off the Blue and Yellow lines, King Street Station; and several hotels are within walking distance, so it's easy to get to and around.

Upon your arrival, the USPTO will issue you a SMART card ID badge. These badges are required to pass through security access checkpoints in the Public Search Facility. Badges are obtained from the USPTO Security Service Center in room 1C51 on the lobby level of the Madison Building at the Alexandria campus from 8 A.M. to 4:30 P.M. Visitors must present a valid photo ID to be issued an access badge. I recommend you double-check the hours of operation by calling toll-free 1-800-786-9199 or locally 571-272-3275. Depending on where in the facility you want to search, the Patent Public Search Facility is typically open from 8 A.M. to 8 P.M. It's closed weekends and federal holidays.

Computer workstations enable you to search for patents issued from 1790 to the current week of issue using the patent examiner systems web-based Examiner Search Tool (WEST) and Examiner Automated Search Tool (EAST), the USPTO website, and related applications. Full document text may be searched on U.S. patents issued since 1971 and scanned images of each page from 1920 to 1970. U.S. patent images from 1790 to the present may be retrieved for viewing or printing. Some foreign patent documents may be searched using EAST and WEST. On March 15, 2001, the USPTO published its first set of patent applications under the American Inventors Protection Act, a 1999 law making far-reaching changes to the U.S. patent system.

"Publication of patent applications before a patent is granted is one of the most fundamentally significant changes to the U.S. patent system in over 100 years," said Nicholas Godici, former acting Undersecretary of Commerce and acting director of the USPTO. "Published applications will become an important reservoir of reference materials for patent examiners and a valuable resource to the public as the volume of published applications increases."

Fast Facts

Copyright, a form of intellectual property law, protects original works of authorship, including literary, dramatic, musical, and artistic works such as poetry, novels, movies, songs, computer software, and architecture. Copyright does not protect facts, ideas, systems, or methods of operation, although it may protect the way these things are expressed.

Published patent applications may be viewed as images or text searched at www.USPTO.gov/patft/index.html. New applications are published every Tuesday. Publication of patent applications is now required for the vast majority of filings made on or after November 29, 1999. Publication occurs after expiration of an 18-month period following the earliest effective filing date. The earliest effective filing date may be influenced by a number of factors, including foreign filing. Previously, U.S. patent applications were held in confidence until a patent was granted, while other major patent offices around the world have a history of publishing patent applications.

If you're going to file for foreign patents, you need to advise the USPTO of this when you apply for a U.S. patent. If you have no intention of going for foreign patents, the USPTO will keep your application under wraps until a patent is awarded, if this happens.

The Scientific Library of the Patent and Trademark Office. Near the Patent Public Search Facility is the Scientific Library of the Patent and Trademark Office, located on the ground-floor level of the Remsen office building. The Scientific Library makes publicly available over 120,000 volumes of scientific and technical books in various languages, about 90,000 bound volumes of periodicals devoted to science and technology, the official journals of 77 foreign patent organizations, and over 12 million foreign patents. The hours are from 8 A.M. to 5 P.M. Whether you do a manual or computer search, be sure to look through every possible class and subclass the patent office personnel suggest or you feel are pertinent, and then add some for good measure.

Internet search. You can also conduct searches *pro se*. Go to www.USPTO.gov and have at it. IBM also hosts a search site, www.ibm.patent.com, and Google facilitates patent searching at www.google.com/patents?hl=en.

To search foreign patents, there is only one free site. It is run by the World Intellectual Property Office (WIPO) at pctgazette.wipo.int/eng. The site provides access to various intellectual property data collections hosted by the WIPO, including Madrid, PCT, and JOPAL (nonpatent reference) data. The WIPO also supports fully searchable information retrieval and display. Access to the Digital Library is available to the general public free of charge. The services are operational and are updated on a daily, weekly, and monthly basis, respectively.

Be aware that these databases are intended for use by the general public. Due to limitations of equipment and bandwidth, they're not intended to be a source for bulk downloads of USPTO data. Bulk data can be purchased from the office at cost. The USPTO monitors who uses these databases. If someone generates an unusually high number of daily database accesses (e.g. searches, pages, or hits), whether generated manually or in an automated fashion, the USPTO may deny access to these servers without notice, according to Pamela Rinehart, Manager, Research and Administration and Patents Webmaster.

> **Fast Facts**
>
> An effective logo is reflective of brand identification and brand improvement and is also novel, simple, telegenic, charismatic, and promotable on multiple levels.

Patent and Trademark Depository Libraries

Every inventor should conduct, or at least watch, at least one hands-on patent search to fully understand and appreciate the process. Obviously, not everyone can visit the Patent and Trademark Office's Public Search Facility in Alexandria, Virginia. If you can't make the trip, you may inspect copies of patents at a Patent and Trademark Depository Library (PTDL), a nationwide network of prestigious academic, research, and public libraries. The USPTO does not have regional offices; it has the PTDLs. In addition to being research centers, the USPTO uses these as sites for outreach programs. For example, when the American Inventor Protection Act passed, officials put on seminars at the PTDLs to explain it to the intellectual property community.

PTDLs are the best deal in town. They provide the public with a local link to the USPTO, expert reference assistance, patent and trademark databases, seminars and workshops, and USPTO searching resources. Most of the services are offered for free or at a very low cost.

PTDLs continue to be one of the USPTO's most effective mechanisms for publicly disseminating patent information. PTDLs receive current issues of U.S. patents and maintain collections of patents issued earlier. The scope of these collections varies from library to library, ranging from patents of only recent years to all or most of the patents issued since 1790.

The patent collections in the PTDLs are open to the general public, and I've always found the librarians very willing to take the time to help newcomers gain effective access to the information contained in patents. In addition to the patents, PTDLs usually have all the publications of the U.S. Patent Classification System, including the *Manual of Classification*, *Index to the U.S. Patent Classification*, *Classifications Definitions*, and *Official Gazette of the United States Patent and Trademark Office*.

At each PTDL, you can conduct a manual search using the computerized database, CASSIS. This permits access to the weekly USPTO publication, the *Official Gazette*. CASSIS is limited in its range and capabilities. If you do find relevant prior art through CASSIS, which is not always easy, the PTDL should be able to make copies off microfilm for you.

The complete list of Patent and Trademark Depository Libraries is in Appendix C. There's no charge for you to search their patent collections. Because of variations among the PTDLs in their hours of service and the scope of their patent collections, be sure to contact the library in advance about its collection and hours.

411

The PTDL program oversees a national network of 88 libraries located in all 50 states, the District of Columbia, and Puerto Rico. The PTDLs conduct seminars, briefings, and training classes locally and nationally.

As mentioned earlier, a PTDL branch may have a specialized collection. To see the inventory of what's available, go to www.USPTO.gov and look under PTDLs.

Even though I live near enough to the Alexandria, Virginia, Public Search Facility, I often opt to do my work at the University of Maryland's PTDL, located within its Engineering and Physical Sciences Library. Crowded with books and not much larger than a small meeting room, the library offers only a couple chairs. However, here I can do my search work and have access to a very extensive collection of technical publications outside the PTDL that I enjoy browsing for ideas and technologies. Such "extras" are not available at the main government facility, and I consider them a bonus.

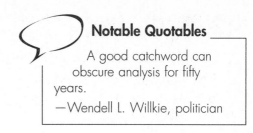

Notable Quotables

A good catchword can obscure analysis for fifty years.
—Wendell L. Willkie, politician

Electronic Databases

The USPTO provides basic patent and trademark electronic search products to all PTDLs. Many PTDLs also subscribe to WEST (Web Examiner's Search Tool). Partnership PTDLs in Sunnyvale, California; Detroit, Michigan; and Houston, Texas, offer both text and image retrieval of patents and trademarks. Here's more of what you can expect to find (note that the databases available from the USPTO's website outlined in the following list may not be available for general access at all PTDLs):

- **Optical Disk Products at PTDLs**—Describes USPTO electronic search products regularly provided to PTDLs.

- **Trademark Search System (X-Search)**—Available at PTDL Partnership sites in Sunnyvale, California; Detroit, Michigan; and Houston, Texas.

- **USPTO Internet Search Systems**—Search the U.S. Patent Database and Trademark Acceptable Identification of Goods and Services Manual.

- **Trademark Electronic Search System (TESS)**—Provides access to the same text and image database of trademarks as currently provided to examining attorneys at the USPTO via the X-Search system.

- **USPTO Web Patent Database**—Provides the full text of all U.S. patents issued since January 1, 1976, and full-page images of each page of every U.S. patent issued since 1790.

Bright Ideas

A workman left a soap-mixing machine on too long. He was so embarrassed by his mistake that he ran outside and tossed the residue into a stream so his boss wouldn't see it. Imagine his surprise when the incriminating evidence of his mistake floated to the surface. Ivory, the soap that floats, was born.

PTDL Publications

You'll typically find these publications and documents at a Patent and Trademark Depository Library:

◆ Patent and Trademark Depository Library Program—Describes the mission, history, operation, and services of the PTDLs.

◆ List of PTDL libraries—Includes the address and telephone number of all current PTDLs.

Fast Facts

Established in 1995, the U.S. Patent and Trademark Museum strives to educate the public about the patent and trademark systems and the important role intellectual property protection plays in our nation's social and economic health. The Museum is operated for the USPTO by the National Inventors Hall of Fame. It houses both permanent and changing exhibits, as well as a Museum Gift Shop. The museum is located in the Atrium of the Madison Building, 600 Dulany Street, Alexandria, Virginia, and is easily accessible from the King Street and Eisenhower Avenue Metro stations. It's open Monday through Friday from 9 A.M. to 5 P.M., Saturday from noon to 5 P.M., and closed on Sundays and federal holidays. There is no admission fee.

◆ Optical Disk Products at PTDLs—Lists optical disk products available for public used at all PTDLs.

◆ Patents: The Collection for All Reasons—Describes the ways in which this unique resource can be used.

◆ The Seven-Step Strategy—Outlines a suggested procedure for patent searching.

◆ Conducting a Trademark Search at a PTDL—Outlines a suggested procedure for trademark searching.

◆ Examples and descriptions of patent and trademark document types.

◆ Patent Document Kind Codes (also available as a PDF document).

◆ USPTO Search Facilities Hours and Location.

◆ Document Disclosure Program.

◆ International Schedule of Classes of Goods and Services (also available as a PDF document).

A librarian can usually assist you in finding a list of those who make a living searching patents. Don't be put off if a librarian is reluctant to give a specific recommendation; they are not permitted to provide legal advice nor personally recommend any patent professionals or search organizations.

411

You may be able to take advantage of cutting-edge technologies and facilities that Sandia National Laboratories has to offer. Contact Corporate Business Development and Partnerships Center Organization 1300, Mail Stop 0185, Sandia National Laboratories, PO Box 5800, Albuquerque, NM 87185; 505-845-7730; fax: 505-844-3513; net_admin@giss.tt.sandia.gov; www.sandia.gov.

Patent Search Steps

Here is a brief guide to manual searches at the PSF and PTDLs for U.S. patents. No matter where you decide to conduct a search, you must take certain steps in any patent search.

1. If you know the patent number, go to the *Official Gazette*, available at patent search facilities and in many public library reference rooms, to read a summary of the patent.

2. If you know the patentee or assignee, look at the *Patent/Assignee Index* to locate the patent number. This is available at any of the patent search facilities. In Crystal City, it is on microfiche and in card catalogues.

3. If you know the subject, start with the *Index to the U.S. Patent Classification*.

4. Once you've jotted down the class(es) and subclass(es) out of the *Index*, check the information in relation to the hierarchy in the *Manual of Classification* to see if it is close to what you need. The *Manual of Classification* is available at all patent search facilities.

5. Using the class/subclass numbers you have found, look at the U.S. Patent Classification Subclass and Numeric Listing, and copy the patent numbers of patents assigned to the selected class/subclass. If you are at the Crystal City facility, take the class/subclass numbers into the stacks of patents

Notable Quotables

Inventing is a combination of brains and materials. The more brains you use, the less material you need.

—Charles F. Kettering, inventor, electric cash register

and begin "pulling shoes." (To pull shoes is to physically remove patent group-ings from the open shelves.)

6. Then, using the *Official Gazette* again, look at the summaries of those patents. (At the Crystal City facility, you won't have to go back to this publication because the actual patents are there.)

7. Upon locating the relevant patents, examine the complete patent in person or on microfilm, depending on where you conduct the search.

8. Print copies of all relevant prior art. Your patent attorney will want to cite some of it in your application.

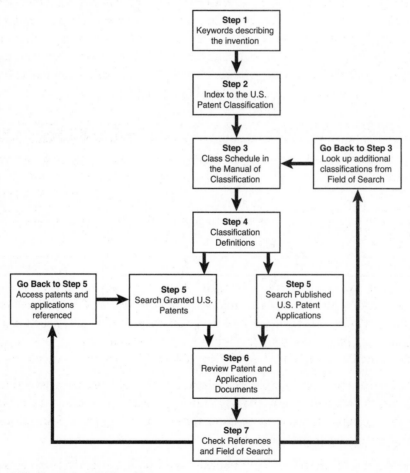

U.S. Patent Search Flow Chart.

(Courtesy of the U.S. Patent and Trademark Office)

Patent Classification System

Patents are arranged according to a classification system of more than 465 classes and over 200,000 subclasses. The *Index to the U.S. Patent Classifications* is an alphabetical list of the subject headings referring to specific classes and subclasses of the U.S. patent classification system. The classifications are intended as an initial means of entry into the USPTO's classification system and should be particularly useful to those who lack experience in using the classification system or who are unfamiliar with the technology.

The classifications are to searching a patent what the card catalog is to looking for a library book. It's the only way to discover what exists in the field of prior art. Before you begin your search, use the classifications to plot your direction. First, look for the term you feel best represents your invention. If you can't find a match, look for terms of approximately the same meaning, for example, describing a similar function, effect, or application. By doing some homework before you begin searching, such as familiarizing yourself with the *Index* and locating the class and subclass numbers for terms that pertain to your invention, you'll save time.

Bright Ideas

Allured by photography, music teachers Leopold Godowsky and Leopold Mannes co-invented an easy-to-use, practical color film. They supported themselves by teaching music and putting on concerts, and in their spare time they mixed up concoctions in Mannes's kitchen. Their work caught the attention of Kodak, and the company offered them full-time, well-paid jobs. In 1935, Kodak introduced Kodachrome film, the result of their work.

Once you have recorded the identifying numbers of possibly pertinent classes and subclasses, refer to the *Manual of Classification*, a loose-leaf USPTO volume listing the numbers and descriptive titles of more than 300 classes and 95,000 subclasses used in the subject classification of patents, with an index to classifications. This manual is also available at the Patent and Trademark Depository Libraries and at www.uspto.gov.

The classifications are arranged with subheadings that can extend to several levels of indentation. A complete reading of a subheading includes the title of the most adjacent higher heading and so on until there are no higher headings. Some headings reference other related or preferred entries.

New classes and subclasses are continuously based on breaking developments in science and technology. Old classes and subclasses are rendered obsolete by technological advance. In fact, if you have suggestions for future revisions of the classifications or if you find omissions or errors, you are encouraged to alert the USPTO. Send your suggestions to Editor, U.S. Patent Classification, Office of Documentation, U.S. Patent and Trademark Office, Washington, DC 20231.

How to Order Copies of Prior Art

If you can't get a copy of a specific patent(s) through a PTDL or www.USPTO.gov, you may order copies of original patents or cross-referenced patents contained in subclasses comprising the field of search from the Patent and Trademark Office. Mail your request to Commissioner for Patents, PO Box 1450, Alexandria, VA 22313-1450.

Payment may be made by check, coupons, or money. Expect a wait of up to four weeks when ordering copies of patents by mail from the USPTO.

For the convenience of attorneys, agents, and the general public in paying any fees due, deposit accounts may be established in the USPTO with a minimum deposit of $310. For information on this service, call 571-272-6500.

411

BountyQuest is an Internet destination where companies post large cash rewards for vital information. I saw one this morning for $10,000. The rapidly growing, high-stakes patent arena is the source of BountyQuest's first rewards, where access to fugitive information helps resolve today's raging patent controversies. BountyQuest opened for business in 2000 and is privately held. I have no experience with the company and list it as a piece of intellectual candy. For more information, visit www.bountyquest.com.

What to Do with Your Search Results

Study the results of the patent research. You may be out of luck if a previously patented invention is very similar to yours; you may even be an *infringer* on another's invention. On the other hand, one or more patents may describe inventions that are intended for the same purpose as yours but are significantly different in various ways. Look these over and decide whether it is worthwhile to proceed. Consult a patent attorney if you have any doubt.

def•i•ni•tion

An **infringer** is one who misappropriates another person's intellectual property.

If the features that make your invention different from the prior art provide important advantages, you should discuss the situation with your attorney to determine whether a fair chance exists of obtaining a patent covering these features.

I've found from experience that a good patent attorney can often get some claim to issue, albeit not always a strong one. A patent for patent's sake is usually possible. Whether it will be worth the paper it is printed on is another matter. Do not make this decision lightly, because the patent process is not cheap. The average utility patent costs about $2,500.

DIY Trademark Searches

Trademark searching is so streamlined and foolproof today that it can all be done from your personal computer via the Internet. There's no need to hire a search firm. In fact, Greentree Information Services, my searcher of choice, no longer accepts assignments to search trademarks because it's now something people can do for themselves.

For details on trademark searches, see Chapter 17.

The Last Word

When determining which search method is best for you, consider how much time and money you can spare and how well you can do the job yourself. Finding out early that the Mother of All Ideas is old news can save you a lot in developmental and legal costs, not to mention time.

Conversely, you just might find out that your idea is the next sliced bread.

The Least You Need to Know

- When you search for gold, sometimes you get the gold; sometimes you get the shaft. Don't be surprised if your search reveals a crowded field of invention.
- Patent searching—there's no need to pay retail.
- Patent and Trademark Depository Libraries (PTDLs) are very user-friendly.
- There's no need to pay for a federal trademark search. You can do it yourself easily.

How to Hire a Patent Attorney

In This Chapter

- Yes, you need a patent attorney
- No, you shouldn't do utility patents yourself
- It's a buyer's market
- What to look for under the hood
- Where you can save major dollars

America's creative genius is truly an invaluable national asset which in my view arises from our independent spirit. An important part of this great resource continues to reside in the independent inventor community. Clearly these entrepreneurial innovators are helping ensure that American industry remains competitive in the global marketplace.

—John K. Williamson, assistant general counsel, intellectual property, PPG Industries

The art of drafting a patent isn't brain surgery, but it does take an expertise most inventors don't possess. Even those skilled in the arcane language of the patent process may not be up-to-date on USPTO regulations with regard to the prosecution of a patent application or the handling of office actions. This process is not without red tape, and as with any bureaucracy, things are always in transition.

Do You Need a Patent Attorney?

Yes. Count on it. If you think it's expensive to use a patent attorney, see what it costs you if you *don't* hire one and mess up your patent. While it's perfectly legal for you to draft and prosecute your own patents (i.e., working *pro se*), I strongly recommend that you hire patent counsel for all patent work except design patents.

411

Intellectual Property Owners (IPO) is a nonprofit association that serves the owners of patents, trademarks, copyrights, and trade secrets. Founded in 1972 and based in Washington, D.C., it has a diverse membership: more than a hundred Fortune 500 member companies, including GE, 3M, IBM, AT&T, and PPG Industries, as well as several hundred independent inventors and patent attorneys and a few universities. IPO's National Inventor of the Year Award recognizes America's most outstanding inventors. Winners epitomize the American tradition of technological leadership and "Yankee ingenuity." For information and a membership application, call 202-466-2396, e-mail info@ipo.org, or visit www.ipo.org.

Time after time, without equivocation, the value of my patents has been enhanced by the contribution of a savvy patent attorney, someone who knows how to define invention and navigate the waters of prior art. The fact is, anyone can get a patent on almost anything. What good patent counsel will do is increase the odds that a patent awarded adequately protects your invention.

"Patent writing should be done by those specifically skilled in the art," says Tomima Edmark, inventor of Topsy Tail, the invention that turned a ponytail inside out and made over $80 million in worldwide sales. "Writing your own patent application is a big mistake."

Calvin D. MacCracken, who holds 80 U.S. patents and 250 foreign patents, advises in his *Handbook for Inventors*, "Writing your own patent is long, hard work …. If you can somehow afford a good patent attorney to do the whole job, that may well produce a better patent …."

(Note: I'm referring to utility patents here. For advice on design patents, please refer to Chapter 14. I don't recommend patent counsel for design patents, nor spending money on a search of prior art. Plant patents are covered in Chapter 15.)

411

To find a patent attorney or patent agent licensed to practice before the USPTO, go to https://oedci.uspto.gov/OEDCI/GeoRegion.jsp. Currently, the USPTO recognizes 9,339 active agents and 28,933 active attorneys. Information concerning a practitioner's status as an attorney is based on records provided to the USPTO's Office of Enrollment and Discipline and might not reflect the practitioner's status in a State Bar. If you're interested in a practitioner's status in a State Bar, contact that State Bar for specific information.

Do-It-Yourself Could Do You In

Use step-by-step, do-it-yourself books or computer programs only as primers. These books have a wonderful tutorial benefit, but it's reckless and foolhardy for those not skilled in patent specification preparation, particularly claim drafting, to do it for themselves.

"Applying for a patent seems easy. Just describe what your invention is all about, fill out a form, pay the filing fee, and presto! You're done," quips Dinesh Agarwal, Esq., a skilled and artful patent attorney of mine from Alexandria, Virginia. Dinesh, a 25-year patent attorney, was selected among Virginia's "Legal Elite" (Best Lawyers—Intellectual Property) in 2004 and 2006.

"But wait," he says. "Did you include a 'written description' of the invention? Did you provide 'enablement'? Did you disclose the 'best mode' for carrying out the invention?" Multiple statutory provisions and rules apply to a patent application that matures into a patent.

Dinesh continues, "A patent is a form of contract. It is a contract between you and Uncle Sam. Would you sign an important contract without the benefit of legal counsel? Would you think of buying real estate without a qualified surveyor or real estate lawyer? You should not apply for a patent without hiring a patent attorney. A patent confers upon an inventor property rights similar to real estate or owning an automobile. You just can't see or touch it. It's called 'intangible' personal property rights."

According to Dinesh, a patent attorney can …

◆ Navigate the complex maze of laws/regulations that can affect your rights.

◆ Stop you from becoming a villain to your own invention, e.g., engaging in activities that might bar you from obtaining a patent.

Competent patent counsel can also determine, early on …

◆ The scope and content of protection to which you may be entitled under the law.

◆ Whether your product might infringe on a third party's patent.

◆ How to avoid infringement of a third party's patent.

◆ Whether you should license or purchase a third party's patent.

◆ How to build your intellectual property (ip) portfolio.

◆ How to use patented technology without paying royalties.

◆ How best to protect your invention inexpensively and mark your products as "Patent Pending."

◆ The state of technology in a desired area.

◆ How to improve upon an existing technology.

◆ How to avoid mistakes of others in a desired technical area.

◆ The potential competition in a desired technical area.

He or she can also …

◆ Draft the application to satisfy the applicable statute and regulations.

◆ Draft the application to receive the proper scope of legal protection.

◆ Draft the application to avoid pitfalls or landmines that might later blow up when, for example, you're about to dominate the market.

◆ Shepherd your application through the USPTO corridors for proper review and consideration.

◆ Deal with the incredibly busy examiners who will approve (or disapprove) your application.

◆ Obtain patent protection in foreign countries. (A U.S. patent is effective only in the United States.)

- Maintain enforceability of the patents.

- Negotiate licenses and royalties with third parties.

- Deal with potential infringements by third parties.

In summary, a patent attorney can assist you in determining, early on, how to use your invention as a sword or a shield.

A patent is a form of lottery ticket. It's the Big Spin. The invention it covers may hit pay dirt. Therefore, you want to make every effort to ensure a patent has teeth and cannot be easily attacked. Patent attorneys aren't perfect, but if you are working together with your attorney, your claims will more likely be stronger.

You can do your own income tax. For people who don't make a lot of money, this may be the most cost-effective way to deal with the IRS. But those who have substantial earnings or estates hire CPAs. They don't do their income tax with a self-help book—they have too much at stake. Wealthy people use CPAs to level the playing field and give themselves every benefit of the law. Inventors should do the same through the counsel of a patent attorney.

Here's another way to look at it: if you bought a state lottery ticket and hit the big prize, such as a multistate purse, would you purchase a do-it-yourself book on income tax or would you hire the best CPA to help you keep as much of the money as possible under the law?

Patents are invaluable if a product hits the mother lode, and therefore must be afforded every advantage. So even if you really know your stuff, I recommend that you have competent counsel review your work. There's no guarantee that a licensed practitioner won't make a mistake, but if he does, he'll know how to correct it—and he carries malpractice insurance. Do you?

Bottom line: smart inventors use experienced advisers to ensure they obtain the strongest protection available on their inventions.

Bright Ideas
As a visitor to Labrador in the early 1900s, Clarence Birdseye was impressed by the quality of the fish and game the Eskimos froze. In 1924, he started the Freezing Company, and this kicked off the frozen fruit and vegetable industry. Birdseye was granted a patent in 1930 for his method of packaging frozen food.

Is That Your Final Answer?

Ask the lawyers you interview some important questions:

Do you draft the patent, or does an assistant do it?

How long will it take you to complete the job (that is, write the initial application and have it filed)?

Are you up-to-speed on The American Inventors Protection Act enacted November 29, 1999, as Public Law 106-113?

Are there any hidden charges in addition to service fees and disbursements, including government fees? Lawyers like clients to pick up their overhead plus fees. Some lawyers charge for incoming faxes. Refuse to pay for fax traffic between you and your patent firm if you're located in the same city.

What is the charge for photocopies? This can be a profit center for some patent lawyers. This isn't as bad as it used to be, though. Some state legal ethic codes, e.g., Virginia's, allow lawyers only to recover their costs.

If the price is too high, cut a better deal. If there are co-inventors, get one copy and have one of the inventors copy and distribute the material. Services that specialize in copying patent files for law firms charge as much as $1 per page, which the patent attorney then marks up. You can buy black-and-white copy service less expensively at Kinko's or Staples.

> **Inventions Wanted**
>
> Family-owned Faultless Starch/Bon Ami (www.faultlessinventors.com) has been making consumer products since 1887. Some of the products include Kleen King®, Magic®, Hot Iron Cleaner®, Weed Popper®, Garden-Claw®, and Weasel Edger®. The company invites outside submissions and even sponsors an annual invention contest with prizes. This contest is overseen by the Inventors Club of Kansas City.

How are telephone consultations billed? Am I going to be charged every time I ask a question? I set these ground rules early in any relationship with counsel.

May I have a list of references and their phone numbers? You'll want to talk to other independent inventors and see if they were satisfied.

What kind of guarantee comes with the work? In other words, you want to be sure you don't get eaten alive by fee creep, which can be caused by interferences and appeals at the USPTO. It may take two or three years to prosecute a patent, depending on the amount of office action involved. Nail down the price up front, because a lawyer's hourly rate most likely will have gone up by the time the work has been completed.

If your lawyer directs your search and drawing initiatives and mistakes are made, your lawyer will stand behind the work. The lawyer simply points out the mistakes to the subcontractors and takes it out of their hides.

Levy's Rules for Hiring a Patent Attorney

Consider the following points when retaining counsel. Read them carefully; they could save you time and money:

Be sure your patent attorney is registered by the Patent and Trademark Office. The USPTO keeps a register of 9,339 active agents and 28,933 active attorneys qualified to practice before it. To be listed, a person must comply with the regulations prescribed by the USPTO, which requires proof that the person is of good moral character and of good repute, and that he or she has the legal, scientific, and technical qualifications necessary to give inventors valuable service. Individuals much demonstrate certain qualifications by passing an exam. Those admitted must have a college degree in engineering or science, or the equivalent of such a degree.

To find a patent attorney or patent agent in your city or state licensed to practice before the USPTO, go to https://oedci.uspto.gov/OEDCI.

In actuality, far fewer people are practicing patent law than it would seem from the list. The USPTO list may contain lawyers and patent agents who have gone to the other side of the grass or are no longer in business.

Hire a patent attorney who's a specialist in your technology. You wouldn't want a dermatologist to do your heart surgery. Nor would you want an electronic patent specification written by an attorney whose specialty is mechanical engineering. Satisfy yourself of the lawyer's expertise. Interview more than one candidate. Patent counsel should be able to help you broaden your claims by probing your mind to be sure you've considered all possible embodiments and improvements. Only those versed in your field of invention will be able to do this effectively.

Be wary of lawyers who pitch themselves as agents to help sell your invention. You're hiring patent counsel, not a salesman.

Hire patent counsel who understands the ins and outs of The American Inventors Protection Act enacted November 29, 1999, as Public Law 106-113. This is complicated stuff for the brightest of them.

Notable Quotables

When patterns are broken, new worlds can emerge.

—Tuli Kupferberg, poet and free-formist

Shop around. It's a buyer's market. If the lawyer is inflexible, go elsewhere.

Request an estimate. Patent attorneys are able to give close estimates when they understand the scope of work. Once you have an acceptable price, ask your attorney to agree in writing and cap it off. Otherwise, you may find your budget busted. Make a package deal whenever you can. You are selling money, not buying services.

Don't embarrass yourself by insisting that the lawyer sign a confidentiality agreement before you'll disclose your invention. Patent lawyers don't steal ideas. If you're preoccupied about this, get over it. It's unethical for a patent lawyer to steal ideas, and it's a great way to get disbarred.

Know who will do your work, especially if you're dealing with a large firm. The big firms need litigation and hefty retainers to make money. They don't make enough to pay the light bills drafting claims and prosecuting patents for independent inventors.

You want to be important to the attorney. Years ago, I found one lawyer putting our work on hold while he took care of business for a more senior attorney at the firm. You also don't want your work rushed. Thought must be given when going for as wide a set of claims as possible. Be sure your work won't be farmed out to a less experienced attorney in the firm.

Bright Ideas

In the early 1920s, R. A. Watkins, owner of a small printing plant in Illinois, was approached by a man who wanted to sell him the rights to a homemade device made of waxed cardboard and tissue on which messages could be printed and then easily erased by lifting up the tissue. Watkins wanted to think about the proposition overnight and told the man to return the next day. In the middle of the night, Watkins's phone rang; it was the inventor calling from jail. The man said that if Watkins would bail him out, he could have the device. Watkins agreed and went on to acquire both the U.S. patent rights and the foreign rights to the device, which he called the Magic Slate.

If possible, hire your own patent searcher. Lawyers don't search patents. They hire specialists to do that for them and then mark up the bills. Large firms typically have people on staff who go to the USPTO every day; others use freelancers. You'll save a lot of money making a direct hire. (See Chapter 12 for more on hiring patent searchers.)

If the attorney allows you to handle this process, he may ask that he be indemnified from problems that could arise from a less-than-satisfactory search. For example, your searcher could miss a key piece of prior art. Your attorney also won't render a written opinion unless you pay extra for it.

I look at it this way: if I hire a highly qualified searcher who also does work for the law firms, then I am willing to take that risk in return for the savings. I usually do not need a written opinion to figure out if the prior art precludes me from getting protection. The search results will show this. But if I do need an opinion, I pay for it.

If possible, hire your own patent draftsman, too. Lawyers don't draw. They hire specialists and then mark up their bills. Larger firms frequently have draftsmen on staff; others use freelancers. Here, again, you'll save money if you make the call.

If several lawyers show up for a meeting, ask who they are, what their purpose is, and whether you're paying for them. If you are, be very sure they're needed. One lawyer should be capable of handling the patent.

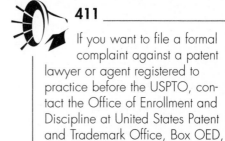

411

If you want to file a formal complaint against a patent lawyer or agent registered to practice before the USPTO, contact the Office of Enrollment and Discipline at United States Patent and Trademark Office, Box OED, PO Box 1450, Alexandria, VA 22313-1450; 571-272-4097; fax: 571-273-0074.

Another Money-Saver

The more groundwork you lay for the patent attorney, the better shape you'll be in on a couple fronts:

♦ It will take the attorney less time to work up the specifications and claims if he doesn't start with a blank paper.

♦ Give the practitioner the benefit of your ideas for claims. One of the greatest contributions an inventor can make to the drafting of claims is to point out how the competition might end-run them to get around the patent.

No one knows your invention better than you do. Develop an in-depth description of your invention, and draft all the claims you can think of. Don't worry about how to justify them. It's important that the patent attorney have an idea of the invention's scope and reach.

The Least You Need to Know

♦ Patent attorneys are *required.*

♦ Do-it-yourself isn't the best plan when it comes to patents. Get an attorney.

◆ Shop around for the best patent attorney for you—it's a buyer's market.

◆ Steer clear of large law firms where you might not get the best service.

◆ Hire your own patent searcher and draftsman. You'll save money.

Part 5

Uncle Sam Wants (to Protect) YOU!

The United States of America has had more than 200 years of Patent and Copyright laws on its books. Is it possible that early lawmakers James Madison, George Read, Rufus King, Benjamin Franklin, Alexander Hamilton, George Washington, and Thomas Jefferson could have foreseen the importance of their hard work as it advances America's sciences and useful arts into the twenty-first century?

Imagine how brilliant and omniscient the drafters of the U.S. Constitution and successive statutes were when they thought to write, in Article 1, Section 8, that Congress shall have the power to "promote the Progress of Science and useful Arts, by securing for limited Times to Authors and Inventors the exclusive Right to their respective Writings and Discoveries."

The golden eggs laid by inventors, gadgeteers, cranks, tinkerers, thinkers, imagineers, and entrepreneurs that continue to hatch American industries have been protected and nurtured by a vital—albeit imperfect—system of intellectual property laws that has stood the test of time.

Part 5 focuses on the methods of protection available to you, thanks to our forefathers—patents, trademarks, copyrights, trade secrets. This information isn't meant to take the place of competent legal advice, but rather to familiarize you with the terrain as you continue on your quest to commercialize your ideas.

14

How to Apply for a Utility Patent

In This Chapter

◆ The nonprovisional patent

◆ Staking claim on your invention

◆ Prototypes—necessary or not?

◆ Patenting computer programs

> We need to thank our creative inventors for not only our good life, but a healthy one in a great land of opportunity. When I look back at the thousands of inventors that I have helped, I see not only the successful companies, but all the lives that they have touched for the better.
>
> —Lawrence J. Udell, executive director, California Invention Center, Center for New Venture Alliance, Intellectual Property International, Ltd.

If you've invented an elevator-winding device, an apparatus for attaching tag pins, a tape-drive mechanism, a 3-D digitizer, a preschool toy, a U-joint mount, or simply a better mousetrap, you might want to consider the kind of protection a nonprovisional utility patent can provide. It's the strongest position you can take.

Manufacturers get a warm and fuzzy feeling from broad utility patents. A utility patent on an invention will really pump up your concept's shine and get everyone's attention. The more bulletproof you can make your invention, the better. A strong utility patent can give your licensee a monopoly on making, using, and selling the invention. That's what it's all about.

Before deciding whether to proceed with the filing of any patent application, you have to consider a patent search (see Chapter 12). Once you've made that decision, dive into this chapter to see the options available to you.

(Note that the USPTO no longer runs its Document Disclosure program. It was discontinued on February 1, 2007.)

Provisional Application for a Utility Patent

Since June 8, 1995, the United States Patent and Trademark Office has offered the option of filing a provisional application for patent. This is designed to provide a lower-cost first patent filing in the United States. Applicants are entitled to claim the benefit of a provisional application in a corresponding nonprovisional application filed not later than 12 months after the provisional application filing date.

A provisional application for patent is a U.S. national application for patent filed in the USPTO under 35 U.S.C. § 111(b). It allows filing without a formal patent claim, oath, or declaration or any information disclosure (prior art) statement. It provides the means to establish an early effective filing date in a later-filed nonprovisional patent application filed under 35 U.S.C. § 111(a). It also allows the term "Patent Pending" to be applied in connection with the description of the invention.

A provisional application for patent has a pendency lasting 12 months from the date the provisional application is filed. The 12-month pendency period cannot be extended. Therefore, if you file a provisional application, you must file a corresponding nonprovisional application for patent (nonprovisional application) during the 12-month pendency period of the provisional application to benefit from the earlier filing of the provisional application. In accordance with 35 U.S.C. § 119(e), the corresponding nonprovisional application must contain or be amended to contain a specific reference to the provisional application within the time period and in the manner required by 37 CFR 1.78.

Nonprovisional Application for a Utility Patent

A nonprovisional application for a patent is made to the Assistant Commissioner for Patents and includes several elements, in the following order.

Bright Ideas
Jacob Schick, a retired U.S. Army colonel and inventor, was inspired to develop a razor that worked without soap or water. After World War I, Schick devoted himself to inventing an electric razor. His wife mortgaged their Connecticut home to finance the venture. The patented design that resulted used a series of slots to hold the hairs while a series of moving blades cut off the hairs.

A Letter of Transmittal

First up, a transmittal letter. This should be filed with every patent application to instruct the USPTO on the services you desire in the processing of your application. In this cover letter, inform the director of your name, address, e-mail address, and telephone number; the type of application; the title of your invention; and the contents of the application.

Specification

Next, the specification. This must include a written description of the invention and of the manner and process of making and using it. The specification is required to be in such full, clear, concise, and exact terms as to enable any person skilled in the art or science to which the invention pertains, or with which it is most nearly connected, to make and use it.

The specification must set forth the precise invention for which you're seeking patent protection, in such a way as to distinguish it from other inventions and from what is old. It must describe completely a specific embodiment of the process, machine, manufacture, composition of matter, or improvement invented and must explain the method of operation or principle whenever applicable. Write the best embodiment you contemplate for your invention.

In the case of an improvement to an invention, the specification must particularly point out the part(s) of the process, machine, manufacture, or composition of matter to which your improvement relates. The description should be confined to the specific improvement and to such parts that cooperate with it or as may be necessary to complete understanding or description of it. The pages of the specification, including claims and abstract, should be numbered consecutively, starting with page 1. The page numbers should be centrally located above or, preferably, below the text.

Fast Facts

During the last century, inventors were prolific. Here are some important twentieth-century inventions and their approximate dates of conception, according to *The World Book:* safety razor: 1901; air-conditioning: 1902; airplane: 1903; helicopter: 1907; television: 1920s; modern plastics: 1930s; xerography: 1938; transistor: 1947; and compact disc: 1982.

Title. You'll need to give your invention a title. It should be as short and specific as possible (it may not exceed 500 characters in length) and should appear as the heading on the first page of the specification, if it does not otherwise appear at the beginning of the application.

Also include any cross-references to related applications, if you know of any. Include, too, references to a microfiche appendix, for computer program listings, if any. The total number of microfiche and total number of frames should be specified.

Background of the Invention. The specification should set forth the background of the invention in two parts:

♦ *Field of the Invention.* This section should include a statement of the field of endeavor to which the invention pertains. This section may also include a paraphrasing of the applicable U.S. patent classification definitions or the subject matter of the claimed invention. This section may also be titled "Technical Field."

♦ *Description of the Related Art (or Prior Art).* This section should contain a description of information known to you, including references to specific documents, that are related to your invention. This section should also contain, if applicable, references to specific art-related problems involved in the prior art that your invention solves.

Summary of the Invention. This section should present a summary of the substance or general idea of the claimed invention. The summary may point out the advantages of the invention or how it solves previously existing problems, preferably those problems identified in the "Background of the Invention" section. A statement of the object of the invention may also be included. The summary should precede the detailed description.

Abstract of the Disclosure. The purpose of the abstract is to enable the USPTO and the public to determine quickly from a cursory inspection the nature and gist of the technical disclosures of the invention. The abstract points out what is new in the art to which the invention pertains. It should be in narrative form and generally limited to a single paragraph on a separate page.

Claims. The specification must conclude with a claim particularly pointing out and distinctly claiming the subject matter you regard as your invention.

More than one claim may be presented, provided the claims differ substantially from each other and are not unduly multiplied.

411

Since October 27, 2000, the USPTO has been accepting electronic patent filings. EFS-Web is not a patent application authoring tool, but simply a means of allowing you to electronically submit patent applications and related documents as PDF attachments. You choose the tool, process, and workflow with which you want to author your documents; the only requirement is that you must convert them to PDF files before submitting them via EFS-Web.

One or more claims may be presented in dependent form, referring to and further limiting another claim or claims in the same application. Any dependent claim that refers to more than one other claim ("multiple dependent claim") shall refer to such other claims in the alternative only. A multiple dependent claim shall not serve as a basis for any other multiple dependent claim. For fee calculation purposes under 37 CFT § 1.16, a multiple dependent claim will be considered to be that number of claims to which direct reference is made therein. For fee calculation purposes, any claim depending from a multiple dependent claim will be considered that number of claims to which direct reference is made in that multiple dependent claim.

The claim or claims must conform to the invention as set forth in the remainder of the specification. The terms and phrases used in the claims must find clear support or antecedent basis in the description so that the meaning of the terms in the claims may be ascertainable for reference to the description.

Drawings

A patent application must contain drawings if drawings are needed to understand the subject matter you're patenting. The drawings must show every feature of the invention as specified in the claims. Omission of drawings will cause an application to be considered incomplete. An application for a design patent must contain at least one drawing.

When drawings are included, there must be a brief description of the several views of the drawings, and the detailed description of the invention must refer to the different views by specifying the numbers of the figures. It also must refer to the different parts by use of reference letters or numerals (preferably the latter). (For specific guidelines to drawings, see Chapter 16.)

Oath or Declaration

All the actual inventors must sign this document. An oath may be administered by any person within the United States, or by a diplomatic or consular officer of a foreign country who is authorized by the United States to administer oaths. A declaration does not require any witness or person to administer or verify its signing. Thus, use of a declaration is preferable.

The document must identify the application to which it is directed. It must give the name, city, either state or country of residence, country of citizenship, and post office address of each inventor, and it must state whether the inventor is a sole or joint inventor of the invention claimed. Additionally, designation of a correspondence address is needed on the oath or declaration. Providing a correspondence address helps ensure prompt delivery of all notices, official letters, and other communications.

Fee payment. Last but not least, don't forget to include your check. Fees for patent applications are subject to change, so always double-check before filing. Having made improper payments in the past, which caused delays and penalties, I now call several times before writing a check to the USPTO. For up-to-date fees, call 571-272-1000. Please remember that two sets of fees exist—one for a small entity and one for other than a small entity. If you find that you need additional guidance filing your application, hire a patent attorney.

Bright Ideas

Charles Goodyear had no formal education. When his family hardware business failed and he couldn't clean up the mess, he was put in debtors' prison. Ironically, it was there that he started experimenting to find a more stable rubber. On June 15, 1844, Goodyear was awarded Patent No. 3,633 for "Improvement In India-Rubber Fabric." His invention never made him any money, and in 1860, he died in poverty. Twenty-eight years later, tires emblazoned with his name rolled out of Frank Seiberling's factory, named for the man who invented the process of vulcanizing.

Models Not Generally Required

Now that you know what *is* required for your utility patent application, let's go over what's *not* required: models. Models were once required in all cases admitting a model, as part of the application, and these models became part of the record of the patent. Such models are no longer generally required (the description of the invention in the specification, and the drawings, must be sufficiently full and complete and capable of being understood to disclose the invention without the aid of a model), and will not be accepted unless specifically called for by the examiner.

If the invention relates to a composition of matter, you may be asked to furnish specimens of the composition or of its ingredients or intermediates, for the purpose of inspection or experiment.

But if you want to license your invention, you'd better have a looks-like/works-like prototype to show. Companies don't license ideas; they need to see prototypes—or, at the very least, an operational breadboard.

411

Here are some patent blogs you may enjoy perusing: anticipatethis.wordpress.com, inventivestep.net, www.stus.com/stus-category.php?cat=TOP&sub=IPL, www.infringement.blogs.com, and www.patentlysilly.com.

Solamente Ingles, Por Favor

All application papers must be prepared and submitted in English, or a translation into English will be required along with the required fee. All application papers must be legibly written on only one side, either by a typewriter or mechanical printer in permanent dark ink or its equivalent in portrait orientation on flexible, strong, smooth, nonshiny, durable, and white paper.

Fast Facts

The Camp Invention program is a nationally acclaimed summer-enrichment experience for children in grades 1 through 6. The National Inventors Hall of Fame Foundation program was developed in partnership with the USPTO and fosters creativity and inventive-thinking skills through hands-on activities, brainstorming, and open-ended exploration. It introduces students to science, technology, mathematics, and engineering concepts in an engaging and age-appropriate manner. Get more information at www.campinvention.org or by calling 571-272-1000.

The Rules of the Game

The papers must be presented in a form with sufficient clarity and contrast between the paper and the writing to permit electronic reproduction.

The application papers must all be the same size—either 21cm by 29.7cm (DIN size A4) or 8½ by 11 inches (21.6cm by 27.9cm), with a top margin of at least ¾ inch (2cm), a left-side margin of at least 1 inch (2.5cm), a right-side margin of at least ¾ inch (2.0cm), and a bottom margin of at least ¾ inch (2.0cm), with no holes made in the submitted papers. The spacing on all papers must be 1½ or double-spaced, and the application papers must be numbered consecutively (centrally located above or below the text) starting with page 1.

The application for a patent is not forwarded for examination until all required parts, complying with all the necessary rules, are received. If any application is filed without all the required parts for obtaining a filing date (incomplete or defective), you will be notified of the deficiencies and given a time period to complete the application filing (a surcharge may be required), at which time a filing date as of the new date of such a completed submission will be given to you. If you do not correct the omission within a specified time period, the application will be returned or otherwise disposed of; the filing fee, if submitted, will be refunded minus a handling fee set forth in the fee schedule.

Now that you have all the parts of the application ready to go, keep the following in mind:

◆ Send or deliver all parts of the complete application together; otherwise, each part must be signed and a letter must accompany each part, accurately and clearly connecting it with the other parts of the application.

◆ All applications received in the USPTO are numbered in serial order, and you'll be informed of the application serial number and filing date by a filing receipt.

◆ The filing date of an application for patent is the date on which a specification (including at least one claim), and any drawings necessary to understand the subject matter sought to be patented are received in the USPTO. Or in the case of a previously incomplete or defective application, it's the date on which the last part completing the application is received.

411

Opportunities exist to pick up technologies and sell or license your patents online. I cannot vouch for the following services, but I include them for their interest and potential. PatentAuction.com is an auction site for patents, trademarks, and copyrights from all over the world. Yet2.com claims a database of more than $2.5 billion in licensable technology. Its funding comes from a stellar cast of world-class companies, including AGFA, 3M, BASF, P&G, DuPont, General Mills, and Ciba. NewIdeaTrade.com invites companies, individuals, universities, and government agencies to promote; buy; sell; and license new ideas and inventions, patents, copyrighted works, trademarks, and other intellectual property.

I Do Solemnly Swear ...

Your oath or declaration is required by law for a nonprovisional application. You must swear that you believe yourself to be the original and first inventor of the subject matter of the application, and you must make various other statements required by law and various statements required by Patent and Trademark Office rules. You must swear the oath before a notary public or other officer authorized to administer oaths. A declaration may be used in lieu of an oath. Oaths or declarations are required for applications involving designs, plants, and utility inventions and for reissue applications. A declaration does not need to be notarized.

When filing a continuation, or divisional application, a copy of an oath or declaration may be used;. or a continued prosecution application may be filed that requires neither a new oath or declaration, nor a copy of an oath or declaration from a prior application.

You (or the person entitled by law to make application on your behalf) must sign the oath or declaration in person. The full first and last name with middle initial or name, if any, of each inventor is required. The post office address and proof of citizenship of each inventor are also required.

Sample forms are available by calling the USPTO General Information Services at 1-800-786-9199 or 571-272-1000, or by accessing the USPTO website at www.uspto. gov under the "USPTO Forms" section. The paperwork in a complete application will not be returned for any purpose whatsoever, nor will the filing fee be returned. If you've not kept copies of the papers, the office will furnish copies to you for a fee.

Patentability of Computer Programs

Can computer programs be patented? The answer is not simple.

Under certain tests, the USPTO awards patent protection to a piece of software. The former Court of Customs and Patent Appeals (CCPA), known today as the Court of Appeals for the Federal Circuit, has held that computer processes are statutory unless they fall within a judicially determined exception.

The original cases that went to the U.S. Supreme Court from the CCPA provided guidance to the USPTO on the patentability of computer-related inventions and software. However, the USPTO and some patent attorneys disagree on the interpretation of the cited court cases.

As if this situation weren't murky enough, in recent years, a spate of cases are prompting the USPTO to review its guidelines.

As a standalone invention, a software program *per se* may not be patentable, but in view of new court decisions, the USPTO interpretation of existing case law may change.

If you want to patent a computer software program, it just may be possible. Consult a patent lawyer who stays current with the case law. Or watch for news about this in the *Official Gazette* or the *Manual of Patent Examining Procedure*.

Just the Fax, Please

Among those documents that the USPTO *will not* accept by fax are ...

◆ New or continuing patent applications of any type.

◆ Assignments.

◆ Issue fee payments.

◆ Maintenance fee payments.

- Declarations or oaths under 37 CFR 1.63 or 1.67.

- Formal drawings.

- All papers relating to international patent applications.

- Papers to be filed in applications subject to a secrecy order under 37 CFR 5.1–5.8 and directly related to the secrecy order content of the application.

Your fax submissions may include a certificate for each paper stating the date of transmission. A copy of the facsimile submission with a certificate faxed with it will be evidence of transmission of the paper, should the original be misplaced. The person signing the certificate should have a reasonable basis to expect that the paper would be transmitted on the date indicated. Here's an example of a preferred certificate:

Certification of Facsimile Transmission

I hereby certify that this paper is being facsimile transmitted to the Patent and Trademark Office on the date shown below.

_____

Type or print name of person signing certifying.

_____

Signature

_____

Date

When possible, the certification should appear on a portion of the paper being transmitted. If the certification is presented on a separate paper, it must identify the application it relates to and the type of paper being transmitted (such as amendment, notice of appeal, and so on).

If the USPTO loses or misplaces the facsimile submission, the submission will be considered filed on the date of the transmission, if the party who transmitted the paper …

1. Informs the USPTO of the previous facsimile transmission promptly after becoming aware that the submission has been misplaced or lost.

2. Supplies another copy of the previously transmitted submission with the Certification of the Transmission.

3. Supplies a copy of the sending unit's report confirming transmission of the submission. If a copy of the report is not available, the party who transmitted the paper may file a declaration under 37 CFR 1.68, which attests to the previous timely transmission on a personal knowledge basis or to the satisfaction of the commissioner.

If all these criteria cannot be met, the USPTO will require you to submit a verified showing of facts. Such a showing must indicate to the satisfaction of the commissioner the date the USPTO received the submission.

Bright Ideas

Sylvan N. Goldman, son of Jewish immigrants, was born in 1898 and grew up in the Oklahoma Territory. After some ups and downs, by the mid-1930s, he owned half of the Piggly Wiggly grocery chain. In 1936, Goldman wondered how to help his customers carry more groceries and then got an idea. He and mechanic Fred Young started to tinker. Their first shopping cart was a metal frame that held two wire baskets. The frame was designed to be folded to nest the baskets. By 1940, shopping carts were engrained in American life. Supermarket checkouts were redesigned and the layout of aisles was changed. In 1947, the folding cart gave way to the single-basket carts we use today.

The Least You Need to Know

- A provisional patent costs less and does less to protect your invention.

- A nonprovisional patent has teeth that grip. This patent is what you ultimately want for the greatest protection of your invention.

- It's important to keep your application in the proper order.

- Done wrong, claims can turn steak into dog food.

- If you opt *not* to build prototypes, I hope you like to eat patents, because no one pays for paper.

- You can now patent computer programs, but the USPTO and the courts are still developing the guidelines and controlling authority.

Chapter 15

Flower Power! Applying for a Plant Patent

In This Chapter

- ◆ Patented plants = money trees
- ◆ What you can protect
- ◆ How to make application
- ◆ Where to find answers to your questions

There is a demand for an expanding plant pallet and American inventors are meeting it. Innovative and unique flora that bloom profusely all year, free of pests or slow growing, no prune plants that offer flowers, fragrance, berries and fall color, the plant inventor has found a way to create it, often resulting in a vastly improved, aesthetically pleasing landscape with lower maintenance costs and the need for fewer pesticides.

—Joel M. Lerner, landscape columnist, *The Washington Post*

Question: What do the following plants have in common: a hybrid tea rose named Ruiyel, a lantana named Mongen, an azalea named Panfilia, a chrysanthemum named Golden State, and a nectarine tree named Western Pride?

Answer: They were all awarded U.S. patents.

The USPTO has issued more than 19,000 plant patents to date. Henry Bosenberg received Plant Patent No. 1 in 1931 for a climbing rose. In 1997, Plant Patent No. 10,000 was awarded to breeder David Lemon in a ceremony at the U.S. Botanical Garden in Washington, D.C., for his Regal geranium named Lois. Today, Art Unit 1661 (the Art Unit within the USPTO that handles plants) averages circa 750 patents a year.

Plant Patents: A Growing Business

Plant patents can bring financial gains to their inventors and the companies that commercialize such intellectual property. Seed companies and plant breeders sell patented "designer plants" through catalogues and in nurseries to homeowners and landscapers.

> ### Bright Ideas
>
> Plant Patent No. 11,616 was awarded for an azalea that was named after USPTO examiner Jim Ron Feyrer. It seems that Robert Edward Lee, its *pro se* inventor, of Independence, Louisiana, liked Jim and honored him by designating his azalea by the name Jim Ron Feyrer.

Tied in first place for the number of plant patents awarded by the USPTO between January 1, 1977, and January 1, 2009, are Yoder Brothers (a.k.a. Aris Horticulture) and Paul Ecke Ranch, at 958 patents each. Bear Creek Gardens owns 282 patents. Ball has 225. To see the full ranking, go to www.uspto.gov/go/taf/plant.htm#PartB.

Even the Queen of England has patents. She owns two patents for ash trees, applied for through the Canadian Department of Agriculture.

There are some 3,400 species of trees, shrubs, and bushes in the rose family. A USPTO search reveals over 2,000 patents on roses. Here's how a patent abstract reads, in part, for a bush in the rose family (not an actual rose!) invented by David Austin. It is Plant Patent No. 11,211, *Physocarpus opulifolius* CV "monlo"—a new and distinct selection of Ninebark that offers a unique combination of an outstanding cold-hardy shrub with intense foliage color throughout the seasons, peaking in summer to a maroon red and contrasting with the creamy-white flowers.

Spring Meadow Nursery, holder of more than 50 plant patents, awarded from 1998 to 2009, shows in a catalog when a royalty is paid. For example, write-up for *Physocarpus opulifolius* "Monlo" (PP11211) states that 57¢ of the price is royalty. This plant was developed by Kordes Nursery and introduced by Monrovia Nursery. The same catalog lists a 30¢ royalty on each sale of "Abelia confetti" (PP8472), and so forth. This is the first time I've ever seen an inventor royalty broken out and shown as part of the price in a public document.

Forgene, Inc., received a patent on a white spruce tree that can grow at twice the normal rate. Neil Nelson, inventor of the Super Tree, as it's called, said the patent marks the first time in U.S. patent history that the USPTO has awarded a general patent for a tree.

Other trees have been given patent protection as plant patents, but until the Nelson patent, the USPTO had never issued a *general* patent on a tree. "This patent was issued in recognition of the milestone genetic improvement incorporated in these hybrid trees," said Nelson.

Fast Facts

Plants become patentable in 1930. In 1931, Henry F. Bosenberg obtained Plant Patent No. 1 for "a climbing rose." In 1932, James Markham obtained the first patent awarded for a tree, a peach tree.

Beyond the Garden Walls

The U.S. Patent Office issued three new plant–related utility patents to Portland-based Exelixis Plant Sciences, Inc. Utility plant patents are handled by Art Unit 1638. Some plants can qualify for both plant and utility patents.

The patents were awarded for a promoter to regulate the expression of genes in plants, a novel protein to detect a new strain of grapevine leaf-roll virus infection in grape plants and a strain of bacillus that has been effective in combating plant fungal and bacterial infections. Exelixis, formerly Agritope, has had 15 U.S. and 7 foreign patents issued. Applications for 39 other patents are pending.

411

Many plant patent owners use Royalty Administration International as their agent. For more information, or to see if they represent a certain patentee, get in touch with these experts in plant ip: 10175 Six Mile Cypress Parkway, Suite 3, Ft. Myers, FL 33912; 1-800-472-4724; Sam Rizzi, manager.

Floyd Zaiger and Family (Zaiger Genetics) have achieved international prominence for their fruit and rootstock hybridizing program. Known around Art Unit 1661 as nice people, the Zaigers have introduced several hundred varieties over the past five decades and hold over 100 U.S. plant patents on varieties developed for home orchard as well as commercial use.

Multinational corporations (e.g., Georgia-Pacific, International Paper, Boise Cascade, and Union Camp) are actively looking for ways to increase the density of trees whose wood is destined for use as paper pulp and in construction. Genetic engineering efforts are underway to reduce branching in trees grown specifically to make furniture, increase growth rates in wood burned for fuel, change fruit trees for modified taste, vary the ripening characteristics of fruit, and so on. A company is even trying to develop a caffeine-free coffee plant. If this could be done, there would be no need for the expensive process required to produce decaf coffee. If plants are your "field" of invention, this challenge could bring you lots of "beans" if you're able to do it.

Inventions Wanted

Have an idea for a dorm room product? If so, Bed Bath & Beyond wants to see it. In partnership with Edison nation, the retailer is looking for products that address innovation in space, organization, storage, cleaning, lighting, comfort, and decorating. For details, go to www.bedbathandbeyond.com/studentsofInvention. asp?utm_source=e&utm_medium=e&utm_term=e&utm_content=headerfooter&utm_name=StudentsofInvention.

Who Can Apply for a Plant Patent?

If you have invented or discovered and asexually reproduced a distinct and new variety of plant, other than an edible tuber-propagated plant or a plant found in an uncultivated state, the government makes it possible for you to patent it.

The grant, which lasts for 20 years from the date of filing the application, protects your right to exclude others from asexually reproducing, selling, or using the plant so reproduced.

Patent-Protected Grounds

Your protection is limited to …

♦ A living plant organism that expresses a set of characteristics determined by its single genetic makeup or genotype, which can be duplicated through asexual reproduction but cannot otherwise be "made" or "manufactured."

♦ Sports, mutants, hybrids, and transformed plants are comprehended; sports or mutants may be spontaneous or induced. Hybrids may be natural, from a planned breeding program, or somatic in source. While natural plant mutants might have naturally occurred, they must have been discovered in a cultivated area.

♦ Algae and macro fungi are regarded as plants, but bacteria are not.

> **Bright Ideas**
>
> Luther Burbank, a horticulturist and plant breeder, developed, discovered, or improved some 800 varieties of trees, vegetables, fruits, and flowers. His most successful "invention" was the Burbank potato, developed in 1872. He is also known for the Santa Rosa plum and the Shasta daisy.

While the USPTO does accept utility applications having claims to plants, seeds, genes, and so on, the topic is well beyond the scope of this book. To obtain information, contact the USPTO Information Services Division, at 1-800-786-9199, or a registered patent attorney who specializes in plants.

Infringement

Proving infringement has been difficult because so much has depended on coloration. However, today patent applicants are including the molecular biology of their plants, to make future identification in infringement cases easier to prove.

The infringers are people who take cuttings from original plants, perhaps bought legally at a nursery, and replicate them to their own benefit. For example, someone could buy one patented apple tree, take it back to his or her orchard, and breed acres of them over time, thereby robbing the inventor of royalties.

Turning to Trademarks

Breeders are starting to use trademark protection more to protect their patents after their patents expire. Let's look at an example.

There's a very popular apple from Australia called the Pink Lady Apple, or Kripps Pink, if you want the technical name. The patent is more than halfway through its term of 20 years. The patent owner (assignee) is working hard now to establish the trademark Pink Lady so that when the patent "turns into a pumpkin," he will be able to fend off the competition through brand equity. Perhaps people will want the Pink Lady Apple brand, just as label-conscious consumers buy watches, cars, clothing, and so on.

Fast Facts _____

Within families of plants, you'll find tons of species. For example, the composite family has about 20,000 species. The orchid family, more than 20,000 species. The pea family, about 17,000. The lily family, about 4,000. The mustard family, about 3,000. The morning-glory family, 1,800 species.

The Cost of Doing Business

Approximately 50 percent of all plant patents are filed *pro se*—that is, by their inventors without the assistance of patent counsel. This is because there's only one claim, and it's illustrated and described. In other words, what you see is what you get. It's not unlike the design patent in that regard. If inventors want to get into the molecular biology of their plants, they typically hire a botanist to draft the description and may have a patent attorney check it for format.

Figure the price of photography and printing of two images of the plant. Pictures or watercolor drawings are required if color is a distinguishing characteristic of the new variety. If you don't submit color photographs or drawings, the examiner may require them.

For the most current fees, check the USPTO website at www.uspto.gov or call 1-800-786-9199 or 571-272-1000. Fees change annually around October.

Fast Facts

A proponent of the legislation that would make plants patentable, inventor Thomas Alva Edison sent a telegram to Congress that read, in part: "Nothing that Congress could do to help farming would be of greater value and permanence than to give to the plant breeder the same status as the mechanical and chemical inventors now have through patent law. There are but a few plant breeders. This will, I feel sure, give us many Burbanks." (He was referring to horticulturist and plant breeder Luther Burbank, mentioned earlier.)

Making Application

An application for a plant patent consists of the same parts as other applications, with the addition of a plant color-coding sheet. As with the utility patent, the term of a plant patent is 20 years from the date the application was filed in the United States, or from the date the earliest such application was filed if the application contains a specific reference to an earlier filed application under 35 U.S.C. 120, 121, or 365(c).

The Application

Your application for a plant patent and any responsive papers pursuant to the prosecution duplicate copies are no longer required. The original should be signed.

Specification

The specification should include a complete detailed description of the plant and the characteristics that distinguish it over related known varieties. It should also include its antecedents, expressed in botanical terms in the general form followed in standard botanical textbooks or publications dealing with the varieties of the kind of plant involved (evergreen tree, dahlia plant, rose plant, apple tree, and so forth) instead of a mere broad nonbotanical characterization, as is commonly found in nursery or seed catalogs.

Notable Quotables

All mankind is divided into three classes: those who are immovable, those who are moveable, and those who move.

—Benjamin Franklin

Here are some of the factors you must ascertain for a reasonably complete botanical description for the claimed plant:

◆ Genus and species

◆ Habit of growth

◆ Cultivar name

◆ Vigor

◆ Productivity

◆ Precocity (if applicable)

◆ Botanical characteristics of plant structures (buds, bark, foliage, flowers, fruit, and so on)

◆ Fertility (fecundity)

◆ Other characteristics that distinguish the plant, such as resistance(s) to disease, drought, cold, dampness, fragrance, coloration, regularity and time of bearing, quantity or quality of extracts, rooting ability, timing or duration of flowering season, etc.

The amount of detail required in a plant patent application is determined on a case-by-case basis and by the similarity of the prior art plants to the plant being claimed. The examiner will evaluate the completeness of the application. The examiner's judgment may be tempered by the level of activity in a specific market class. The botanical description of a plant in a market class with a high level of commercial activity may require greater detail, substance, and specificity than that for a plant in a market class of little activity.

Fast Facts

If a plant label has a patent number written on it, you need permission to propagate it even for your own use. Most hybridizers will give you permission to propagate a rose for your own use, but not for profit. Asexual propagation without the written permission of the patent holder is against federal patent laws.

Here's how to frame your specification for submission to the USPTO:

◆ *Title of the Invention.* The title of the invention must include the name of the claimed plant.

◆ *Cross-Reference to Related Applications (if any).* Related applications include …

1. A utility application from which the claimed plant is the subject of a divisional application.

2. A continuation (co-pending, newly filed application) or CPA to the same plant filed when a parent application has not been allowed to a sibling cultivar.

3. An application not co-pending with an original application that was not allowed.

4. Co-pending applications to siblings or similar plants developed by the same breeding program, and so forth.

The Claim

A plant patent is granted on the entire plant. It follows, therefore, that only one claim is necessary and only one is permitted.

The Oath: I Do Solemnly Swear ...

Together with the required oath or declaration, you must include a statement that you (and your co-inventors, if any) have asexually reproduced the new plant variety. If the plant is a newly found plant, the oath or declaration must also state that the plant was found in a cultivated area.

Drawings

While you are permitted to submit watercolor drawings, the USPTO basically gets photographs from everyone these days. So if you go that route, send them in duplicate, not mounted on chipboard or any other subsurface. They should be printed on a full-size piece of paper. The sizes required are 8½×11 or A4 (European size).

Specimens—Send Me No Flowers

Specimens of the plant variety, its flower, or its fruit should not be submitted unless specifically called for by the examiner.

411

The Plant Variety Protection Act (Public Law 91577), passed December 24, 1970, provides for a system of protection for sexually reproduced varieties, for which protection was not previously provided, under the administration of a Plant Variety Protection Office within the Department of Agriculture. If you have any questions about the protection of sexually reproduced varieties, address them to Commissioner, Plant Variety Protection Office, Agricultural Marketing Service, National Agricultural Library Building, Room 0, 10301 Baltimore Boulevard, Beltsville, MD 20705-2351.

Cost: Green Fees

Fees change annually, so be sure to call the USPTO (1-800-786-9199 or 571-272-1000) or visit the USPTO website (www.uspto.gov) and double-check the prices before taking any action.

If you qualify as a small entity, the USPTO reduces the filing and issue fees by half.

If you have any questions relating to plant patents and pending plant patent applications, contact the Patent and Trademark Office.

Provisions and Limitations

Patents to plants that are stable and reproduced by asexual reproduction, and not a potato or other edible tuber-reproduced plant, are provided for by Title 35 United States Code, Section 161, which states:

> Whoever invents or discovers and asexually reproduces any distinct and new variety of plant, including cultivated sports, mutants, hybrids, and newly found seedlings, other than a tuber propagated plant or a plant found in an uncultivated state, may obtain a patent therefore, subject to the conditions and requirements of title. (Amended September 3, 1954, 68 Stat. 1190)

The provisions of this title relating to patents for inventions apply to patents for plants, except as otherwise provided.

Plant patents must also satisfy the general requirements of patentability. The subject matter of the application is a plant that you developed or discovered and has been found stable by asexual reproduction.

To be patentable, the following is also required:

◆ The plant was invented or discovered and, if discovered, the discovery was made in a cultivated area.

◆ The plant is not a plant excluded by statute, where the part of the plant used for asexual reproduction is not a tuber food part, as with potato or Jerusalem artichoke.

◆ The person or persons filing the application are those who actually invented the claimed plant (that is, they discovered or developed and identified or isolated the plant, and asexually reproduced the plant).

◆ The plant was not sold or released in the United States more than one year prior to the date of the application.

◆ The plant was not shown to the public (by description in a printed publication more than one year before the application for patent with an offer to sale, or by release—even as a gift—or sale of the plant) more than one year prior to application for patent.

◆ The plant is shown to differ from known, related plants by at least one distinguishing characteristic, which is more than a difference caused by growing conditions, fertility levels, and so on.

◆ The invention would not have been obvious to one skilled in the art at the time of invention by applicant.

If you have any doubt about the patentability of a specific plant, consult a qualified legal authority prior to making application, to ensure that the plant satisfies statutory requirements and is not exempted from plant patent protection.

Inventorship

An inventor is any person who contributed to either step of invention. For example, if you discovered a new and distinct plant and asexually reproduce it, you would be a sole inventor. If you discovered or selected a new and distinct plant, and a second person asexually reproduced the plant and ascertained that the clones of the plant were identical to the original plant in every distinguishing characteristic, the second person would properly be considered your co-inventor. If either step is performed by a staff, every member of the staff who performed or contributed to the performance of either step could properly be considered a co-inventor. Thus, a plant patent may have many inventors.

However, if you direct that the asexual reproduction be performed by a custom propagation service or tissue culture enterprise, those performing the service for you would not be considered co-inventors.

Asexual Reproduction

Asexual reproduction is the propagation of a plant to multiply the plant without the use of fusion of gametes, to ensure that an exact genetic copy of the plant is reproduced. Any known method of asexual reproduction that renders a true genetic copy of the plant may be used. Acceptable modes of asexual reproduction include but are not limited to rooting cuttings, grafting and budding, apomictic seeds, bulbs, division, slips, layering, rhizomes, runners, corms, tissue culture, and nucellar embryos.

The purpose of asexual reproduction is to establish the stability of the plant. This second step of the invention must be performed with sufficient time prior to application for patent rights to allow the thorough evaluation of propagules or clones of the claimed plant for stability, thus ensuring that such specimens retain the identical distinguishing characteristics of the original plant.

Helpful Hints

When you're making application for a plant patent, please …

- Make every attempt not to present a name for the plant that has already been used or is confusingly similar to a plant of the same market or botanical class. Search old catalogs and available international register listings before assigning a name to a plant.

- File all drawings (and photos) in duplicate. Be sure that two sets of drawings (the USPTO no longer accepts mounted drawings) accompany the application when filed, and that these are of reasonable fidelity to the specified colors of the plant. Be sure that the scale and clarity of the drawings are appropriate to allow for adequate reproduction, even if reduced in scale upon publishing.

- Include a transmittal sheet that itemizes the contents of the application as filed.

- File each individual application in a separate envelope, and be sure to include all the parts of each application in the same envelope. Request that a filing receipt bearing the serial number of the application be returned to you.

- Model the application after a recent patent of acceptable format and content that describes a plant related to or in the same market class as the claimed plant, if one is available.

- Check that the oath or declaration is required for a plant patent application. Ensure that you've signed the oath or declaration in permanent ink. Check that your mailing address is correct and complete.

Fast Facts

Subclass 307 contains 131 patents on red poinsettias. Subclass 330 contains 112 patents on red geraniums. Subclass 198 contains 213 patents on yellow flesh, freestone, standard-size peaches.

- Where color is a distinguishing characteristic of the plant, specify the color of the plant as defined by reference to an established color dictionary (e.g., Pantone) recognized in this country. The color reference most commonly used is the Royal Horticulture Society of England Colour Chart (RHS Colour Chart).

- Be sure any drawings filed are complete, are correctly mounted, and reasonably correspond with the colors of the plant that are specified and the true and characteristic plant coloration.

- Include the appropriate filing fee with your application, to avoid processing delays.

- Direct preexamination questions concerning the application to the examiner, by telephone, to expedite prosecution.

- Include your current telephone number with all correspondence.

Mail new patent applications to:

The Honorable Commissioner for Patents of Patents and Trademarks
Box: Patent Application
Washington, DC 22031

The Least You Need to Know

- Plant patents protect for 20 years from the date of filing.

- You can get a utility patent on plants.

- Fifty percent of plant patents are filed *pro se*.

◆ To be patentable, a plant must be found stable by asexual reproduction.

◆ Any known method of asexual reproduction that renders a true genetic copy of the plant may be used.

◆ The USPTO no longer accepts mounted drawings of plants for which application is made. Photographs, in duplicate, are fine.

Chapter 16

Applying for a Design Patent

In This Chapter

- A design patent is inexpensive ip insurance
- It's all about form over function
- You don't need a lawyer to apply
- The Crest Fluorider™ story
- Design patents versus utility patents
- Elements of a design patent

> Good design keeps the user happy, the manufacturer in the black and the aesthete unoffended.
>
> —Raymond Loewy, the father of industrial design

Design patents are a way to protect ornamental and cosmetic aspects of your inventions—*not* their function. Perhaps the most celebrated design patent ever granted is Number 11,023, issued on February 18, 1879, to Auguste Bartholdi on his design for a statue, "Liberty Enlightening the World," one we call the Statue of Liberty.

So if your product has a unique appearance—and this is important to its success—a design patent can be a worthwhile investment. And it's not an expensive one.

Think of the distinctive designs of a Mazda Miata, an iMac computer monitor, a bottle of Classic Coke, and Casio's G-Shock watch, to mention a few products. Without a doubt, the look of these products contributes to their popularity. Design patents are taken out on such products to foil knock-off artists who, although not necessarily pretending to market the authentic item, trade on the goodwill and dress of the original product by causing confusion in the consumer's mind.

Insurance Against Me-Too Competitors

A design patent doesn't have the teeth of a utility patent, but if you want an inexpensive way to legally place a "Patent Pending" or "Patented" label on your product, or add protection to an invention covered by a utility patent, this patent may be for you.

The range of ornamental appearances that have been patented during the more than 150 years design patents have existed is very impressive. Over 550,000 designs have received design patent protection since the first one was granted to George Bruce for "Printing Type" on November 9, 1842.

Form over Function

You can get design patents on just about anything: baby bibs, sweatbands, tissue box holders, rearview mirrors, dishes, toys, vending machines, telephones, pencils and pens, and even internal combustion engines.

Volkswagen licensed Infogrames, the French entertainment conglomerate, to do the computer game *Beetle Buggin'*. The legal copy reads, "Trademarks, design patents, and copyrights are used with the approval of the owner Volkswagen AG." In this case, the German automobile manufacturer appears to be using the design patent to keep people away from its intellectual property (ip).

Rubbermaid has design patents on containers. Totes protects umbrella handle designs. Parker Pen takes them out on writing instruments. Ford has design patents on quarter panels and other car parts. (Patenting the design of car door panels and the like can prevent competitors from selling replacement parts modeled after the factory parts.)

An industry that relies heavily on design patents is cosmetics. The appearance of a perfume bottle, for example, is critical to a brand's success. Design attracts the consumer long before he or she has experienced the scent.

The chances to get a design patent are high. It's just a matter of comparing drawings. If the examiner finds something different, he awards a patent. The level of obviousness is fairly low.

Bright Ideas
Gertrude B. Elion, 1988 Nobel Laureate in Medicine and Scientist Emeritus with Burroughs-Wellcome Company, is credited with the synthesis of two of the first successful drugs for leukemia, as well as Imuron, an agent to prevent the rejection of kidney transplants, and Zovirax, the first selective antiviral agent against herpes virus infections. Researchers who discovered AZT, a breakthrough treatment for AIDS, used Elion's protocols. In 1991, she became the first female inductee into the National Inventors Hall of Fame.

Most lawyers I have interviewed say that design patents are so easy to obtain that they do not even conduct searches of prior art for their clients. Rejections are that rare." Ninety-nine percent of them issue.

Putting the Competition on Notice

For little expense and effort, a design patent permits you to legally post a NO TRESPASSING sign in the form of a notice that reads "Patent Pending," "Patent Applied For," or "Patented." By the way, you do not have to notify with the words "Design Patent Pending" or "Design Patent Applied For," or even give the design patent number when it issues. It's best to keep 'em guessin'. If your competitors know it is a design patent, their decision to end-run you will be much easier to make and carry out.

411
You can gain access to $25 billion worth of federally funded research and development that annually takes place at more than 700 federal laboratories and centers. Uncle Sam wants to transfer federal technologies and expertise into commercial applications that will improve the U.S. economy. Your key to this wealth of information is available at flc2.federallabs.org/index.html.

Design patents are intended to protect the ornamental and cosmetic aspects of products—but not their function. The disclosure and description of the invention in a design application is entirely in the drawing, not in the words. The single claim in a design patent is for "the appearance of a *(whatever the product is usually called)* as shown *(in the drawing)*."

Lawyers Need Not Apply

I do not use patent counsel to prepare and file design patent applications. Unlike complicated utility and plant patents, where patent lawyers are invaluable, design applications are easy and uncomplicated to draft and process. Paying a lawyer to handle design patents is tossing money out the window, as far as I'm concerned.

The application form is simple, esoteric language is not required to draft claims, and searches are unnecessary. A design patent search doesn't even require reading—it's all in the line drawings or photographs.

> **Fast Facts**
>
> In 1791, Samuel Mulikin became the first inventor to hold multiple patents. Thomas Jennings, believed to have been the first African American patentee, received a patent in 1821 for "dry scouring of clothes." Mary Kies invented a device for "weaving straw with silk or thread." She was the first woman to obtain a U.S. patent, in 1809.

The visual element is your biggest expense (plus USPTO fees). If you do the application and filing yourself, it will cost you (at the date of this writing) $230 (this includes the basic filing fee, search fee, and examination fees) as a small entity, plus $430 if it issues. This totals $660. Then you have the formal drawings that are required whether you apply *pro se* or through a law firm. This can cost you some serious dollars if many drawings are required.

If you retain a law firm, your cost could be between $650 and $1,000. You can be sure the lawyer will mark up the drafting prices by a minimum of 100 percent.

A design patent is good for 14 years, and there are no maintenance fees.

How to Find a Draftsman

The best way to find draftsmen is through recommendations by other inventors. If this isn't possible, ask a librarian at a Patent and Trademark Depository Library (PTDL) to see if there is one in your area. (See Appendix C for a complete listing of PTDLs.) Other options include references from engineering schools and, when all else fails, the Yellow Pages.

Years ago, the USPTO had a list of bonded patent draftsmen. In those days, it was easy to find someone through this qualified roster. These draftsmen were bonded because they frequently had to make modifications to original drawings. But since January 1, 1991, no one has been allowed to alter original drawings. If you want to make a change to a drawing on an application today, you must submit a new drawing.

"But they accept copies today," says Robert MacCollum, a draftsman from Silver Springs, Maryland, whose career spans 36 years. "In fact, they encourage it," he adds. They also allow submissions via the Internet. Bob thinks online submissions have been allowed to cut down on paper. He hastens to point out, however, that original drawings are still necessary for foreign filings. "The reason for this is that they may have to print them out for 20 countries," he says.

Depending on the complexity of the invention, MacCollum charges between $50 and $150 per sheet, the high end being rare. Design drawings can typically be done with one or two sheets. Utility drawings can require many more. The most sheets he has ever needed for an application was 20.

If you opt to submit photographs, you may well be able to shoot them yourself.

To make the drawings, draftsmen need reference art or models of the invention. "Some inventors have sent me videotapes of product which I drew off a television monitor. I recall once having to run outside my home and sketch a loading device attached to a flatbed truck. It took me all afternoon to do this and get it to scale." But his most unusual memory was the time a Taiwanese furniture maker actually sent him three outdoor benches as reference art. When asked what he did with them afterward, he responded, "They came and got them."

Fast Facts

Design patents are an important method for protecting games. Inventors cannot protect "game play," but they can seek design patent protection for their board layouts. In other words, no one can stop a game publisher from selling a path game, but how that path and its squares are designed and laid out on the board, from an ornamental standpoint, is protectable.

Design Patents Can Be Valuable

In the early 1980s, we spent $500 to learn that lawyers were not necessary in such matters. At the time, I had been using a large law firm for utility patents and, naturally, released our first design patent to them. I did not know any better.

The lawyer said he would "write it up." I was asked to provide the draftsman with a prototype of the design. It was a tricycle with a mainframe shaped like a toothpaste tube. It ultimately became Proctor & Gamble's Crest Fluorider™, a premium offering.

When U.S. Design Patent No. 273,774 issued, I saw the claim for the first time. I had been used to reading complicated claims on our mechanical patents. Many were so arcane I had trouble comprehending them. Not this time. In the case of our "Child's Riding Vehicle," the claim was one line. It read: "The ornamental design for a child's riding vehicle, as shown and described."

The Crest Fluorider® program was very successful for us, so the $500 legal expense was a wash. But the design patent was soon to become very important—and not vis-à-vis a competitive premium, but between us inventors and P&G.

There was little chance the trike would be knocked off. No other toothpaste brand had $12 million to invest in the production and promotion of such a product. P&G ordered 30,000 units just to put up on displays in supermarkets nationwide. The design patent benefited us when P&G used our proprietary design throughout the pages of a juvenile coloring book it distributed to dental offices.

The Cincinnati consumer goods manufacturer did not want to pay us for the use of our design on the cover and inside this book. The P&G lawyers saw it as fair use. But when we presented our design patent award, they immediately changed their tune. We agreed on a one-time payment for the right to emblazon our design on the 1 million books the company had already published and distributed. By the way, we owned the mark Fluorider™, too.

Defining Design

The USPTO defines a design as the visual ornamental characteristics embodied in or applied to an article of manufacture. Because a design is manifested in appearance, the subject matter of a design patent application may relate to the configuration or shape of an article (e.g., the Black & Decker Snake Light, a Bose Wave radio, and so on), to the surface ornamentation applied to an article (e.g., the swirls on a Coke bottle, and so on), or to the combination of configuration and surface ornamentation (e.g., Jean-Paul Gaultier eau de toilette, and so on).

A design for surface ornamentation is inseparable from the article to which it is applied and cannot exist alone. It must be a definite pattern of surface ornamentation, applied to an article of manufacture. Patent law permits design patents to be granted to anyone who has invented a new, original, and ornamental design for a manufactured product. A design patent protects only the appearance of the article, not its structural or utilitarian features.

An ornamental design may be embodied in an entire article or only a portion of an article, or may be ornamentation applied to an article. If your design is directed to just surface ornamentation, it must be shown applied to an article in the drawings, and the article must be shown in broken lines, as it forms no part of the claimed design. Draftsmen skilled in the art will know the regulations.

 411

The principal statutes of the U.S. Code that govern design patents are available on the USPTO website, www.uspto.gov, and are set forth in Chapter 1500 of the Manual of Examining Procedure. To purchase the manual, contact the Superintendent of Documents, U.S. Government Printing Office, Washington, DC 20402; 202-512-1800.

Claims

A design patent application may have only a single claim. If you have designs that are independent and distinct, they must be filed in separate applications because they cannot be supported by a single claim. Designs are independent if there is no apparent relationship between two or more articles. For example, a pair of sunglasses and a car side mirror are independent articles and must be claimed in separate applications.

Designs are considered distinct if they have different shapes and appearances, even though they are related articles. For example, two vases having different surface ornamentation creating distinct appearances must be claimed in separate applications. However, modified forms, or embodiments of a single design concept, may be filed in one application. For example, vases with only minimal configuration differences may be deemed a single design concept, and both embodiments may be included in a single application.

Fast Facts

The U.S. Patent Office had already granted more than 500 automotive patents by 1895, only a couple years after Charles and Frank Duryea demonstrated the first practical American car. By the 1920s, thousands of patents covered a wide range of automobile innovations, and the industry employed almost 5 million workers.

Improper Subject Matter for Design Patents

A design for an article of manufacture that is dictated primarily by function lacks ornamentality and is not proper statutory subject matter (for example, a mechanism).

Similarly, a design for an article of manufacture that is hidden in its end use and whose ornamental appearance is of no commercial concern prior to reaching its end use lacks ornamentality and is not proper statutory subject matter (for example, the inside of an exhaust muffler).

In addition, for a design to be patentable it must be "original." Clearly, a design that simulates a well-known or naturally occurring object or person is not original as required by statute. Furthermore, subject matter that could be considered offensive to any race, religion, sex, ethnic group, or nationality is not proper subject matter for a design patent application.

The Difference Between Design and Utility Patents

In general terms, a *utility patent* protects the way an article is used and works, while a *design patent* protects the way an article looks. Both design and utility patents may be obtained on an article if invention resides in both its utility and ornamental appearance.

While utility and design patents afford legally separate protection, the utility and ornamentality of an article are not easily separable. Articles of manufacture may possess both functional and ornamental characteristics.

Invention marketing services exist to help inventors license and commercialize their inventions or to otherwise profit from their ideas. While some organizations are legitimate, most are not (see Chapter 2). The dishonest types are often fast to recommend that you pursue a patent for your idea because this is a profit center for them.

To put the odds in their favor that a patent will issue, they'll have you go for a design patent and may not tell you the difference between a design patent and a utility patent. They will, however, charge you as if it was a utility patent and then make you think that what issues is invaluable. Dishonest brokers will automatically recommend patent protection for your idea with little regard for the value of any patent that may ultimately issue.

> **Notable Quotables**
>
> Handling rejection must be part of your regular diet, and success your occasional dessert.
>
> —Roger Lehmann, co-inventor, P.J. Sparkles

Be wary of any agent who is willing to promote your invention or product without making a detailed inquiry into the merits of your idea and giving you a full range of options that may or may not include the pursuit of patent protection.

411

Under the best of conditions, trying to identify and reach people within a huge bureaucracy like the USPTO can be a challenge. To reduce frustration and increase your chances for success, you need the Information Directory. This useful 140+-page resource contains the complete office telephone directory, divided into organizational and alphabetical sections. It is a must in every serious inventor's resource library. For a free copy of the Information Directory, call 1-800-786-9199 or 571-272-1000, or pick up one at the Public Search Facility (Walk-In Counter), 600 Dulany Street, Alexandria, VA 22313.

Elements of a Design Patent Application

The elements of a design patent application should include the following:

- Preamble, stating your name, title of the design, and a brief description of the nature and intended use of the article in which the design is embodied

- Description of the figure(s) of the drawing

- Feature description

- A single claim

- Drawings or photographs

- Executed oath or declaration

Here is what an application looks like laid out:

Sample Specification

I, (Name) _____ have invented a new design for a (Title) _____ as set forth in the following specification:

FIG. 1 is a _____ view of a _____ showing my new design;

FIG. 2 is a _____ view thereof;

FIG. 3 is a _____ view thereof;

FIG. 4 is a _____ view thereof;

FIG. 5 is a _____ view thereof; and

FIG. 6 is a _____ view thereof.

I claim: The ornamental design for a _____
_____ as shown.

If you have questions regarding a design patent application and its forms, contact the Design Patent Practice Specialist of Technology Center 2900 at 571-272-2900.

The filing fee is also required. Contact the USPTO at 1-800-786-9199 or go online to be sure the fees have not changed. Small entities (an independent inventor, a small business concern, or a nonprofit organization) get the filing fee reduced by half if they file a Statement Claiming Small Entity Status.

For a detailed explanation of each of the above elements, please refer to the USPTO Guide to Filing a Design Patent Application at www.uspto.gov/web/offices/pac/design/index.html#views.

The Least You Need to Know

- Design patents are an inexpensive form of protection.

- Design patents do not have the teeth of a utility patent.

- You don't need legal counsel to apply for a design patent.

- The forms are as easy as A-B-C to complete.

- Beware! Many agents use design patents as a profit center.

Chapter 17

Mark Your Words

In This Chapter

◆ The name game

◆ Licensing trademarks—a $141 billion business

◆ Funny foreign faux pas

◆ How to apply for federal trademarks

Swiss watches. Chinese tea. Australian outback. Egyptian pyramids. Yankee ingenuity.

Only one of these captures the dreams and possibilities of tomorrow. Yankee ingenuity is the substance upon which America's rich enterprise history is built, and there is no better definition of that substance than the American inventor. Inventing is more than the "American Dream." Combined with hard work, inventing is the future of America—and it belongs to anyone who will chase their dreams.

—Andy Gibbs, founder, PatentCafe.com

What do Kleenex®, Ford®, Furby®, IBM®, Barbie®, Mr. Clean®, Poppin' Fresh®, and the Gerber Baby have in common with the distinctive buildings that house McDonald's®, and Fotomat®, as well as the Campbell's soup can?

They are all registered trademarks and are very important to their owners as tools to sell their products and services.

There Is Nothing in the World Like a Brand

Don't underestimate the contribution a good *trademark* can make to your licensing effort. It always creates fast product identification and can help communicate the item's story. I spend a good amount of time coming up with the most appropriate trademark for every product we develop.

For example, my pitch to Proctor & Gamble that it license our unique big-wheel trike design would not have had the same impact without our trademark, Fluorider®. Proctor & Gamble placed our unique ride-on in 33,000 supermarkets under this trademark.

When we invented and patented a toy truck that transformed from a conventional-wheel configuration to an in-line configuration via a variable geometry chassis, Remco licensed the trademark Switchblade® as part of the deal.

And our line of Micro Machines® built around authentic state police cruisers, motor-cycles, and aircraft was contingent upon our licensing to the manufacturer our trade-mark, Troopers®.

> **Fast Facts**
>
> The Hershey's Kisses® trade-mark was first registered in 1921; the famous Kiss design, however, was not reg-istered until 1983. The Starkist® trademark was registered in 1940. Its well-known symbol, Charlie®, was registered in 1970. The Denver Broncos® trademark of a stylized wild stal-lion was registered in 1998.

Trademarks can also be very important as a source of additional income in case the trademark on the principal invention becomes valuable. For example, if your invention hits pay dirt under a trademark you control, you may have opportunities to license collateral merchandise—an arena your licensee may or may not participate in with you.

For example, today's Caterpillar® is more than earth-moving equipment. It is also a line of rugged foot-wear. Furby® had its trademark licensed for much more than toys. It was on everything from pencils to popcorn. The licensing business today is over $140 billion.

"The right licensing deal with the right company can bring in meaningful royalty income with no cost of sales," says Michael Ross, senior vice president and publisher of Britannica. "This revenue goes right to the bottom line. Accountants and CEOs love this kind of revenue."

Trademarks Can Take Many Forms

A trademark includes any word, name, symbol, device, or combination—used or intended to be used—in commerce to identify and distinguish the goods of one manufacturer or seller from goods manufactured or sold by others, and to indicate the source of the goods. In short, a trademark is a brand name. A trademark can be …

- A coined word (Trix®, Acura®)

- An everyday word with no connection to the product it promotes (Ivory®, Apple®)

- A phrase (All the News That's Fit to Print®, Catch the Wave®)

- A word that describes a quality or product function (Blockbuster®, Marks-a-Lot®)

- A coined word that suggests product performance (Timex®, Jell-O®)

- A foreign word with or without significance to the item (Volkswagen®, Dos Equis®)

- The name of a product's inventor or company founder (Ford®, Piaget®)

- The name of a celebrated person selected for a positive image (Lincoln®, Raleigh®)

- A name from literature (Peter Pan®, Atlas®)

- Initials (CVS®, MCA®)

- Numbers (7-11®, 66®)

- A combination of letters and numbers (WD-40®, S-500)

- A pictorial mark (Gerber Baby, Playboy Bunny)

- A distinct color (John Deere green, Toro red)

- A sound (NBC chimes)

- A scent (since 1990)

Bright Ideas
What may be the oldest registered trademark was reportedly first used in commerce in England in 1790, according to Trademark Office records. Serial Number 70021734 was filed on August 15, 1892. It was a logo for Gordon's®, consisting of a boar's head resting on a roll. The registrant was Gordon and Company, a British spirits maker.

Dollars and Scents

Clark's Oh-Sew-Easy Needles of Goleta, California (invented by Clark Osewez), was awarded the first fragrance trademark registration for its line of sewing threads perfumed with "a high impact fresh floral fragrance reminiscent of plumeria blossoms."

Explaining the decision, J. David Sams, chief administrative law judge of the USPTO's Trademark Trial and Appeal Board, offered, "If it looks like a trademark and quacks like a trademark, it is a trademark."

In reviewing the Oh-Sew-Easy application, the board found that no one else was using "high impact … plumeria blossoms" fragrance or any fragrance whatsoever in the marketing of sewing thread. That made the use of a fragrance distinctive.

Supreme Court Makes a Colorful Decision

Since the 1950s, Qualitex Company has used a distinctive green-gold color on the pads it makes and sells to dry-cleaning firms for use on dry-cleaning presses. In 1989, Jacobson Products, a Qualitex rival, began to sell its own press pads to dry-cleaning firms; its pads were a similar green-gold color.

411

Here are some interesting trademark blogs you may enjoy reading: www.property-intangible.com, www.vegas-trademarkattorney.com, www.schwimmerlegal.com, seattle-trademarklawyer.com, and www.likelihoodofconfusion.com.

In 1991, Qualitex registered the special green-gold on press pads with the USPTO as a trademark (Registration No. 1,633,711). Furthermore, it brought a trademark-infringement suit, challenging Jacobson's use of the green-gold color.

The case made it all the way to the U.S. Supreme Court, which, in a unanimous opinion delivered by Justice Breyer on March 28, 1995, determined that a color may sometimes meet the basic legal requirements for use as a trademark.

Lost in the Translation

Your item may one day be marketed overseas, so when selecting a trademark, do your best to see what it means in other languages and how it will translate. Why is this important? Here are some of my favorite bloopers:

◆ *No va* in Spanish means "It does not go." This caused a major *problema* for Chevy south of the border, down Mexico way, when it introduced its Nova line of cars.

- Coors put its slogan "Turn It Loose" into Spanish, where it read "Suffer from Diarrhea." Shares of Dos Equis went up!

- Scandinavian vacuum manufacturer Electrolux used the following in an American campaign: "Nothing sucks like an Electrolux®." 'Nuf said.

- Clairol introduced its "Mist Stick®" curling iron into Germany, only to find out that "mist" is slang for cow manure. Not too many people had a use for a "Manure Stick."

- Coca-Cola® was brought into China as "Kekoukela." To their surprise it meant "Bite the wax tadpole," or "female horse stuffed with wax," depending on the dialect. After researching 40,000 characters, Coke® decided upon "kokou kole," or "happiness in the mouth."

The Morton® Umbrella Girl trademark, first used in 1914, was registered in 1946. The logo seen on the container today was introduced in 1968. Also trademark protected is the slogan, "When it rains it pours."

- Coke® was not the only Chinese trademark gaffe. Pepsi's "Come Alive With the Pepsi Generation" was translated to read "Pepsi Brings Your Ancestors Back from the Grave."

- Frank Perdue's slogan, "It takes a strong man to make a tender chicken," was translated into Spanish as "It takes an aroused man to make a chicken affectionate." Ouch!

◆ Parker introduced a ballpoint pen in Mexico. The ads were supposed to have read: "It won't leak in your pocket and embarrass you." Instead, the company thought the word for embarrass was *embarazar* (to impregnate), so the ad read: "It won't leak in your pocket and make you pregnant."

◆ When American Airlines wanted to advertise its new first-class leather seats in the Latin American markets, it translated "Fly In Leather" literally, which meant *en Español* "Fly Naked" *(Vuela en cuero).*

These are good for a laugh, within the context of this book, but these mistakes cost their companies lots of money, not to mention embarrassment.

Even though your licensee will probably do diligence on any trademark you recommend or assign to it, you should also take care to avoid potential problems by considering everything from federal and common law searches to how the mark may translate into foreign languages. And be sure to share your conclusions with your licensee.

All About Trademarks

The primary function of a trademark is to indicate the origin of a product or service; however, trademarks also guarantee the quality of the goods bearing the mark and, through advertising, create and maintain a demand for the product. Trademark rights are acquired only through use of the trademark; this use must continue if the rights you can acquire are to be preserved.

Registration of a trademark in the USPTO does not in itself create or establish any exclusive rights, but it is recognition by the government of your rights to use the mark in commerce to distinguish your goods from those of others.

Types of Trademarks

There are escalating levels of protection available under trademark laws. You have choices.

Common law trademark ™:

◆ No registration or fee is required.

◆ Rights accrue from the use of the mark on a product or service.

◆ Trademarks may carry the ™ symbol.

State trademark ™:

- Registration and a small fee are required.

- Protection is granted according to state law.

- Protection is granted only within the state.

- Trademarks may carry the ™ symbol.

Federal trademark ®:

- Higher fees and a slow-paced process are involved.

- You must use or intend to use the mark in interstate commerce.

- Protection is national, in all 50 states.

- Exclusivity is guaranteed.

- Visibility of use is high.

- The trademark lasts indefinitely as long as renewal fees are paid and the mark remains in commerce.

- U.S. Customs can use it to block importation of goods that infringe the mark.

- After the mark has been registered with USPTO, the ® may be placed on it.

Federal registration of trademarks falls under the jurisdiction of the USPTO. In fiscal year 2008, the USPTO received 401,392 applications, from which it issued a record 274,250 trademark registrations.

The average time between filing an application and its disposition (in other words, registration, abandonment, or issuance of notice of allowance) was 13.9 months at the end of fiscal year 2008.

The current team is one of the most experienced ever in the Trademark Office. I call the examiners often and have never once been disappointed or frustrated. You would never know it is a bureaucracy.

411

For a comprehensive overview of U.S. trademark law, go to Cornell Law School's website, www.law.cornell.edu/topics/trademark.html. There are no subscription fees, and the pages aren't cluttered with commercial messages or banner advertising. It's a nonprofit activity of the Cornell Law School.

What Kinds of Federal Marks Are Available?

Besides the trademark, you can apply for other kinds of marks from the office. Let's look at them:

Trademark. A "trademark," as defined in section 45 of the 1946 Trademark Act (Lanham Act), "includes any word, name, symbol, or device, or any combination thereof adopted and used by a manufacturer or merchant to identify his goods and distinguish them from those manufactured or sold by others." Examples of trademarks include Coca-Cola, Barbie, Ford, and *Men Are from Mars, Women Are from Venus.*

Service mark. A mark used in the sale or advertising of services to identify the services of one person and distinguish them from the services of others. Titles, character names, and other distinctive features of radio or television programs may be registered as service marks, notwithstanding the fact that they, or the programs, may advertise the goods of the sponsor. Examples of service marks include American Express and Mr. Goodwrench.

Certification mark. A mark used upon or in connection with the products or services of one or more persons other than the owner of the mark to certify regional or other origin, material, mode of manufacture, quality, accuracy, or other characteristics of such goods or services. The mark also may indicate that the work or labor on the goods or services was performed by members of a union or other organization. Examples of certification marks of quality include Underwriters Laboratories' UL symbol and 100 Percent Pure Florida's Seal of Approval. Examples of certification marks of service include the Automobile Association of America's Approved Auto Repair and the Motion Picture Association of America's movie ratings.

Collective mark. A trademark or service mark used by the members of a cooperative, an association, or another collective group or organization. Marks used to indicate membership in a union, an association, or another organization may be registered as collective membership marks. Examples of collective marks include the National Collegiate Athletic Association, the National Rifle Association of American Member, the Automobile Association of America, and Sigma Delta Chi.

> **Notable Quotables**
>
> Advertising may be described as the science of arresting the human intelligence long enough to get money from it.
>
> —Stephen Leacock, humorist, essayist, teacher

Trade and commercial name. Marks differ from trade and commercial names used by manufacturers, industrialists, merchants, agriculturists, and others to identify their businesses, vocations, occupations, or other names or titles lawfully adopted by persons, firms, associations, companies, unions, and other organizations. The latter are not subject to registration unless actually used as trademarks. Examples of trade and commercial names include Coca-Cola Company, HY-Grade Auto Supply, and Sony Corporation of America.

Do You Need a Federal Trademark Registration?

While federal registration is not necessary for trademark protection, registration on the Principal Register (the strongest position a mark can have) does provide certain advantages:

♦ A constructive date of first use of the mark in commerce. This gives you nation-wide priority as of that date, except with certain prior users or prior applicants.

♦ The right to sue in federal court for trademark infringement.

♦ Recovery of profits, damages, and costs in a federal court infringement action and the possibility of treble damages and attorneys' fees.

♦ Constructive notice of a claim of ownership. This eliminates a good-faith defense for a party adopting the trademark subsequent to your date of registration.

♦ The right to deposit the registration with U.S. Customs to stop the importation of goods bearing an infringing mark.

♦ *Prima facie* evidence of the validity of registration, your ownership of the mark, and your exclusive right to use the mark in commerce in connection with the use of goods or services specified in the certificate.

♦ The possibility of incontestability, in which case the registration constitutes con-clusive evidence of your exclusive right, with certain limited exceptions, to use the registered mark in commerce.

♦ Limited grounds for attacking a registration when it's five years old.

♦ Availability of criminal penalties and treble damages in an action for counterfeit-ing a registered trademark.

♦ A basis for filing trademark applications in foreign countries.

Marks Not Subject to Registration

A trademark cannot be registered if it …

- ◆ Consists of or comprises immoral, deceptive, or scandalous matter or matter that may disparage or falsely suggest a connection with persons living or dead, institutions, beliefs, or national symbols, or may bring them into contempt or disrepute.

- ◆ Consists of or comprises the flag or coat of arms or other insignia of the United States, of any state or municipality, of any foreign nation, or any simulation thereof.

- ◆ Consists of or comprises a name, portrait, or signature identifying a particular living individual except by his written consent or the name, signature, or portrait of a deceased president of the United States during the life of his widow, if any, except by the written consent of the widow.

> **Bright Ideas**
>
> B.V.D. underwear takes its name from the men who started the company in 1876—Bradley, Voorhees, and Day.

- ◆ Consists of or comprises a mark that so resembles a mark registered in the USPTO, or a mark or trade name previously used in the United States by another and not abandoned, as to be likely when applied to the goods of another person, to cause confusion, to cause mistake, or to deceive.

Registerable Marks

The trademark, if otherwise eligible, may be registered on the Principal Register unless it consists of a mark that, when applied to your goods/services, is merely descriptive or deceptively misdescriptive of them, except as indications of regional origin, or is primarily merely a surname.

Such marks, however, may be registered on the Principal Register, provided they have become distinctive as applied to your goods in commerce. The commissioner may accept as *prima facie* evidence that the mark has become distinctive as applied to your goods/services in commerce, proof of substantially exclusive and continuous use thereof as a mark by you in commerce for the five years preceding the date you filed the application for registration.

All marks capable of distinguishing your goods and not registerable on the Principal Register, which have been in lawful use in commerce for the year preceding your filing for registration, may be registered on the Supplemental Register. A mark on this register may consist of any trademark, symbol, label, package, configuration of goods, name, word, slogan, phrase, surname, geographical name, numeral, device, or any combination of these.

411

To keep up with the business of brand licensing, subscribe to *Li©ense! Global* magazine, a controlled-circulation publication sent free to those who qualify. Find out more at www.licensemag.com or by calling 212-951-6600.

Searches for Conflicting Marks

You are not required to conduct a search for conflicting marks prior to applying with the USPTO. However, some people find it useful, and I *highly recommend* it. The application fee, which covers processing and search costs, will not be refunded even if a conflict is found and the mark cannot be registered. In evaluating your application, an examining attorney will conduct a search and notify you if a conflicting mark is found.

To determine whether there is a conflict between two marks, the examiner determines whether there would be likelihood of confusion—that is, whether relevant consumers would be likely to associate the goods or services of one party with those of the other party as a result of the use of the marks at issue by both parties. The principal factors to be considered in reaching this decision are the similarity of the marks and the commercial relationship between the goods and services identified by the marks. To find a conflict, the marks need not be identical, and the goods and services do not have to be the same.

You can do a search in several ways. You can hire a patent attorney, engage the services of a professional trademark search firm, or do it yourself.

Law Firm Trademark Search

Your patent attorney will gladly handle a trademark search. Lawyers rely on the services of a professional trademark search firm and then add a premium of 40 to 100 percent or more, depending on what the market will bear and the firm's overhead. If you decide to hire counsel, get an estimate first. Also find out how much the law firm charges for copies. Avoid surprises.

A lawyer will most likely give you a search that goes much wider than the USPTO. If your lawyer is on the ball, he or she would typically purchase a search by Thomson & Thomson, the world leader in trademark services. For information, call toll-free 1-800-356-8630 or visit www.thomson-thomson.com.

Professional Trademark Search

While you can do your own trademark search via the USPTO's website and Internet search engines, trademark lawyers can provide a much deeper search and should be considered for more serious products.

Making Your Application

If you find the mark available, go to the Trademark Electronic Application System (TEAS) at http://teas.uspto.gov/V1.22. TEAS allows you to fill out a form and check it for completeness over the Internet. Using e-TEAS, you can then submit the form directly to the USPTO, making an official filing online.

Or using PrinTEAS, you can print out the completed form for mailing to the USPTO. It's your choice.

DIY Trademark Search

If you decide to go it alone, you can approach your search in a number of ways.

You may visit the Trademark Office's Public Search Room, located on the first floor of the Madison East building, 600 Dulany Street, Alexandria, VA 22314. The staff there is very helpful, and once you learn the layout, you can breeze through the search process.

Trademark information on CD-ROM has been distributed to the Patent and Trademark Depository Libraries (PTDLs). These products include TRADEMARKS Registrations, which contains all currently registered U.S. trademarks; TRADEMARKS Pending Applications; and the TRADEMARKS Assignment File, which contains ownership information.

By the way, these products are available for sale to the public and may be ordered from the USPTO's Office of Electronic Information Products, PO Box 1450, Alexandria, VA 22313-1450; 571-272-5600; ipd@uspto.gov.

If you want to be as thorough as possible, back up the USPTO search with Thomson & Thomson. Do this yourself and avoid the lawyer's markup. For good measure, I always run my proposed trademarks through several Internet search engines (e.g., dogpile.com, altavista.com, yahoo.com, etc.) to see if something turns up that might cause interference for me.

Establishing Trademark Rights

Trademark rights arise from either (1) actual use of the mark or (2) the filing of a proper application to register a mark in the USPTO stating that you have a bona fide intention to use the mark in commerce regulated by the U.S. Congress. (See the following "Types of Applications for Federal Registration" section for a discussion of the terms *commerce* and *use in commerce*.)

Federal registration is not required to establish rights in a mark, nor is it required to begin use of a mark. However, federal registration can secure benefits beyond the rights acquired by merely using a mark. For example, the owner of a federal registration is presumed to be the owner of the mark for the goods and services specified in the registration and to be entitled to use the mark nationwide.

Two related but distinct types of rights are at work in a mark: the right to register and the right to use. Generally, the first party that either uses a mark in commerce or files an application in the USPTO has the ultimate right to register that mark. The USPTO's authority is limited to determining the right to register. The right to use a mark can be more complicated to determine. This is particularly true when two parties have begun using the same or similar marks without knowledge of one another, and neither has a federal registration. Only a court can render a decision about the right to use, such as issuing an injunction or awarding damages for infringement.

Note that a federal registration can provide significant advantages to a party involved in a court proceeding. The USPTO cannot provide advice concerning rights in a mark. Only a private attorney can provide such advice.

Terms of a Trademark

Unlike copyrights or patents, trademark rights can last indefinitely if the owner continues to use the mark to identify its goods or services. The term of a federal trademark registration is 10 years, with 10-year renewal terms.

However, between the fifth and sixth year after the date of initial registration, the registrant must file an affidavit setting forth certain information to keep the registration alive. If no affidavit is filed, the registration is cancelled.

Types of Applications for Federal Registration

You may apply for federal registration in three principal ways:

Anyone who has already commenced using a mark in commerce may file based on that use (a "use" application).

Anyone who has not yet used the mark may apply based on a bona fide intention to use the mark in commerce (an "intent to use" application). For the purpose of obtaining federal registration, *commerce* means all commerce that may lawfully be regulated by the U.S. Congress—for example, interstate commerce or commerce between the United States and another country. The use in commerce must be a bona fide use in the ordinary course of trade and not made merely to reserve a right in a mark. Use of a mark in promotion or advertising before the product or service is actually provided under the mark on a normal commercial scale does not qualify as use in commerce. If you file based on a bona fide intention to use in commerce, note that you will have to use the mark in commerce and submit an allegation of use to the USPTO before the USPTO will register the mark.

> **Bright Ideas**
>
> The Seven-Up Company registered "The Uncola" as a trademark over the objections of the Coca-Cola Company, which made the case that no entity should be permitted exclusive rights to a term that was the equivalent of *noncola*.

Additionally, under certain international agreements, anyone may file in the United States based on an application or registration in another country.

Who May File an Application?

The application must be filed in the name of the owner of the mark: usually an individual, corporation, or partnership. The owner of a mark controls the nature and quality of the goods or services identified by the mark.

The owner may submit and prosecute its own application for registration or may be represented by an attorney. The USPTO cannot help select an attorney.

Fast Facts

When selecting a trademark, avoid the likelihood of confusion with similar marks by remembering S.A.M.—sound, appearance, meaning. If your mark is similar to another in any of these areas, you might want to reconsider it.

Foreign Applicants

If you do not live in the United States, you must designate, in writing, the name and address of a domestic representative—a person residing in the United States "upon whom notices of process may be served for proceedings affecting the mark."

This person will receive all communications from the USPTO unless you are represented by an attorney in the United States.

Where to Send the Application and Correspondence

Mail your application to the Commissioner of Trademarks:

> Commissioner for Trademarks
> PO Box 1451
> Alexandria, VA 22313-1451

Or you can file your trademark application online using TEAS. TEAS allows you to fill out and submit your application directly to the USPTO over the Internet. You can pay by credit card, through an existing USPTO deposit account, or via electronic funds transfer.

Use of the ™, ℠, and ® Symbols

Anyone who claims rights in a mark may use the ™ (trademark) or ℠ (service mark) designation with the mark to alert the public to the claim. *It is not necessary to have a registration, or even a pending application, to use these designations.* The claim may or may not be valid.

The registration symbol, ®, may be used only when the mark is registered in the USPTO. It is improper to use this symbol at any point before the registration issues.

Omit all symbols from the mark in the drawing you submit with your application; the symbols are not considered part of the mark.

Examination

After the USPTO determines that you've met the minimum filing requirements, an application serial number is assigned and the application is forwarded to an examining attorney. This may take a number of months. The examining attorney reviews the application to determine whether it complies with all applicable rules and statutes and includes all required fees.

A complete review includes a search for conflicting marks and an examination of the written application, the drawing, and any specimen.

If the examining attorney decides that a mark should not be registered, the examining attorney will issue a letter (office action) explaining any substantive reasons for refusal and any technical or procedural deficiencies in the application.

The examining attorney may also contact you by telephone if only minor corrections are required. If a correction or modification can be done by phone, that's how the examiners prefer to handle it. I have always found trademark examiners to be most helpful and professional. Unlike many bureaucrats, they tend to favor less paper.

You must respond to any objections within six months of the mailing date of the letter or the application will be abandoned. If your response does not overcome all objections, the examining attorney will issue a final refusal. You may then appeal to the Trademark Trial and Appeal Board, an administrative tribunal within the USPTO.

A common ground for refusal is likelihood of confusion between your mark and a registered mark. Marks that are merely descriptive in relation to your goods or services, or a feature of the goods or services, may also be refused. Marks consisting of geographic terms or surnames may also be refused. Marks may be refused for other reasons as well.

Publication for Opposition

If there are no objections, or if you overcome all objections, the examining attorney will approve the mark for publication in the *Official Gazette*, a weekly publication of the USPTO, and the USPTO will send you a Notice of Publication indicating the date of publication.

In the case of two or more applications for similar marks, the USPTO publishes the application with the earliest effective filing date first. Any party who believes it may be damaged by the registration of the mark has 30 days from the date of publication to file an opposition to registration. An opposition is similar to a formal proceeding in the federal courts but is held before the Trademark Trial and Appeal Board. If no opposition is filed, the application enters the next stage of the registration process.

Issuance of Certificate of Registration or Notice of Allowance

If your application was based on the actual use of the mark in commerce prior to approval for publication, the USPTO will register the mark and issue a registration certificate about 12 weeks after the date the mark was published if no opposition was filed.

If instead the mark was published based on your statement of having a bona fide intention to use the mark in commerce, the USPTO will issue a Notice of Allowance about 12 weeks after the date the mark was published, again provided no opposition was filed. You then have six months from the date of the Notice of Allowance to either use the mark in commerce and submit a Statement of Use or request a six-month Extension of Time to File a Statement of Use. You may request additional extensions of time only as noted in the instructions.

If the Statement of Use is filed and approved, the USPTO will issue the registration certificate.

Bobbi's Traps and Tips

In 2009, through a serendipitous chain of events involving what amounted to a nuisance lawsuit over a trademark, I met Roberta Jacobs-Meadway, partner in the Philadelphia-based ip law firm Eckert Seamans. She was hired to handle our defense. The lawsuit was a distraction. Meeting our defense counsel and her team was an attraction.

Bobbi, a gifted trial attorney, displayed the legal knowledge, advocacy skills, and the experience of the finest practitioners. She and her colleagues handled the plaintiffs with the air of Red Adair extinguishing and capping a blazing, erupting oil well.

After the case was over, I asked Bobbi to contribute some advice to this chapter. So here are Bobbi's Traps and Tips.

Traps

Beware of fraud on the Trademark Office. An application may be void and a registration subject to cancellation if goods identified in the application/registration have not been sold before the declaration of use is made, even if other goods have been sold under the mark and even if the goods are sold after the date of the declaration of use.

Beware of the naked license. Trademark rights can be lost if there is no control over the nature and extent of use of the mark by permitted users.

Beware of abandonment. Three years nonuse gives rise to a presumption of abandonment of rights, but rights in a mark can be lost if the mark is still in use but the form is altered over time. That is, if the mark is registered in special form and the form changes, the registration may not be able to be maintained, and the rights provided by registration will then be lost.

Beware of the territorial nature of trademark rights. Having a mark protected in the United States provides no rights in countries where the goods may be manufactured. If another owns the mark in China or India or Brazil, barriers may be raised to manufacture and export, as well as to sell in that jurisdiction.

Beware of inadvertent infringement. Rights can be acquired based on the filing of an intent to use application with no market presence. Trademark infringement is not an intentional tort. Willfulness may impact on the quantum of damage, but not on the availability of damages or injunctive relief. Common law rights may be claimed in nontraditional trademarks, including sounds, colors, product configurations, and packaging.

Tips

Things to do to avoid issues later:

Do a reasonable trademark search before becoming wedded to a name. Don't look only at the Trademark Office website, although that is a good place to start. Spend some time in the marketplace getting a sense of what is there, how it is displayed, what it is called, and how else it can be identified.

Think creatively about what may be subject to intellectual property protection. Protection can be layered, and the same article may be subject to protection under copyright, trademark, trade dress, patent, design, utility, and publicity rights. If you would be upset if some aspect were copied, look for some means of protection.

Act early to protect intellectual property rights. Trademark applications can be filed on the basis of intent to use. Copyright applications can be made for unpublished works. Patent rights can be lost if you wait too long to file for protection.

Ignore the urban myths. No rights are secured by mailing the work to yourself in a certified envelope. And there's no right to copy any particular number of words or notes or images.

Have written agreements in place with anyone who is working on the project and has any creative input. Make certain it is clear who owns what, who can do what, what payments are owed, and who's responsible for what. Understand with any person who is going to participate in the project what the cost is of getting involved, what the cost is of being involved, and what the cost is of getting out of the deal. Finally, pay attention to intellectual property issues involving indemnifications, warranties, and insurance.

Correspondence and Information

All correspondence about trademark matters should be addressed to Commissioner for Trademarks, PO Box 1451, Alexandria, VA 22313-1451, unless you have the name of a particular examiner or other official.

Here are some phone numbers and web pages you may find useful:

◆ Automated (Recorded) General Trademark or Patent Information: 1-800-786-9199 or 571-272-1000; www.uspto.gov.

◆ The Trademark Electronic Search System (TESS;tess2.uspto.gov/bin/gate.exe?f=tess&state=4004:fogquj.1.1): Search the USPTO database before filing your application to determine whether anyone is already claiming trademark rights in a particular mark.

◆ Trademark Electronic Application System (TEAS; www.uspto.gov/teas/index.html): TEAS allows you to fill out an application form and submit it directly to the USPTO over the Internet. You can pay by credit card, through an existing USPTO deposit account, or via electronic funds transfer.

Bright Ideas
John S. Pemberton, a druggist in Atlanta, brewed the first kettle of Coca-Cola in 1886. Its main ingredients were coca, the dried leaves of a South American shrub, and cola, extracted from the kola nut. The American public coined the abbreviated name Coke. Coke was registered as a federal trademark in 1920.

- The Trademark Application and Registration Retrieval System (TARR; tarr. uspto.gov): From this page, you may retrieve information about pending and registered trademarks obtained from the USPTO's internal database by simply entering a valid trademark serial number or registration number.

- Assignment Branch: 571-272-3350.

- Certified Copies of Registrations: 571-272-3150.

- Information Regarding Renewals [Sec. 9], Affidavits of Use [Sec. 8], Incontestability [Sec. 15], or Correcting a Mistake on a Registration: 571-272-9500.

- Information Regarding International Applications and other documents under the Madrid Protocol: 571-272-8910.

- Trademark Trial and Appeal Board: 571-272-8500.

The Least You Need to Know

- Trademarks can be more important than patents.

- You don't need a federal trademark registration, but it adds to your punch.

- Save money, and do the search and application yourself online. Try it; you'll like it.

- Get a jump on things with an intent-to-use application.

Chapter **18**

Securing Your Copyrights

In This Chapter

- Copyright: a no-brainer to obtain
- What can and cannot be protected
- Understanding what © really means and how long it lasts
- Ways to register your copyright
- Forms and their functions

> The vitality of thought is in adventure. Ideas won't keep. Something must be done about them. When the idea is new, its custodians have fervor, live for it, and, if need be, die for it.
>
> —Alfred North Whitehead, British mathematician, logician, and philosopher

What do Hal David's hit song "Do You Know the Way to San Jose?"; John Gray's best-seller *Men Are from Mars, Women Are from Venus*; the film *The Graduate*; the printed matter on a can of Diet Coke; and this book have in common?

If you said they are all protected by copyright, you are correct.

All About Copyrights

Copyrights are very different from patents and trademarks. A patent primarily prevents inventions, discoveries, or advancements of useful processes from being manufactured, used, or marketed by anyone other than the patentee. A trademark is a word, name, or symbol to indicate origin and, in so doing, distinguish the products and services of one company from those of another.

Copyright protects "original works of authorship" that are fixed in a tangible form of expression. The fixation need not be directly perceptible as long as it may be communicated with the aid of a machine or device.

Copyrightable works can fall into the following categories:

- Literary works

- Musical works, including any accompanying words

- Dramatic works, including any accompanying music

- Pantomimes and choreographic works

- Pictorial, graphic, and sculptural works

- Motion pictures and other audiovisual works

- Sound recordings

- Architectural works

> **Notable Quotables**
>
> It doesn't matter if you try and try and try again, and fail. It does matter if you try and fail, and fail to try again.
>
> —Charles F. Kettering, inventor, car ignition system

These categories should be viewed broadly. For example, computer programs and most "compilations" may be registered as "literary works"; maps and architectural plans may be registered as "pictorial, graphic, and sculptural works." Barbie and Ken, Mattel dolls, are copyrighted as sculptural works.

Copyright does not protect ideas, concepts, systems, or methods of doing something. Copyrights protect the form of expression rather than the subject matter of the writing. You may express your ideas in writing or drawings and claim copyright in your description, but be aware that copyright will not protect the idea itself as revealed in your written or artistic work.

The Copyright Office

Copyrights are not handled by the Patent and Trademark Office. For this, we move across the Potomac River from the USPTO's Alexandria, Virginia, headquarters to Washington, D.C., up Independence Avenue, and to Capitol Hill to the Library of Congress, on the fourth floor of the James Madison Memorial Building. This august institution is primarily responsible for administering copyright law.

In fiscal year 1999, the Copyright Office transferred over 950,000 copyright deposit copies, valued at more than $36 million, to the Library of Congress for its collections.

The Library of Congress, of which the Copyright Office is a part, was established in 1800. It has about 115 million items in its collections, including over 25 million books and other printed matter. The special collections include over 35 million charts, maps, photos, etc. There are also about 5,700 incunabula (books printed before 1501).

You may visit the Copyright Public Information Office at 101 Independence Avenue SE, Washington, D.C., or call 202-707-3000. Recorded information on copyright is available 24 hours a day, 7 days a week. Information specialists are on duty to answer queries by phone or in person from 8:30 A.M. to 5 P.M. Monday through Friday, except holidays. Mail should be addressed to Register of Copyrights, Copyright Office, Library of Congress, Washington, DC 20559-6000.

411

Here are some interesting blogs dedicated to copyrights and copyright law: williampatry.blogspot.com, copyrightlitigation.blogspot.com, researchcopyright. blogspot.com/2009/07/copyright-information-make-money-with.html, permissions-please.today.com/2009/07/22/web-site-copyrights, and www.twm-kd.com/computers/copyrights-intellectualy-property-and-piracy.

What Would an Inventor Copyright?

Copyright protection is available to you for both published and unpublished works. I slap copyright notices on many things I create—proposals, instruction sheets, game content, game boards, package copy, video presentations, sculptures, drawings, photographs, etc. I do not go through the formal process of registering everything, but I typically place the copyright notice on appropriate products, which is legal.

If a licensee opts to use my copyrighted material, I insist that my copyright notice appear on the package or the elements to which it pertains. I typically make it a part of the license agreement. Few object. A couple times, I was told that a product could have only one copyright notice and that it had to be the company's. A call to the Library of Congress settled it. Products can list as many copyrights as are appropriate. For example, there can be one on the artwork, another on the package text and trade dress, yet another on the instructions, etc.

Securing a Copyright

The way in which copyright protection is secured under the present law is frequently misunderstood. In years past, it was required that you fill out forms and send them to the Library of Congress, together with a check and a number of copies of the original work. Today no publication, registration, or other action in the Copyright Office is required to secure copyright under the new law.

> **Fast Facts**
>
> In 1783, Connecticut became the first state to pass a copyright statute. "An Act for the Encouragement of Literature and Genius" was enacted because of the advocacy of Dr. Noah Webster.

Under present law, copyright is secured "automatically" when the work is created, and the work is "created" when it is fixed in a copy or phonographically recorded for the first time. In general, "copies" are material objects from which a work can be read or visually perceived either directly or with the aid of a machine or device, such as books, manuscripts, sheet music, film, videotape, or microfilm.

Registration is recommended for a number of reasons. You might want to register your work to have the facts of your copyright on the public record and have a certificate of registration. Registered works may be eligible for statutory damages and attorney's fees in successful litigation. Finally, if registration occurs within five years of publication, it is considered *prima facie* evidence in a court of law.

Copyright does not protect names, titles, slogans, or short phrases. In some cases, these may be protected as trademarks. Contact the U.S. Patent and Trademark Office at 1-800-786-9199 for further information. However, copyright protection may be available for logo artwork that contains sufficient authorship. In some circumstances, an artistic logo may also be protected as a trademark.

Fast Facts _____

On August 18, 1787, James Madison submitted to the framers of the Constitution a provision "to secure to literary authors their copyrights for a limited time." On May 31, 1790, the first copyright law was enacted under the new U.S. Constitution. A term of 14 years with privilege of renewal for an additional 14 years was offered. On June 9, 1790, the first copyright entry, John Barry's *The Philadelphia Spelling Book,* was registered in the U.S. District Court of Pennsylvania.

Who May File an Application?

The following persons are legally entitled to submit an application form:

The author. This is either the person who actually created the work or, if the work was made-for-hire, the employer or other person for whom the work was prepared.

The copyright claimant. The copyright claimant is defined in Copyright Office regulations as either the author of the work or a person or organization that has obtained ownership of all the rights under the copyright initially belonging to the author. This category includes a person or organization that has obtained by contract the right to claim legal title to the copyright in an application for copyright registration.

The owner of exclusive right(s). Under the law, any of the exclusive rights that make up a copyright and any subdivision of them can be transferred and owned separately, even though the transfer may be limited in time or place of effect. The term *copyright owner,* with respect to any one of the exclusive rights contained in a copyright, refers to the owner of that particular right. Any owner of an exclusive right may apply for registration of a claim in the work.

The duly authorized agent of such author, other copyright claimant, or owner of exclusive right(s). Any person authorized to act on behalf of the author, other copyright claimant, or owner of exclusive rights may apply for registration.

There is no requirement that applications be prepared or filed by an attorney. Don't throw away your money!

Mary Berghaus Levering, associate registrar for National Copyright Programs, says it currently takes between six and eight months to process copyright applications.

Notice of Copyright

Before you publicly show or distribute your work, notice of copyright is required. The use of the copyright notice is your responsibility and does not need any special advance permission from or registration with the Copyright Office.

The notice for visually perceptible copies should contain these three elements:

◆ The symbol © or the word *Copyright*, or the abbreviation *Copr.*

◆ The year of first publication of said work. In the case of complications or derivative works incorporating previously published material, the year of first publication of the compilation or derivative work is enough. The year may be omitted where a pictorial, graphic, or sculptural work, with accompanying text (if any), is reproduced in or on greeting cards, postcards, stationary, jewelry, dolls, toys, or any useful article.

◆ The name of the owner of copyright in the work, an abbreviation by which the name can be recognized, or a generally known alternative of the owner:

Example: © 2010 Stuart Gottdenker

You should affix the notice in such a way as to give it reasonable notice of the claim of copyright.

How Long Does Copyright Last?

The Sonny Bono Copyright Term Extension Act, signed into law on October 27, 1998, amended the provisions concerning duration of copyright protection and generally extended them for an additional 20 years. Specific provisions are as follows:

For works created after January 1, 1978, copyright protection will endure for the life of the author plus an additional 70 years. In the case of a joint work, the term lasts for 70 years after the last surviving author's death. For anonymous and pseudonymous works and works made-for-hire, the term will be 95 years from the year of first publication or 120 years from the year of creation, whichever expires first.

For works created but not published or registered before January 1, 1978, the term endures for the life of the author plus 70 years, but in no case will expire earlier than December 31, 2002. If the work is published before December 31, 2002, the term will not expire before December 31, 2047.

For pre-1978 works still in their original or renewal term of copyright, the total term is extended to 95 years from the date that copyright was originally secured.

For further information, see Circular 15a or the Copyright Office's website, www.loc.gov/copyright.

What Is *Not* Protected by Copyright?

Several categories of material are generally not eligible for federal copyright protection. These include, among others …

♦ Works that have not been fixed in a tangible form of expression (for example, choreographic works that have not been notated or recorded, and improvisational speeches or performances that have not been written or recorded)

♦ Titles, names, short phrases, and slogans; familiar symbols or designs; mere variations of typographic ornamentation, lettering, or coloring; and mere listings of ingredients or contents

♦ Ideas, procedures, methods, systems, processes, concepts, principles, discoveries, or devices, as distinguished from a description, explanation, or illustration

♦ Works consisting entirely of information that is common property and contains no original authorship (for example, standard calendars, height and weight charts, tape measures and rulers, and lists or tables taken from public documents or other common sources)

Submitting Copyright Registrations

You have two options when it comes to submitting registrations for copyright:

♦ Online

♦ By mail

Let's look at both options so you can determine which is best for you.

Striking the Right CORDS

In 1993, the Copyright Office began developing CORDS (Copyright Office Electronic Registration, Recordation, and Deposit System) as its fully automated, innovative system to receive and process digital applications and digital deposits of copyrighted works for electronic registration via the Internet. Today the system is called eCO.

You can use eCO to register basic claims to copyright, even if you intend to submit a hard copy (or copies) of the work(s) being registered. Basic claims include literary works, visual arts works, performing arts works, sound recordings, motion pictures, and single serial issues. At this time, the following types of registration are not available in eCO:

♦ Renewals

♦ Corrections

♦ Mask works

♦ Vessel hulls

♦ Groups of serial issues

♦ Groups of newspaper/newsletter issues

♦ Groups of database updates

♦ Groups of contributions to periodicals

For information about registering these types, see the Copyright Office website.

One of the requirements for establishing an eCO account is to provide an e-mail address. That e-mail address is not available on the public record.

Currently eCO accepts basic registrations only, including any single work, a collection of unpublished works by the same author and owned by the same claimant, or multiple published works contained in the same unit of publication and owned by the same claimant. For example, a compact disc containing 10 songs or a book of poems.

Registering a claim to copyright via eCO involves three easy steps:

1. Complete an application.

2. Pay the associated fee. (Pay online with a credit or debit card or ACH transfer via Pay.gov, or with a deposit account.)

3. Submit your work.

When payment is complete, you will see the "Payment Successful" screen. If not, refer to the "Troubleshooting" section.

You may submit an application and payment in eCO and then create and print a shipping slip to be attached to the hard copy(ies) of your work for delivery to the Copyright Office via mail or courier.

Submitting Registrations by Mail

To register a work by mail, send the following ...

♦ A properly completed application form

♦ A nonrefundable filing fee of $35 (effective August 1, 2009) for each application

♦ A "best edition" of your work

... in the same envelope or package to:

> Library of Congress
> Copyright Office
> 101 Independence Avenue SE
> Washington, DC 20559-6000

Copyright Office fees are subject to change. For current fees, check the Copyright Office website at www.copyright.gov/docs/fees.html, write the Copyright Office, or call 202-707-3000.

In Search of Copyright Records

The Copyright Office's records are open to the public. Moreover, on request, the Copyright Office will search its records for you for $65 for each hour or fraction of an hour the search takes. For information on searching the Office records concerning the copyright status or ownership of a work, request Circular 22, "How to Investigate the Copyright Status of a Work," and Circular 23, "The Copyright Card Catalog and the Online Files of the Copyright Office."

Copyright Office records in machine-readable form catalogued from January 1, 1978, to the present, including registration and renewal information and recorded documents, are now available for searching online. You can examine

---

Bright Ideas

Isaac Singer introduced the installment plan, an innovation that changed American life. Beginning in 1856, a Singer sewing machine could be bought for $5 down and $5 per month. The plan was an immediate success. In only a few months, sales tripled.

these files through LOCIS (Library of Congress Information System). Connect to LOCIS at www.loc.gov/copyright/rb.html.

Investigating the Copyright Status of a Work

You have several ways to investigate whether a work is under copyright protection and, if so, determine the facts of the copyright. You could examine a copy of the work (or, if the work is a sound recording, examine the disc, tape cartridge, or cassette in which the recorded sound is fixed, or the album cover, sleeve, or container in which the recording is sold) for such elements as a copyright notice, place and date of publication, author, and publisher. You could also make a personal search of the Copyright Office catalogs and other records. Or you could have the Copyright Office make a search for you.

The Copyright Office is located in the Library of Congress, James Madison Memorial Building, 101 Independence Avenue SE, Washington, D.C. Most records are open to public inspection and searching from 8:30 A.M. to 5 P.M. Monday through Friday (except legal holidays). The various records freely available to the public include an extensive card catalog, an automated catalog containing records from 1978 on, record books, and microfilm records of assignments and related documents. Other records, including correspondence files and deposit copies, are not open to the public for searching. However, they may be inspected upon request and payment of a search fee. Log on to www.copyright.gov/docs/fees.html for more info.

If you want to search the Copyright Office's public files yourself, you will be given assistance in locating the records you need and in learning searching procedures. If the Copyright Office staff actually makes the search for you, a search fee will be charged. The search will not be done while you wait.

Fast Facts _____

Copyright protection was given to dramatic works in 1856.

The Copyright Office is not permitted to give legal advice. If you need information or guidance on matters, such as disputes over the ownership of a copyright, suits against possible infringers, the procedure for getting a work published, or the method of obtaining royalty payments, you might have to consult an attorney.

Application Forms

All copyright application forms are now available online at www.copyright.gov/forms. Here are the forms you'll most likely require:

Form TX (text) for published and unpublished nondramatic literary works. This comprises the broadest category, covering everything from novels to computer programs, game instructions, and invention proposals.

Form VA (visual arts) for published and unpublished works of the visual arts. This would be for artwork you may have developed as an adjunct to your invention, charts, technical drawings, diagrams, models, and works of artistic craftsmanship.

On the website, you will find additional forms:

Form CA (supplementary) for application for supplementary copyright registration. Use this when an earlier registration has been made in the Copyright Office and some of the facts given in that registration are incorrect or incomplete. Form CA allows you to place the correct or complete fact on record.

Form RE (renewal) for renewal registration. Use this when you want to renew a copyright.

As of this writing, the cost is $35 per registration for a basic claim in an original work of authorship (electronic filing). For a current and comprehensive list of all services and fees, go to www.copyright.gov/docs/fees.html.

> **Bright Ideas**
>
> The country's first feature film, D. W. Griffith's *Birth of a Nation*, was registered for copyright protection in 1915. "God Bless America," by Irving Berlin, was registered in 1939. Mattel's Barbie doll was registered in 1958. Registration of the Ken doll followed in 1960.

For Further Information

Circulars, announcements, regulations, other related materials, and all copyright application forms are available from the Copyright Office website at www.loc.gov/copyright.

Circulars and other information (but not application forms) are available from Fax-on-Demand at 202-707-2600.

For general information about copyright, call the Copyright Public Information Office at 202-707-3000. The TTY number for the deaf or hearing impaired is 202-707-6737. Information specialists are on duty from 8:30 A.M. to 5 P.M. Monday through Friday (EST) except federal holidays. Recorded information is available 24 hours a day. Or if you know which application forms and circulars you want, request them from the Forms and Publications Hotline at 202-707-9100, also available 24 hours a day. Leave a recorded message.

For information by mail, write to:

> Library of Congress
> Copyright Office
> Publications Section, LM-455
> 101 Independence Avenue SE
> Washington, DC 20559-6000

The Least You Need to Know

- Basic copyright protection is free. Just put a copyright notice on your work.

- U.S. copyrights last for the life of the author plus 70 years. No one else can profit from or copy your ideas without your permission during this time frame.

- If you want to file a formal registration for greater protection, you don't need a lawyer. It's a simple process though the Library of Congress Copyright Office.

- To file for a basic claim costs $35 if done online. All the forms you need are on the Library of Congress's website.

Chapter **19**

I've Got a Secret

In This Chapter

- ◆ Do you have a trade secret?
- ◆ Keeping your trade secrets *secret*
- ◆ Ways to expose a trade secret without liability
- ◆ A look at the Uniform Trade Secrets Act (UTSA)

> A sekret ceases tew be a sekret if it iz once confided it iz like a dollar bill, once broken, it iz never a dollar again.
>
> —Josh Billings, *Affurisms* (1865)

Your invention may have a trade secret associated with it—that is, a plan or process, tool, mechanism, or compound known only to you and your partners and/or employees to whom it is necessary to confide it.

A company's trade secrets are its crown jewels. Trade secrets are not patented because, by doing so, they would no longer be secret and the owner would lose any competitive business advantage the secret afforded.

Arguably the most celebrated and legendary trade secret is the Coca-Cola formula. When people refer to it, they mean the ingredient called 7X, a mixture of fruit oils and spices that gives the syrup its signature flavor. It is very important to the Coca-Cola Company to keep its formula secret. In 1977, the Indian government demanded Coca-Cola reveal the formula if it wanted to market its product in the subcontinent. The Atlanta, Georgia–based company said rather than reveal its secret, it would sacrifice this huge market opportunity.

In fact, the formulas for Coca-Cola, Silly Putty, and Sea Monkeys have never been patented. They are protected through trade secrets.

Trade Secret Basics

The most common kinds of trade secrets include chemical formulas or recipes and manufacturing processes or techniques. Trade secrets are potentially unlimited in duration. The protection provided by a trade secret is lost only if someone else discovers the information either independently or by analyzing or dissecting a product through reverse engineering.

> **Bright Ideas**
>
> At age 83, Benjamin Franklin invented bifocals because he hated wearing two pairs of glasses.

Trade secrets do not need to be registered with or granted by any government agencies. If you want to keep something as a trade secret, just take reasonable steps to keep your secret, well, secret.

In the Court

Trade secret protection is a state right under the Uniform Trade Secret Act (UTSA) or similar state laws. Drafted by the National Conference of Commissioners on Uniform State Laws, the UTSA mainly provides relief if information is leaked to your competitors.

To warrant such relief through a court of law, the trade secret must be shown to be both commercially valuable and far enough removed from general knowledge that it is reasonably difficult to discover, such as in a vault or protected by a similar measure. Also, a company must show that it has been diligent in keeping its information secret.

Because patented inventions are made publicly available upon granting of the patent, patent protection and trade secret protection are mutually exclusive; however, because patent applications are kept confidential until and unless they are approved, save for the new 18-month publication rule, an invention can remain a trade secret if the patent application is rejected.

Copies of the UTSA can be ordered from the National Conference of Commissioners on Uniforms State Laws, 676 North St. Clair Street, Suite 1700, Chicago, IL 60611. Forty states have enacted various statutes modeled after the UTSA; therefore, the UTSA should not be relied upon without consulting with intellectual property counsel.

> **Notable Quotables**
>
> Everybody steals in commerce and industry. I've stolen a lot myself. But I know how to steal. They don't—and that's what's the matter with them.
>
> —Thomas Alva Edison

Can Independent Inventors Have Trade Secrets?

Sure you can, but simply classifying product development information as a trade secret is not enough. Furthermore, information known to the public or information that can be easily gathered from reading trade publications, scientific journals, and so forth is not considered a trade secret.

The biggest problem you have is how to keep your trade secrets under wraps. The most frequent disclosure of trade secret information is by current and former employees.

On May 23, 2001, *The Los Angeles Times* reported that software company Avant Corporation agreed to pay $27 million in fines, with the possibility of more to come, after its CEO and six other current and former executives pleaded *no lo contendere* to criminal charges in the theft of computer code from a competitor where Avant's founders had worked.

At the annual conference of the Risk & Insurance Management Society on May 14, 2001, Bradford C. Lewis of Fenwick & West, LLP, told a panel in reference to trade secrets: "It's a much more informal process, but you do have to take specific steps within your organization in order to qualify for trade secrecy protection."

You can lose the rights to trade secret protection when you are pitching a product concept and you share trade secrets as part of your sale's strategy. If you have not taken careful and deliberate steps to protect the trade secret, you may have compromised your secret. In this case, you'd want the potential licensee to sign a hold confidential document.

> **Notable Quotables**
>
> We must look forward to the future, as that is where most of us will be spending the rest of our lives.
>
> —Charles F. Kettering, inventor, spark plug

If the document you sign with the prospective licensee acknowledges your trade secret and promises (on behalf of the company and its employees) to hold your information confidential, then the use or sharing of same could be interpreted as willful and malicious misappropriation.

Protecting Your Secrets

The best advice for keeping your trade secret a secret is to not reveal anything of its nature until and unless you have appropriate documentation agreed to and signed off on by an officer of the reviewing entity. Your nondisclosure document should be drafted by an attorney who specializes in trade secrets. Don't just assume that a patent counsel can handle it.

Fast Facts

On August 1, 2000, the Patent Office issued U.S. Patent No. 6,097,812 on a cryptographic system. The patent application was filed on July 25, 1933, and assigned to the United States of America as represented by the National Security Agency, Washington, D.C. The system was used to crack enemy codes during World War II. The government kept the lid on it all these years. Of course, today it has been overtaken by modern technology.

The Least You Need to Know

- Trade secrets are not filed with the government.
- Loose lips sink ships, so keep your secrets secret.
- There is no statute of limitations on trade secrets.
- If you have to reveal a trade secret to make the sale, think twice about it. Then if you still want to do it, be sure everyone to whom it is shown signs on the dotted line.
- Get competent legal advice when it comes to protecting your trade secrets.

Chapter 20

Say *Ahhh!* The USPTO Patent Examination Process

In This Chapter

◆ Follow your patent application through the USPTO

◆ How not to slip on appeal

◆ Identifying patent infringement

◆ Patent enforcement insurance

◆ Setting a patent free

The stories of America's inventors abound in genius, insight, and ambition—along with frustration and heartbreak. But they tell much more … they sketch the development of a Nation.

—National Geographic Society

If your patent application passes initial muster, it will be assigned to the appropriate examining group and then to an examiner within the USPTO. Patent applications are handled in the order they're received.

The application examination inspects for compliance with the legal requirements and includes a search through U.S. patents, prior foreign patent documents that are available in the USPTO, and available literature—magazines, newspapers, doctoral dissertations, and so on—to ensure that your invention is new. The examiner then reaches a decision based on the study and the search results.

After a visit to the USPTO, Don Coster of the Nevada Inventor Association observed: "Our patent applications go through a process that is so thorough and so efficient that it is hard to believe unless you see it in action. The application does not go directly to an examiner. It must first be examined for content and completeness. The drawings are checked and screened for things like military sensitivity or unlawful usage. Once accepted as legal and complete, [the application] is classified for the proper art group. This is very critical. If the wrong examiner ends up with it on his or her table, it might be months before he or she even gets a first look at it because applications are taken in the order that they're received .... Those people are so conscientious that it rarely ever happens."

First Office Action

You, if you applied *pro se*, or your attorney will be notified of the examiner's decision through what the USPTO refers to as an "action." An action is actually a letter that gives the reasons for any adverse response or any objection or requirement. The examiner will cite any appropriate references or information that you will find useful in making the decision to continue the prosecution of the application or to drop it.

If the invention is not considered patentable subject matter, the claims will be rejected. If the examiner finds that the invention is not new, the claims will be rejected, but the claims may also be rejected if they depict an object that is found to be obvious. It is not uncommon for some or all of the claims to be rejected on the examiner's first action; very few applications sail through as first submitted.

411

The Rothschild Petersen Patent Model Museum is reportedly the largest privately owned collection of U.S. patent models in the world. Containing nearly 4,000 patent models and related documents, it spans America's Industrial Revolution. Alan W. Rothschild is working to establish a National Patent Model Museum. In the meantime, his collection is housed in a private residence in Cazenovia, New York. Visits are by appointment only. If you're interested in helping, call Alan at 315-655-9367 or e-mail maxertaxer@aol.com. To see the background on his initiative, visit www.patentmodel.org.

Your First Response

Let's say the examiner gives you the thumbs down on all or some of your claims. Your next move if you want to continue pursuing the patent is to respond, specifically pointing out the supposed errors in the examiner's action. Patent examiners have a lot on their plates, and their units are typically understaffed for the amount of work they handle. When you respond to an examiner, keep the following in mind:

Examiners must process a specific number of patents to be considered productive by their superiors for periodic job performance ratings. The bottom line is that as careful as they try to be, they make mistakes that can be reversed with careful and cogent argument by you as a *pro se* inventor, or together with your attorney.

Your response should address every ground of the objection and/or rejection. Show where the examiner is wrong. The mere allegation that the examiner has erred is not enough. Do not be timid about it if you feel he or she has made a mistake.

Upon receiving your response, the examiner will reconsider, and you will be notified if the claims are rejected, or objections or requirements made, in the same manner as after the first office action examination. This second action usually will be the final one.

If you are a *pro se* inventor, feel free to call your examiner on the telephone to discuss your case. His name and number will be on the office action. I have always found examiners to be most hospitable and helpful.

If you are represented by patent counsel, typically the examiners will not entertain your calls or visits without counsel. This is the way it is. I know there are good reasons for it, but I am a bit cynical and feel the rule not to see inventors without their lawyers was done to keep the lawyers' revenue stream coming in! Over the years, I have gone more than a few times to meet with an examiner. My lawyer typically sits there while we make our points. No one is more passionate than the inventor, and who knows the product best? The inventor, of course. But this is the way it is.

Bright Ideas

Galileo invented the thermometer in 1593.

In 1989, Englishman Tim Berners-Lee invented the World Wide Web, an Internet-based hypermedia initiative for global information sharing. He never made money on his invention.

Once, an examiner refused to allow me to come in alone unless I dismissed my patent attorney. So I called the lawyer up, explained the problem, and took him off the case. In this instance, I felt confident that I had the argument and saw no reason to pay patent counsel more money for unnecessary meetings. I went, I saw the examiner, I won the point, and my patent issued. Then I rehired the attorney.

Whether you go alone or with your attorney, don't drop in unannounced. It is to your benefit that the examiner have the time to prepare for your visit and get up-to-speed on the case. Remember that personal interviews do not remove the necessity for response to USPTO actions within the required time, and the action of the USPTO is based solely on the written record.

Final Rejection

On the second or latter consideration, the rejection of claims may be made final. Your response is then limited to appeal and further amendment is restricted. You may petition the director in the case of objections or requirements not involved in the rejection of any claim. Response to a final rejection must include cancellation of, or appeal from, the rejection of each claim so rejected and, if any claim stands allowed, compliance with any requirement or objection as to its form.

> **Notable Quotables**
>
> There are certain things that our age needs. It needs, above all, courageous hope and the impulse to creativeness.
>
> —Bertrand Russell, philosopher and mathematician

In determining such final rejection, your examiner will repeat or state all grounds of rejection then considered applicable to your claims as stated in the application.

The odds? Patents are granted in about two of every three applications filed.

Amending Your Application

The preceding section referred to amendments to an application. Let's examine some details concerning amendments:

- You may amend before or after the first examination and action as specified in the rules, or when and as specifically required by the examiner.

- After final rejection or action, amendments may be made canceling claims or complying with any requirement of form that has been made, but the admission of any such amendment or its refusal, and any proceedings relative thereto, shall not operate to relieve the application from its condition as subject to appeal or to save it from abandonment.

♦ If amendments touching the merits of the application are presented after final rejection, or after appeal has been taken, or when such amendment might not otherwise be proper, they may be admitted upon a showing of good and sufficient reasons why they are necessary and were not earlier presented.

♦ No amendment can be made as a matter of right in appealed cases. After decision on appeal, amendments can be made only as provided in the rules.

♦ The specifications, claims, and drawings must be amended and revised when required to correct inaccuracies of description and definition of unnecessary words, and to secure correspondence between the claims, the description, and the drawing.

All amendments of the drawings or specifications, and all additions thereto, must conform to at least one of them as it was at the time of the filing of the application. Matter not found in either, involving a departure from or an addition to the original disclosure, cannot be added to the application even though supported by a supplemental oath or declaration and can be shown or claimed only in a separate application.

The claims may be amended by canceling particular claims, by presenting new claims, or by amending the language of particular claims (such amended claims being, in effect, new claims). In presenting new or amended claims, you must point out how they avoid any reference or ground rejection of record that may be pertinent.

No change in the drawing may be made except by permission of the examiner. Permissible changes in the construction shown in any drawing may be made only by your draftsman, or you if you did the drawings. A sketch in permanent ink showing proposed changes to become part of the record must be filed for approval by the USPTO before the corrections are made. The paper requesting amendments to the drawing should be separate from other papers.

The original numbering of the claims must be preserved throughout the prosecution. When claims are canceled, the remaining claims must not be renumbered. When claims are added by amendment or substituted for canceled claims, they must be numbered consecutively beginning with the next number following the highest-numbered claim previously presented. When the application is ready for allowance, the examiner, if necessary, will renumber the claims consecutively in the order in which they appear or in the order you've requested.

Time for Response and Abandonment

The maximum period given for response is six months, but the Director of the Office has the right to shorten the period to no fewer than 30 days. The typical response time allowed to a USPTO action is three months. If you want a longer time, you usually have to pay extra money for an extension. The amount of the fee depends on the response time desired.

If you miss any target date, your application will be abandoned and made no longer pending. However, if you can show that your failure to prosecute was unavoidable or unintentional, you can revive your application by filing a petition to the Office of Petitions and including the appropriate fee. The proper response must also accompany the petition if it has not yet been filed.

How to Make Appeals

If the examiner circles his or her wagons and begins to stonewall, there's a higher court you can go to. You can appeal rejections that have been made final to the Board of Patent Appeals and Interferences. This body is headed by the chief administrative patent judge and the vice chief administrative patent judge. Typically, each appeal is heard by only three administrative patent judges. An appeal fee is required, and you must file a brief in support of your position. You can even get an oral hearing if you pay enough.

If the board goes against you, there is yet a higher court, the Court of Appeals for the Federal Circuit. Or you might file a civil action against the Director in the U.S. District Court for the District of Columbia. He won't take it personally; it goes with the territory. The Court of Appeals for the Federal Circuit will review the record made in the USPTO and may affirm or reverse the USPTO's action. In a civil action, you may present testimony in the court, and the court will make a decision.

Bright Ideas

In 1929, David Sarnoff, founder of RCA, asked Russian émigré Vladimir Zworykin, born in Murom, 200 miles east of Moscow, what it would take to develop television for commercial use. "A year and a half and $100,000," he reportedly responded. In reality, it took 20 years and $50 million. Before his death in 1982 at age 92, Zworykin said of his invention: "The technique is wonderful. It is beyond my expectations. But the programs—I would never let my children even come close to this thing."

What Are Interference Proceedings?

Parallel development is a phenomenon that should not be discounted. On numerous occasions, a company executive has said to me, "I've seen that concept twice in the last month," or something to this effect. At times, two or more applications may be filed by different inventors claiming substantially the same patentable invention. A patent can be granted to only one of them. In such cases, the USPTO institutes a proceeding known as an "interference" to determine who the original inventor is and who is entitled to the patent. About 1 percent of all applications filed become engaged in an interference proceeding.

Interference proceedings may also be instituted between an application and a patent already issued if the patent has not been issued for more than one year prior to the filing of the conflicting application and if the conflicting application is not barred from being patentable for some other reason.

The priority question is determined by a board of three administrative patent judges on the evidence submitted. From the decision of the Board of Patent Appeals and Interferences, the losing party may appeal to the Court of Appeals for the Federal Circuit or may file a civil action against the winning party in the appropriate U.S. district court.

The terms *conception of the invention* and *reduction to practice* are encountered in connection with priority questions. *Conception of the invention* refers to the completion of the devising of the means for accomplishing the result. *Reduction to practice* refers to the actual construction of the invention in physical form. In the case of a machine, it includes the actual building of the machine. In the case of an article or composition, it includes the actual carrying out of the steps in the process; actual operation, demonstration, or testing for the intended use is usually required. The filing of a regular application for patent completely disclosing the invention is treated as equivalent to reduction to practice. The inventor who proves to be the first to conceive the invention and the first to reduce it to practice will be held to be the prior inventor, but more complicated situations cannot be stated this simply.

This is why it is important to have evidence that proves when you first had an idea and when the prototype was made. It is critical that you keep careful and accurate records throughout the development of an idea.

If your utility patent is found to be allowable, a notice of allowance will be sent to you or your attorney. Within three months from the date of the notice, you must pay an issue fee.

> **411**
>
> The requirements at the USPTO are subject to change on a frequent basis. It is impossible for most inventors to keep up. Filing an application without sufficient fees may result in the loss of your filing date and/or a surcharge to reactivate the application. Therefore, before filing any application, to check whether new requirements have not been put into place and ensure that you are enclosing the proper fee, call 1-800-786-9199 or 571-272-1000 for assistance from customer service representatives, or visit the USPTO website at www.uspto.gov.

What Rights Does a Patent Give You?

It's a pretty exciting moment when you get your first patent. It comes bound inside a beautiful oyster-white folder that has the U.S. Constitution screened in blue as its background. The large official gold seal of the U.S. Patent and Trademark Office is embossed on it.

Between the covers of that folder is your patent, a grant that gives you, the inventor(s), "the right to exclude others from making, using, or selling the invention throughout the United States" and its territories and possessions for a designated period of time (17 or 20 years, depending on the actions of Congress), subject to the payment of maintenance fees as provided by law.

Having a patent does not guarantee your ability, nor does it explicitly give you the right, to make, use, or sell the invention. Any person is ordinarily free to make, use, or sell anything he or she pleases, and a grant from Uncle Sam is not required. But others may not do so without authorization. You may assign your rights in the invention to another person or company.

If you receive a patent for a new concept and the marketing of said concept is prohibited by law, the patent will not help you. Nor may you market said concept if by doing so you infringe on the prior rights of others.

Maintenance Fees

All utility patents that issued from applications filed on or after December 12, 1980, are subject to maintenance fees that must be paid to keep the patent in force. These fees are due at $3\frac{1}{2}$, $7\frac{1}{2}$, and $11\frac{1}{2}$ years from the date the patent is granted and can be paid without a surcharge during the six-month period preceding each due date. The amounts of the maintenance fees are subject to change.

Be advised that the USPTO does not mail notices to patent owners advising them that a maintenance fee is due. If you have a patent attorney tracking your business, he or she will let you know when the money is due. (And an attorney gets paid every time your business moves across his or her desk.) But if you are doing it by yourself and you miss a payment, it may result in the expiration of the patent. A six-month grace period is provided, during which the maintenance fee may be paid with a surcharge.

Can Two People Own a Patent?

Yes. Two or more people may jointly own patents as inventors, investors, or licensees. Most of my patents are joint ownership. Anyone who shares in the ownership of a patent, no matter how small a part they might own, has the right to make, use, or sell it for his or her own profit unless prohibited from doing so by prior agreement. It is accordingly dangerous to assign part interest in a patent of yours without having a definite agreement hammered out about respective rights and obligations to each other.

Can a Patent Be Sold?

Yes. The patent law provides for the transfer or sale of a patent, or of an application for patent, by a contract. When assigned the patent, the assignee becomes the owner of the patent and has rights identical to those of the original patentee.

411

If you've been ripped off by an invention marketing service, the Federal Trade Commission (FTC) has made it easy for you to file a complaint. Online, go to www.ftc.gov and look under Consumer Protection. Or call 1-877-FTC-HELP (1-877-382-4357). While the FTC does not resolve individual consumer problems, your complaint helps investigate fraud and can lead to law enforcement action.

Assignment of Patent Applications

If you want to assign your patent or patent application to a third party (manufacturer, investor, university, employer, or other entity), you can do so by filing the Assignment of Patent, or Assignment of Patent Application.

You can sell all or part of the interest in a patent. If you prefer, you could even sell it by geographic region. I consider patents valuable properties, personal assets. Never assume that because you have been unsuccessful in selling a patent, it has no value. You might sell it eventually or find someone infringing it, which would turn it into a positive account.

Infringement of Patents

Infringement of a patent consists in the unauthorized making, using, or selling of the patented invention within the territory of the United States during the term of the patent. If someone uses your patent without your permission, it is your right to seek relief in the appropriate federal court.

When I see an apparent infringement of a patent of ours, as has occurred occasionally over the years, the first thing I do is call the company and set up a meeting. I am not litigious. Things can often be worked out between parties. Thus far, I have always been able to do this. Court battles over patents can be long and expensive affairs. Where elephants fight, grass doesn't grow. And if you want to continue working in your particular field, it is wise to avoid making too many corporate enemies.

Several years ago, I saw an infringement of a patent we hold. One call to the company's president and a quick fax of our patent brought immediate relief in the form of a royalty on all items made to date and in the future. Not only that, but I was invited to submit ideas for licensing consideration.

If your friendly approach is turned away, and you are sure of your position, the next step is to get a lawyer and decide whether a temporary restraining order (TRO) is appropriate. A TRO is an injunction to prevent the continuation of the infringement. You may also ask the court for an award of damages because of the infringement. In such an infringement suit, the defendant may raise the question of the validity of the patent, which is then decided by the court. The defendant may also claim that what is being done does not constitute infringement.

Infringement is determined primarily by the language of the claims of the patent, and if what the defendant is making does not fall within the language of any of the claims of the patent, there is no infringement.

The USPTO has no jurisdiction over questions relating to patent infringement. In examining applications for patent, no determination is made as to whether the patent-seeking invention infringes any prior patent.

Bright Ideas
In 1926, Alabama-born Waldo Semon, a research chemist at B.F. Goodrich, in Akron, Ohio, put his assigned work aside and tried dissolving polyvinyl chloride (PVC) to create an adhesive for bonding rubber to metal. "People thought of PVC as worthless back then," Semon said. "They'd throw it in the trash." He never created the adhesive, but while heating PVC in a solvent at a high boiling point, he discovered a substance that was both flexible and elastic. No one knew what to make of it. Today, however, PVC has become the second-best-selling plastic in the world, generating billions of dollars in sales each year.

To Sue or Not to Sue

If you do catch someone infringing your patent, you may decide to sue for damages. This can be a costly exercise. According to Stephen R. May, former manager of Intellectual Property Services Department at Pacific Northwest Laboratory in Richland, Washington, "a full-blown patent lawsuit that actually goes to trial will probably cost a minimum of $75,000 to $100,000, although a very simple case could cost less." In most instances, May reports, the costs can be $250,000 and up.

His advice to inventors: "If you believe someone is infringing your patent, an attorney can draft a 'cease and desist' letter, possibly for as little as a few hundred dollars. This might resolve the matter if the infringer ceases, but in many cases it does not."

The expensive part of any lawsuit is "discovery," in which you and the infringer exchange documents and take depositions of potential witnesses. The photocopying bill alone could run into the thousands of dollars, and the process could last anywhere from six months to several years. Trials tend to run from one to six weeks, with decisions rendered in a matter of days in the case of a jury, or as long as several months if the verdict is by a judge. If you lose, appeals take more time and money.

Each time I get involved with a lawyer to defend a patent or trademark, money seems to disappear from my bank account. So it's best if you can work things out between yourself and the infringer and not hire counsel. Both sides benefit. If you need to hire a lawyer, you might want to try for a contingency deal—i.e., the lawyer might take a third of any recovery instead of charging you.

Fast Facts _____

Rod G. Martin, inventor of the foam helicoid football, offered to license nonexclusive rights to manufacture his proprietary football design to Marvlee, which was found making it without permission. Marvlee declined. So Martin took Marvlee to court for patent infringement. Federal Judge James Ware ruled that Marvlee's grooved foam footballs infringed Martin's U.S. patent. The judge awarded damages of $282,183 plus interest. Finding the infringement to have been willful, Ware added Martin's legal fees. The total judgment against Marvlee came to $1.23 million. The suit to safeguard his intellectual property would never have come to pass had Marvlee agreed to pay Martin a fair royalty.

Patent Enforcement Insurance

The only right a patent gives the inventor is the right to defend it in a court of law. And as mentioned earlier, patent infringement litigation can be costly. How much? Ask Diane B. Loisel, a nurse from Bowie, Maryland. After obtaining a patent for a cap she had invented for use in neonatal respiratory therapy, she claimed that a company to whom she had presented the concept had begun to manufacture and market it without her permission.

Loisel's patent attorney told her that to litigate would cost her $250,000 in legal fees. "If you're going to get a patent, you're going to have to fight," her lawyer had told her previously. "But he never told me it would cost so much money," she said.

To help inventors shoulder the risk and responsibility for enforcing their patents against infringers, insurance companies market policies designed to reimburse the litigation expenses incurred by a patent owner in enforcing his or her U.S. patents.

Fast Facts _____

On March 2, 1861, the fee for obtaining patent protection became $35, of which $15 was to be paid at the time of application, and $20 when the patent issues. In 2009, the fee for submitting a utility application was $1,090 (this includes the filing, search, and examination fee), or $545 for the independent inventor.

Patent attorney Robert W. Faris, a partner in Nixon & Venderhye of Arlington, Virginia, says of this kind of policy, "One of the downsides of this type of insurance is that the insurance company is reimbursed for its expenses out of the settlement or judgment. This means that if the recovery is on the order of the legal expenses incurred for the litigation, the patent owner could come away with practically no financial recovery although his patent rights will have been vindicated."

Faris adds that the program seems pretty risky for the insurance company. "I don't know how they are able to predict with any certainty what the risks would be beforehand. They would have to be only taking on patents whose chances for infringement are very remote."

One such company permits its insured to choose patent counsel. However, before the company will open the tap and start paying bills, the policyholder must provide a written opinion from his or her attorney attesting to the fact that the matter is one that can be litigated, and the policyholder must show proof that the alleged infringement will cause economic damage.

Would Faris recommend patent infringement insurance? "I might well recommend that certain clients look into it because it is the only way some small businesses might be able to enforce their patent rights," he concludes.

He points out that patent infringement insurance does not cover the inventor if his or her U.S. patent infringes an existing patent. In other words, it could protect you (the inventor) from someone infringing your patent, but it is of no help to you if your patent infringes the patent of another inventor.

Abandonment of Patents

Two kinds of abandonment exist:

♦ Intentional—you let it lapse

♦ Unintentional—due to circumstances beyond your control

If the reason for abandonment is your fault—for example, you simply lost track of dates and missed a deadline—you must pay the due fee plus a penalty for your mistake. A costly error! Check the USPTO website (www.uspto.gov) for the latest fee schedule.

If your reason is unintentional—for example, you claim to never have received the notice from the USPTO—you must pay to have your petition considered, plus you still have to pay the required fee. You might want to add a notarized letter to the form explaining your story in detail.

I was involved once in a case in which the USPTO put the wrong zip code on our paperwork, an error that caused a one-month delay and ultimately resulted in our getting slapped with abandonment papers. I was able to cure this with a phone call to a senior USPTO official. It was an open-and-shut case, as far as he was concerned.

Upon seeing proof of the typo, he personally ordered the abandonment to be withdrawn. We never even had to pay the petition fees; there was just no question about who was wrong.

If you have any questions about how to handle a petition, do not hesitate to call the USPTO at 571-272-3282 for the latest information. I have had occasion to revive patents, and the folks who answer this line are extremely helpful.

Mail petitions for revival to:

> Mail Stop Petition
> Commissioner for Patents
> PO Box 1450
> Alexandria, VA 22313-1450

It's a good idea to log all your USPTO correspondence in and out of your office. This helps you keep track of deadlines and gives you a record of paper flow. Losing paperwork or missing a deadline can be both costly and time-consuming.

The Least You Need to Know

♦ If at first you don't succeed, you have options.

♦ Patent examiners are human. They err.

♦ The USPTO is classified as a friendly port.

♦ The written word lives. The spoken word dies. Keep meticulous records, to avoid headaches later.

♦ A missed deadline can cause major problems.

Part 6

People Who Share, People Who Dare

It's been rumored that at the end of every rainbow there's a pot of gold. Well, it's no different as you approach Part 6. As your last stop in the book, it's only fitting that I give you maps to some potential pots of gold.

In the following chapters, you'll learn about financial grants you may qualify for from the federal government. If you don't qualify for or need such financing, you may be able to benefit from access to Uncle Sam's extensive patent portfolio or collaborative R&D opportunities.

One of the last frontiers for the inventor is the toy industry, and you'll learn all about what it offers here, too. Cabbage Patch Kids, Candyland, Furby, G.I. Joe, Mr. Potato Head, Monopoly, Nerf, Tickle Me Elmo!, Trivial Pursuit, Twister, and UNO are just a few of the products created by independent inventors.

It's only appropriate that the final treasure in this book be the friendship of other inventors. To help you meet men and women who share your passion for invention, the last chapter opens the world of inventor organizations and associations—local, regional, and national.

I hope you've enjoyed the journey and found it worthwhile, at times entertaining, and even inspirational. Most importantly, I hope you now see that the success you so dearly crave is the by-product of seemingly endless radical factors that must all coalesce within a certain time frame, and with method. There's no easy answer, no easy way. But if you combine what you've learned in the book with a truly innovative concept and add a dash of your own individuality, you'll position yourself for cashing in on your inventions.

Chapter 21

Hidden Treasures in Uncle Sam's High-Tech Closets

In This Chapter

◆ NIST—100+ years old and going strong

◆ Financial support for enabling technologies

◆ Manufacturing extension partnerships

◆ Federal labs—open for your business

◆ All about grants

The federal government's R&D laboratories, formerly a closed universe of expertise, are aggressively seeking commercial partnerships that further their newly expanded missions. They're out to demonstrate that technology transfer is a two-way street.

—Paul Harris, founding publisher, *Technology Business* magazine

Could yours be the perfect invention to aid U.S. combat soldiers? Would your idea assist astronauts? Have you created a vaccine that could rid the world of a deadly disease? Do you think you could possibly be the next Steve Jobs? Perhaps your ideas or inventions are not as grand as these, but you need a little assistance with funding your idea and making your dream a reality. The federal government may be able to help you.

Numerous federal programs are available to you, and the N.I.H. (Not Invented Here) Syndrome does not apply. It's amazing how many opportunities exist here to blend government resources with your ingenuity.

In this chapter, I highlight the programs I feel hold the most potential benefit to you as an independent inventor—if certain criteria are met. The programs range from financial grants to technology transfer. Let me remind you that government programs involve all kinds of paperwork and red tape. However, if you are able to tolerate working with a large bureaucracy and dealing with its frequent dynamic inaction, one of these programs may hold rewards for you.

The National Institute of Standards and Technology

Founded in 1901, the National Institute of Standards and Technology (NIST) is a nonregulatory federal agency within the U.S. Department of Commerce's Technology Administration. NIST's mission is to promote U.S. innovation and industrial competitiveness by advancing measurement science, standards, and technology in ways that enhance economic security and improve quality of life.

411

Universities have lots of technology available. Check out the Association of University Technology Managers (AUTM), a nonprofit organization with membership of more than 2,300 technology managers and business executives who oversee intellectual property. AUTM's members represent over 300 universities, research institutions, teaching hospitals, and a similar number of companies and government organizations. Visit www.autm.net/index_n4.html for more information.

NIST's fiscal year 2009 resources totaled $1.6 billion. It is based primarily in two locations: Gaithersburg, Maryland (headquarters—578-acre campus), and Boulder, Colorado (208-acre campus). NIST employs about 2,900 scientists, engineers, technicians, business specialists, and administrative personnel. About 2,600 associates and facility users from academia, industry, and other government agencies complement the staff. In addition, NIST partners with 1,600 manufacturing specialists and staff at about 400 Manufacturing Extension Partnership (MEP) affiliated service centers around the country.

NIST laboratories perform research across a wide range of disciplines, affecting virtually every industry. Primary fields of research include chemical science and technology, physics, material science and engineering, electronics and electrical engineering, manufacturing engineering, computer systems, building technology, fire safety, computing, and applied mathematics.

Reflecting its role as the only federal laboratory exclusively dedicated to serving the needs of U.S. industry, NIST offers more than 300 types of calibrations, 1,000 standard reference materials for calibrating instruments and evaluating test methods, 24 standard reference data centers, laboratory accreditation programs, and free evaluation of energy-related inventions.

NIST carries out its mission, in part, through four interwoven programs:

- NIST Laboratories
- Baldrige National Quality Program
- Hollings Manufacturing Extension Partnership
- Technology Innovation Program

NIST Laboratories conducts research that advances the nation's technology infrastructure and is needed by U.S. industry to continually improve products and services.

The Baldrige National Quality Program promotes performance excellence among U.S. manufacturers, service companies, educational institutions, health-care providers, and nonprofit organizations. It also conducts outreach programs and manages the annual Malcolm Baldrige National Quality Award, which recognizes performance excellence and quality achievement.

Hollings Manufacturing Extension Partnership is a nationwide network of local centers offering technical and business assistance to smaller manufacturers.

The Technology Innovation Program provides cost-shared awards to industry, universities, and consortia for research on potentially revolutionary technologies that address critical national and societal needs. (This is a newly created program authorized by Congress.)

To contact NIST with general inquiries about these or any of its programs, call 301-975-3058, e-mail inquiries@nist.gov, or visit www.nist.gov.

Grants and awards supporting research at industry, academic, and other institutions are available on a competitive basis through several different NIST offices. For general information on grants programs, contact Joyce Brigham at 301-975-6329.

The Technology Innovation Program

The Technology Innovation Program (TIP) at NIST was established to help U.S. businesses and institutions of higher education or other organizations, such as national laboratories and nonprofit research institutions, to support, promote, and accelerate innovation in the United States through high-risk, high-reward research in areas of critical national need. These areas need government attention because the magnitude of the problem is large and societal challenges are not being sufficiently addressed.

In January 2009, TIP announced nine projects for award, representing up to $88.2 million in new research. TIP funds $42.5 million of it.

Who Gets Funded?

Under TIP, funding can go to a single company project led by a small or medium-size company (large companies are excluded) or to a joint venture, with the important differences that institutions of higher education can be the lead partner in the venture, and resulting intellectual property may reside with any member of the venture, including universities and nonprofit research institutions. Large companies may participate in a TIP joint venture as an unfunded partner.

TIP can fund single-company projects for up to $3 million over three years and joint ventures for up to $9 million over five years. TIP will fund no more than 50 percent of total project costs, and its funds may be used only for so-called direct costs, not indirect costs (such as overhead), profits, or management fees. No TIP funding may go to a large company.

How Can I Receive Funding?

You must submit a proposal to TIP in response to a notice published in the *Federal Register* announcing a competition and availability of TIP funds (solicitation/RFP). Notices are also posted on the TIP website, www.nist.gov/tip, and at www.grants.gov (Announcement of Federal Funding Opportunity).

In addition, you can have your name added to the TIP mailing list by completing an electronic request at http://tipmailing.nist.gov/forms/mailing_list.cfm or by calling 1-888-847-6478 to receive competition announcements.

Is There a Deadline for Submitting a TIP Proposal?

Yes. The deadline date(s) are included in the *Federal Register* notice announcing the competition and notices posted on the TIP and grants.gov websites.

Once a competition is announced, proposals may be submitted prior to and until the deadline date(s). TIP does not consider unsolicited proposals.

How and Where Do I Submit Proposals?

Proposals may be submitted either electronically or in hard copy. Electronic submissions are encouraged and offer many benefits, including no mailing or copying fees.

Proposals must be submitted to one of two locations only and will not be accepted if submitted directly to any TIP staff member. For electronic submissions, go to www. grants.gov. To submit paper copies, mail to:

Technology Innovation Program
National Institute of Standards and Technology
100 Bureau Drive, Stop 4750
Gaithersburg, MD 20899-4750

Will My Confidential/Proprietary Information Be Protected?

Yes. All individuals who have access to submitted proposals must sign nondisclosure agreements. The government will protect confidential/proprietary information about business operations and trade secrets possessed by any company or participant to the full extent of the law. To the extent permitted by law, TIP will withhold such information from disclosure pursuant to the following statutes, which can be found at www. nist.gov/tip/helpful.html.

For complete details on TIP and how to apply for funding, go to www.nist.gov/tip/comp_09/kit_09/pdfs/kit_09_complete_with_cover.pdf for the 2009 TIP Proposal Preparation Kit.

Manufacturing Extension Partnership

The Manufacturing Extension Partnership (MEP) is another NIST program that may interest you if you want to manufacture and market your invention.

The MEP is a nationwide network of 392 manufacturing extension centers and more than 1,600 field staff providing a wide variety of expertise and services to small manufacturers (under 500 employees) in all 50 states and Puerto Rico. MEP is viewed as a strategic, long-term partner that can help small manufacturers not only resolve their problems but also become high-performance, world-class enterprises.

While part of a national network, each NIST MEP center works directly with area firms to provide expertise and services tailored to their most critical needs, which range from process improvements and worker training to business practices and applications of information technology. Solutions are offered through a combination of direct assistance from center staff and work with outside consultants.

Inventions Wanted

QVC is always on the hunt for new products. Submit a concept to QVC at www.vendor. studiopark.com/submit.asp. Maybe you'll be lucky enough to have your product selected.

NIST MEP centers are staffed by knowledgeable manufacturing engineers and business specialists who typically have years of practical experience gained from working on the manufacturing floor, managing plant operations, or both. NIST MEP center staff also know the local business community and the available local resources and can access additional resources available through the NIST MEP network. As a result, centers help small firms to overcome barriers in locating and obtaining private-sector resources.

NIST MEP centers work with companies that are willing to invest time, money, and/ or human resources to improve their businesses. Typical clients include manufacturers who ...

- Have been unable to locate the proper resources or technologies they need.

- Want expert, impartial advice in helping them evaluate alternative solutions.

- Need help solving a specific problem, such as determining the cause of product defects, modifying plant layout to improve workflow, or establishing employee training.

- Want assistance in reversing negative business situations, such as sales decreases, loss of market share, or cost increases.

Bright Ideas

J. B. Dunlop, one inventor of the pneumatic tire, was a veterinary surgeon.

- Want to implement new technologies or processes that will help establish them as market leaders.

- Seek to improve their ongoing business operations for peak performance.

MEP has proven to be highly effective in helping America's small manufacturers improve their competitiveness. In fiscal year 2008, MEP ...

- Served 31,961 manufacturers.

- Increased or retained $10.5 billion in sales.

- Realized $1.44 billion in cost savings.

- Created 17,316 jobs and retained 39,763 jobs.

For general inquiries about MEP, call 1-800-MEP-4MFG (1-800-637-4634) or 301-975-5020, or visit www.mep.nist.gov.

In Search of Innovation at USG Labs

I have never applied for R&D funds from the federal government, but I have visited many government laboratories in search of new technologies, gizmos, and widgets I could apply to my concepts. You have heard many of the laboratory names—Argonne, Fermi, Lawrence Berkeley, Lawrence Livermore, Los Alamos, Oak Ridge, and Sandia.

I recall visiting Los Alamos National Laboratory in New Mexico and being told that a team from Hasbro had been there the day before. We were both looking into Nitonol (a.k.a. shape memory alloy).

Open for Your Business

Other federally funded research and development centers are open to you as well. Each center has its own website where you can find full details about their programs. A great way to find the labs is via www.usa.gov.

Department of Defense:

- Institute of Defense Analysis (Alexandria, VA)

- Logistics Management Institute (Bethesda, MD)

- National Defense Research Institute (Santa Monica, CA)

- Software Engineering Institute (Pittsburgh, PA)

- Center for Naval Analyses (Alexandria, VA)

- Lincoln Laboratory (Lexington, MA)

- ◆ Aerospace Corporation (El Segundo, CA)

- ◆ Project Air Force (Santa Monica, CA)

- ◆ Arroyo Center (Santa Monica, CA)

National Aeronautics and Space Administration:

- ◆ Jet Propulsion Laboratory (Pasadena, CA)

Department of Health and Human Services:

- ◆ NCI Frederick Cancer Research and Development Center (Frederick, MD)

411

Are you looking for a component? ThomasNet®, powered by Thomas Register® and Thomas Regional®, is an industrial search engine that provides one source for finding the exact product, service, or supplier quickly and efficiently. ThomasNet® provides direct access to the detailed information needed to make a purchasing or specifying decision, including line-item product details, CAD drawings, and more.

National Science Foundation:

- ◆ National Astronomy and Ionosphere Center (Areolbo, PR)

- ◆ National Center for Atmospheric Research (Boulder, CO)

- ◆ National Optical Astronomy Observatories (Tucson, AZ)

- ◆ National Radio Astronomy Observatory (Green Bank, WV)

Knocking around in this chapter, you may find money for your R&D or a home for your invention with the help of an agency or department of the federal government. For example, at the Department of Energy (DOE), people are always on the lookout for energy-saving processes and devices. Some concepts in use today might otherwise never have been commercialized had it not been for the assistance of the DOE.

The Department of Energy

We now move from the NIST campus in Gaithersburg, Maryland, to the Forrestal Building, 1000 Independence Avenue SW, Washington, D.C., home to the Department of Energy (DOE). Uncle Sam, as represented by the DOE, owns title to approximately 1,500 active U.S.-patented inventions and, in some cases, foreign counterparts, although, according to DOE patent counsel Robert J. Marchick, this number is dwindling as the federal labs seek to control their own intellectual property (ip).

Generally, these patents are available for license to you if you can show a satisfactory plan for commercial use of the invention. Licenses are generally for royalties and other fees and may be nonexclusive or exclusive, with or without field-of-use restriction. Exclusive licenses require a determination, after public notice and opportunity for comment, that the invention is not likely to be commercialized on a nonexclusive basis. Technical assistance from the laboratory where the invention arose may be available.

As mentioned, a significant number of inventions made at DOE laboratories are owned and licensed directly by the various laboratories. Many of these inventions are included in the DOE patent databases. For further information on possible licensing of these inventions, contact the appropriate DOE laboratory.

If you want to know what's available in patents the DOE owns, contact Robert J. Marchick, patent attorney, USDOE, at U.S. Department of Energy, Washington, DC 20585; 202-586-4792; or Robert.marchick@hq.doe.gov.

The Industrial Technologies Program

The Industrial Technologies Program (ITP) leads national efforts to improve industrial energy efficiency and environmental performance. The ITP is part of the U.S. Department of Energy's Office of Energy Efficiency and Renewable Energy and contributes to its efforts by partnering with U.S. industry in a coordinated program of R&D, validation, and dissemination of energy efficiency technologies and operating practices.

The ITP works with industry to save energy and money, increase productivity, and reduce environmental impacts by …

   ◆ Conducting R&D on new energy-efficient technologies.

   ◆ Supporting commercialization of emerging technologies.

   ◆ Providing plants with access to proven technologies, energy assessments, software tools, and other resources.

   ◆ Promoting energy and carbon management in industry.

The fiscal year 2009 ITP budget appropriation was $140 million, a $76.8 million increase from the fiscal year 2008 appropriation.

411

Grants.gov is your source to find and apply for federal government grants. The U.S. Department of Health and Human Services is the managing partner for Grants.gov. Learn more about Grants.gov and determine if you are eligible for grant opportunities offered on this site.

The ITP is helping industry identify and pursue technology needs through public- and private-sector partnerships. ITP has initiated "Industries of the Future," a customer-driven strategy to encourage energy- and resource-intensive industries to work together to …

◆ Create broad, industry-wide goals for the future.

◆ Identify specific needs and priorities through industry-led road maps.

◆ Form cooperative alliances to help attain those goals through technology partnerships.

The ITP enables nine energy-intensive U.S. industries—agriculture, aluminum, chemicals, forest products, glass, metal casting, mining, petroleum, and steel—to determine their collective technology and other needs for tomorrow through its widely acclaimed "Industries of the Future" strategy. This strategy ensures that federal R&D and other resources are aligned with industry priorities.

411

The Intellectual Property Office of Singapore hosts one of the most informative ip websites I've seen from any government. It's well worth a visit: www.surfip.gov.sg.

To read up-to-date success stories from the ITP and learn about current opportunities, go to www.doe. gov or request a copy of the ITP's *Energy Technology Solutions*. For up-to-date news on the ITP program, go to www1.eere.energy.gov/industry/newsandevents/ news.html. The Office of Industrial Technologies Program is managed by Robert W. Garland, Director, EE-2F, Room 5F-065, Forrestal Building, Washington, DC 20585; 202-586-7547.

Discontinued DOE Programs

Since the first edition of this book, the following DOE programs are no longer operational:

NICE3: Discontinued in 2001. It had paid for technology demonstrations. It was not replaced.

Inventions and Innovation: Zeroed out around 2004. This was for inventors and small businesses. Under this program, more than 500 inventions received financial support from the DOE, with nearly 25 percent reaching the marketplace. Cumulative sales reportedly reached nearly $710 million. So far, there has been no replacement.

The Small Business Administration

Now let's consider the U.S. Small Business Administration (SBA). Created by Congress in 1953 to help America's entrepreneurs form successful small enterprises, in 2008, the SBA offered management and technical assistance to more than 1 million small business owners. America's 25 million small businesses, the backbone of our economy, employ more than 50 percent of the private workforce, generate more than half of the nation's gross domestic product, and are the principal source of new jobs.

As an independent inventor, you are a small business whether you market your concept or license it to a large manufacturer. As a small business owner and operator, you must know how to manage and finance your enterprises. This is where the SBA may be of assistance, in addition to the Small Business Innovation Research Program (more on this coming up).

Through workshops, individual counseling, publications, and videotapes, the SBA helps entrepreneurs understand and meet the challenges of operating businesses— challenges like financing, marketing, and management.

The SBA's Office of Technology helps strengthen and expand the competitiveness of U.S. small high-technology research and development businesses in the federal marketplace. It assists in achieving commercialization of the results of both the federal research and development programs mandated by the Small Business Innovation Development Act of 1982, the Small Business Research and Development Enhancement Act of 1992, and the Small Business Innovation Research Program Reauthorization Act of 2000. Two programs the SBA administers could be useful to you: the Small Business Innovation Research program and the Small Business Technology Transfer program.

Small Business Innovation Research Program

In 1982, Congress passed the Small Business Innovation Development Act, creating the federal Small Business Innovation Research (SBIR) Program. The purpose of the SBIR program is to increase the opportunity for small firms to participate in federal research and development. In addition to encouraging the participation of small businesses, the program is designed to stimulate the conversion of research findings into commercial application. The act pegged the SBA to run the program, govern its policy, monitor its progress, and analyze its results. The SBIR grant program has awarded over $9.5 billion since it began in 1982.

Ten federal agencies with an extramural budget for research or research and development that exceed $100 million annually presently participate in the SBIR Program:

- Department of Agriculture
- Department of Commerce
- Department of Defense
- Department of Education
- Department of Energy
- Department of Health and Human Services
- Department of Transportation
- Environmental Protection Agency
- National Aeronautics and Space Administration
- National Science Foundation

For information on applying for an SBIR grant, agency research programs, programs, application status, and ideas for potential research projects, contact the agency most aligned with proposed research via www.sbir.gov/contact.htm.

How SBIR Works

Under the SBIR Program, the involved federal agencies request highly competitive proposals from small businesses in response to solicitations outlining their R&D requirements. After evaluating the proposals, each agency awards funding agreements for determining the technical feasibility of the research and development concepts proposed. These awards are distributed in three phases.

Phase I. Awards up to $100,000 are made for research projects to evaluate the scientific and technical merit and feasibility of an idea. Time frame: six months. Two thirds of this work must be done by the small business.

Let's say you have an idea for a device that could, if successful, solve a problem posed by one of the SBIR agencies. There just might be $100,000 in the agency's budget to help you prove the concept.

Phase II. The Phase I projects with the most potential are funded to further develop the proposed idea for up to two years. Phase II awards can be as high as $750,000. Time frame: two years, and this can be exceeded with justification. One half of this work must be done by the small business. In other words, if you need help from a larger partner, you can seek it.

If you are successful in realizing the first stage of your R&D effort, and the sponsoring agency thinks you are onto something, you just might qualify for Phase II funding.

> **Notable Quotables**
>
> Companies that are open to new ideas and are prepared to trade, sell, and buy technology assets from others in a fluid way are in a better position to take advantage of the changing weather and circumstances in their ip gardens.
>
> —Edward Kahn, president, EKMS

Phase III. Once you get into the final stage, or the commercialization process, there are no more federal SBIR funds available. At this point, the federal government encourages you to raise private-sector investment or to license your innovation. While the government may extend follow-up production contracts for your technology, it no longer wants to be your partner. Ideally, the federal seed money has been enough to get you off the ground.

State-Supported SBIR Programs

State governments, anxious to build their own industrial bases, have actively supported the SBIR Program by ...

- Promoting the SBIR to small businesses.

- Providing information and technical assistance to SBIR applicants.

- Providing matching funds to SBIR Phase I and II recipients.

- Helping firms obtain Phase III funding from both private and state sources.

Why do the states do this? They see independent inventors and small businesses as a good investment because, chances are, technologies developed in a particular state will stay in the state once commercialized. Innovation leads to hard goods, goods create jobs, jobs employ people, people pay taxes, and so forth.

Each agency listed earlier has an SBIR office. If you'd like to know about SBIR at a particular agency or be put on the mailing lists for SBIR solicitation, contact the appropriate office or go in through the agency website.: sbir.er.doe.gov/sbir/About/about_sbir.htm.

Scoring and Selection Process

Let's take a close look at one SBIR program. The DOE uses three evaluation criteria for SBIR grant applications:

- ◆ Strength of the scientific/technical approach
- ◆ Ability to carry out the project in a cost-effective manner
- ◆ Impact—each is defined in the solicitation and carries equal weight

Your grant application is considered for funding if, based on comments from expert technical reviewers, it has no reservations with respect to any of the criteria and strongly endorses the grant application with respect to at least two of the three criteria.

SBIR Success Stories

We are all inspired by success stories, so here are some from the SBIR program. These are just the tip of the iceberg. SBIR is a very popular and effective federal program.

Joan Gordon had worked as a medical technologist in a clinical lab in Maine Medical Center, Maine's largest hospital, for more than 30 years when her boss, Clark Rundell, proposed in 2000 that they co-found a company involved in the emerging field of molecular diagnostics and genetic testing. Neither Joan nor Clark had a business background, so SBA's Maine Small Business Development Center stepped in to assist the company with building a business infrastructure, developing marketing strategies, refining products, and determining how to parcel out tasks and responsibilities. While working with the Maine SBDC, Maine Molecular Quality Controls, Inc., accomplished its greatest achievement—its quality-control cystic fibrosis testing was the first in the country ever approved by the Federal Drug Administration. The company has received at least five SBIR Phase I and Phase II grants, totaling more than $2.4 million.

> **Notable Quotables**
>
> Mr. Watson, come here, I want you.
>
> —Alexander Graham Bell, to his assistant (These were the first intelligible words transmitted by telephone.)

With an impressive resumé as a business and entertainment entrepreneur in the music, film, and multimedia areas, Marcus Morton founded Network Foundation Technologies, a high-tech software company focused on video streaming and broadcasting live high-quality video online with Dr. Mike O'Neal in 2000. Pronounced *NiFTy*, the company broadcasts large live events to worldwide audiences. NFT's patented technology used in its NiFTy Online Television product is the most efficient and successful method for enabling distributed video broadcasting over the Internet. The company has attracted more than $5 million in private equity from regional and national investors and was the recipient of SBIR Phase I and Phase IB grant awards from the National Science Foundation. In 2007, Marcus Morton was named the Entrepreneur of the Year by the Louisiana Business Incubation Association.

> **411**
>
> NASA Goddard Space Flight Center has expertise in sensors and detectors, guidance, navigation, and control systems and optics. If you have an Earth application for a NASA technology, call its Innovative Partnerships Program at 301-286-0561.

Founded in 2002, Language Weaver discovered its niche for language translation after the tragedy of September 11, 2001. After receiving an SBIR grant, Language Weaver started receiving government interest. Language Weaver provides translation of documents, newscasts, and other source materials for defense and commercial purposes. Application languages include Arabic, Farsi, Somali, Hindi, Chinese, French, and Spanish. Language Weaver has received $150,000 in SBIR Phase I grants and $1.5 million in SBIR Phase II grants. It has received SBIR grants from the National Science Foundation and the U.S. Army.

Dr. James Daughton, co-inventor of "Magnetoresistive" Random Assess Memory (MRAM), founded Nonvolatile Electronics, Inc. (NVE), to further develop his invention. MRAM is a revolutionary technology that fabricates memory with nanotechnology and uses electron spin. MRAM computer chips could prevent unintentional losses of information, extend battery life, and replace all RAM technology in use today. Research funding from the SBIR programs allowed the NVE to base itself in an industrial park in Minnesota where it employs a staff of 70, rather than in the founder's home. NVE has received 121 SBIR grants, contributing to 35 percent of its revenue. Founders credit these grants with preventing the company from failing and improving its ability to attract capital from other sources. The company received half of its funding from SBIRs and BAAs. The 121 grants from SBIR and STTR have totaled $34.3 million in R&D funding.

In fiscal year 2007, SBIR provided about 5,500 federal R&D grants, totaling $2 billion.

> **Fast Facts** _____
>
> In 2008, 49.7 percent of all patents were of U.S. origin, based on the residence of the first-named inventor. Of the U.S.-origin patents issued in 2008, California claimed a 24.1 percent share (22,202 patents), followed by Texas (6.7 percent, 6,184 patents), New York (6.4 percent, 5,905 patents), Washington (4.5 percent, 4,158 patents), Massachusetts (4.2 percent, 3,897 patents), Michigan (3.9 percent, 3,584 patents), and Illinois (3.9 percent, 3,581 patents). U.S.-origin patents from Hawaii, Alaska, Louisiana, Maine, North Carolina, and Washington had the largest percentage increases in patent receipts from 2007 to 2008.

If you'd like to see more of the award winners, or to have a better idea of whether you would qualify, go to www.sba.gov/sbir/library.html and click on SBIR/STTR Annual Awards. For specific information on SBIR programs, call 1-800-827-5722. This number will connect you with the SBA's Small Business Answer Desk.

Small Business Technology Transfer Program

You might want to consider another competitive SBA program: the Small Business Technology Transfer (STTR) program.

The main difference between the SBIR and STTR programs is that all research and development in the STTR pilot program must be conducted jointly by the small business (that's you!) and a nonprofit research institution. Not less than 40 percent of the work conducted under an STTR program award is to be performed by the small business, and not less than 30 percent of the work is to be performed by the nonprofit research institution.

Following submission of proposals, agencies make STTR awards based on small business/nonprofit research institution qualification, degree of innovation, and future market potential. Small businesses that receive awards then begin a three-phase program.

Phase I. Start-up. Awards may be as much as $100,000 for up to a one-year effort to fund exploration of the scientific, technical, and commercial feasibility of your idea or technology.

Phase II. Awards may be as high as $7.5 million for a two-year effort that expands the results of Phase I. During this period, the R&D work is performed and you begin to consider commercial potential. Only Phase I award winners are considered for Phase II.

Phase III. This is the period during which Phase II innovation moves from laboratory to marketplace. No STTR funds support this phase. You must find funding in the private sector or other non-STTR federal agency funding.

Five federal agencies with an extramural budget for research or R&D presently participate in the STTR Program:

- Department of Defense
- Department of Energy
- Department of Health and Human Services
- National Aeronautics and Space Administration
- National Science Foundation

Federally Funded Research and Development Centers (FFRDCS)

Each of the following R&D centers is supported primarily by Uncle Sam:

- Department of Defense
- Institute of Defense Analysis (Alexandria, VA)
- Logistics Management Institute (Bethesda, MD)
- National Defense Research Institute (Santa Monica, CA)
- Software Engineering Institute (Pittsburgh, PA)
- Center for Naval Analyses (Alexandria, VA)
- Lincoln Laboratory (Lexington, MA)
- Aerospace Corporation (El Segundo, CA)
- Project Air Force (Santa Monica, CA)
- Arroyo Center (Santa Monica, CA)

To receive STTR solicitations, contact the participating agency, and brochures and forms will be sent to you. Or make your request via www.sba.gov/sbir/library.html.

The Least You Need to Know

- ◆ The spirit of innovation and technology transfer is alive and well in Washington, D.C.

- ◆ There is no N.I.H. Syndrome when it comes to the government.

- ◆ Uncle Sam may have technological resources and/or funding to help make your dream a reality.

- ◆ Technology is just a click away—www.fedlabs.org.

Chapter 22

Yes, Inventors, There Is a Santa Claus

In This Chapter

- It's a Barnum-and-Bailey, three-ring enterprise
- Researching at retail
- Success stories
- Networking mecca: the New York Toy Fair
- Analyzing your concept

Over the past sixty or seventy years a symbiotic relationship has grown between the toy and game industry and the community of professional inventors who support it. While there are many wonderfully creative designers working internally in our industry, a large share of the truly innovative totally new concepts has come from the inventing community. A look at the history of our business clearly shows the impact of the independent inventor to the toy and game business.

—Mike Hirtle, head of Global Inventor Relations and Product Acquisition, Hasbro, Inc.

The toy industry, although far less entrepreneurial than it was when I got into the business over 30 years ago, is still a potentially lucrative frontier for the independent inventor. The toy industry is The Greatest Show on Earth. It is a high-wire act without a safety net in which manufacturers walk a financial tightrope that stretches from Christmas to Christmas. Corporate impresarios try their best to top one season's hits the next year, and they rely, in part, on the magic of toy-inventing gurus to make it happen.

In few industries can one find such a blending of creative talents, disciplines, polytechnologies, media, theater, self-interest, circus, idealism, cynicism, masquerade, pomp, exaggeration, and ingenuity as prevails in the toy and game business, a fashion industry where no one wants to get caught with their trends down.

Today the toy inventor needs to think more like a brand manager, says David Berko, a managing partner in East West Innovation, LLC. The former senior executive at Hasbro and Mattel points to the compression of the retail environment as the reason. He observes, "The stakes are now so high that the decision by a toy company whether to move forward or not with a product depends on one or more of the large, mass market retailers deciding to carry the item."

An Industry Overview

According to NPD's Global Toy Trends and Forecasts 2009 report, global toy sales rose by $2.4 billion (U.S.) in 2008 when factoring out changes in currency rates. When counted based on current exchange rates, global sales were off 0.8 percent in 2008, to $78.09 billion.

The United States and Europe represented a combined 57 percent of the world's toy consumption in 2008, a 3-point decrease from 2007.

At the current pace of growth, NPD expects worldwide toy sales to reach $80.3 billion in 2012.

The global toy industry generates $67 billion ($21.6 billion in the United States), according to the Toy Industry Association (TIA).

In 2009, the U.S. toy industry shipped over 3.36 billion units, comprising an estimated 125,000 to 150,000 individual products, with 7,000 new items introduced at the 2009 American International Toy Fair.

Toy manufacturers spent over $837 million on advertising in 2009, with 90 percent of the total going to television spots, according to the TIA.

To illustrate how things have changed since this book was first published in 2001, consider these numbers:

In 2001, Americans spent on average $350 per child each year on toys. In 2008, per the TIA, Americans spent $281 per child, per year.

411

Keep up-to-date on brand licensing trends with these magazines and newsletters: *License!* (www.licensemag.com), *Total Licensing* (www. totallicensing.com), *KidScreen* (www.kidscreen.com), *Toys and Family Entertainment* (www. anbmedia.com), and *Royaltie$* (www.anbmedia.com).

In 2001, grandparents accounted for 14 percent of toy sales. In 2008, grandparents accounted for 23 percent of toy sales.

To sustain their growth, toy companies have had to make some midcourse corrections. Perhaps the most dramatic example is the partnership between Hasbro and Discovery Communications, Inc., to form a 50-50 joint venture, including a television network and website dedicated to children's and family entertainment and educational programming.

411

If you want be a toy inventor, read *The Toy and Game Inventor's Handbook* (Alpha Books, 2003) by Richard C. Levy and Ron Weingartner. While this sounds like self-promotion, there's no better book on the topic. When the book came out, Andrea Morris, publisher of *Playthings* magazine, called it "required reading for all toy industry executives, not just toy inventors." The inventor of Taboo, Brian Hersch, wrote, "This is more than peeking behind the veil. Richard and Ron shine a klieg light on the heretofore private world of toy and game invention, licensing, and marketing." For more information, go to www.greatideagear.com/toybook. And don't miss Ron's blog at toydreamers.blogspot.com.

If You Cannot Get to the North Pole ...

So where do you conduct research to validate your ideas? Go shopping! Walmart is the leading toy retailer in the USA, with 4,500 stores. Toys R Us is another excellent hunting ground. But Walmart has sent a message that it will cut the number of toys it buys and will replace toys with food products and electronics. Target also says it will reduce its selection of toys. Online research is okay to a point, but I like to touch and feel products, and that's best accomplished at retail.

Some stores specialize in used toys. These are wonderful places to find older products you can cannibalize for parts for building prototypes. eBay is also a great source of old toys, if you know what you need.

> ### Inventions Wanted
>
> Have an idea how to use video games to become healthier and more active? Best Buy and Electronic Arts (in association with By Kids For Kids and the United Inventors Association) sponsor Invent-A-Game. Winners receive an EE Series Savings Bond worth $10,000 at maturity. Go to www.bkfk.com/games for details. The 2009 winner was 17-year-old Dan Slutz for his game Rhythm!, a music-based platform game where players battle evil forces utilizing various musical styles as weapons to advance, conquer, and defeat their enemies.

The Toys Legends Are Made From

Dozens of inspiring inventor stories show how timely ideas established businesses or expanded lines dramatically through creativity and imagination. For example, Scrabble was invented in 1931 by Alfred M. Butts, an out-of-work architect who was a lifelong devotee of anagrams and crossword puzzles. The game was originally called Crisscross Words and was renamed Scrabble in 1948. To date, over 100 million Scrabble games have been sold worldwide.

Trivial Pursuit was invented by three young Canadians in 1979. In the game's first year on the market, Selchow and Righter, the game's original U.S. manufacturer, sold 22 million sets at retail prices as high as $40. The next year, it sold 6 million copies, and the next, 5 million. Trivial Pursuit has sold more than 75 million games worldwide.

Remember Dr. Erno Rubik, the Hungarian engineer and mathematician who invented the Rubik's Cube? During its three-year hot streak, this innocent-looking $2\frac{1}{4}$-inch puzzle with more than 43 quintillion possible combinations but only one true solution, sold an estimated 100 million authorized copies, plus another 50 million knock-offs and at least 10 million books explaining how to solve it.

Monopoly was brought to Parker Brothers in 1933 by the late Charles B. Darrow, who developed the game while he was unemployed during the Depression. It was initially rejected as having "52 fundamental errors," but it was later published in 1935 and is now licensed in 33 countries and printed in 23 different languages. Over 300 million Monopoly games have been sold worldwide.

Crayola Crayons celebrated its 107th birthday in 2010. Alice Stead Binney conceived the name Crayola for her husband Edwin's crayons in 1903. She derived it from the French word *craie* ("stick of color") and the word *oleaginous* ("oily"). Each year, the company Binney and Smith produces more than 2 billion Crayola Crayons. That would be enough crayons to circle the globe four and a half times or produce a giant crayon 35 feet wide and 400 feet tall—100 feet taller than the Statue of Liberty. Kids ages 2 through 8 spend an average of 28 minutes a day coloring. The average child in the United States will wear down 730 crayons by age 10.

Cincinnati barber Merle Robbins came up with the card game Uno and licensed it to International Games in 1972. Today Uno, published by Mattel, is sold in 26 countries and is available in 12 languages, with sales of over 80 million units worldwide.

> ### Bright Ideas
>
> Only one museum in the world is devoted to play, Strong National Museum of Play in Rochester, New York. Established in 1998, Strong recognizes toys and games that have stood the test of time and amused generations of children. The National Toy Hall of Fame is housed in Strong. For more information, call 585-410-6340 or visit www.museumofplay.org/index.html.

> ### Notable Quotables
>
> Play is at the heart of learning, so good toys can put learning in the hands of a child.
> —Lynn Cohen and Sandra Waite-Stupiansky, early childhood experts

The Hula Hoop, introduced by Wham-O in 1958, set the standards by which all fads are measured. Within four months of its introduction, more than 25 million Hula Hoops were sold. The Hula Hoop was inspired by children's bamboo exercise hoops from Australia.

A game invented by a wealthy Canadian couple to play aboard their yacht was so popular with their friends that they approached Edwin S. Lowe, most famous for publishing bingo games in the 1920s, to make samples of "The Yacht Game" for them to give as gifts. Lowe liked the game so much that he offered to buy the rights from the couple, and they agreed. He eventually changed the name of the game to Yahtzee. In 1973, Milton Bradley acquired the E.S. Lowe Company. Today Hasbro owns Milton Bradley.

The New York Toy Fair: A Networking Mecca

The New York Toy Fair, the largest toy trade show in the United States, is the best place to see what's in and out and meet who's who in the industry. This is where the pulse of the U.S. toy industry is taken and contacts are made and nurtured.

The 2001 Toy Fair featured 1,942 exhibitors, including 333 foreign companies from 31 countries, and was attended by 17,255 commercial retail buyers from 99 countries. It is also one of the most extensively covered trade shows in the United States; the 2001 Fair hosted over 1,000 national and international print and broadcast reporters. By contrast, the 2009 Toy Fair featured 1,100 exhibitors, including 160 foreign companies from 25 countries, and was attended by 10,000 commercial retail buyers from 85 countries.

The Toy Fair is held in New York City, beginning on the second Monday in February. Exhibits are located at the Jacob K. Javits Convention Center.

(There's also a mass-market show annually in Dallas, but it is more difficult for a new inventor to access because products are exhibited inside closed showrooms. At Javits, the companies have open booths spread across acres of floor space.)

For more information on the Toy Fair, its exact dates, seminars, and more, contact The Toy Industry Association, 1115 Broadway, New York, NY 10010; 212-675-1141; fax: 212-633-1429. Or visit the Toy Fair section of the TIA website at www. toyassociation.org.

Bright Ideas

Hasbro's G.I. Joe, the world's first action figure, was created by the late toy-inventing dynamo Larry Reiner. The original figure was almost a foot tall and carried authentic equipment from head to toe. It bowed at the New York Toy Fair 1964. The first year, Hasbro sold more than $30 million worth of G.I. Joe, "America's Movable Fighting Man." Reiner was the co-inventor of Talking Barney and many other megahits throughout the 1960s, '70s, '80s, and '90s.

The Professional Edge

Most major toy companies, where the big money is made on TV-promoted products, depend on the established, professional inventing community. "The importance of the independent inventor cannot be overstated. In-house inventing is the equivalent of trying to boil water without using a stove. Top-quality toy concepts are almost impossible to create internally, without an in-house inventor-designer staff; which in today's economy is financially prohibitive and extremely difficult to put together," says industry veteran Harvey Lepselter.

You can be a part of the action if you are smart about how you present yourself and your concepts. New inventors are breaking into the business every year. (See Part 3 for advice on how to do this.)

Professional inventors know ingenuity is just the first step, not an end in itself. In the professional, creativity and imagination are guided and tempered by hard business reality and historical perspective. Toy inventing is far from child's play.

If you want to jump-start your career and learn the ropes, the best way is through a toy broker. While not all toy manufacturers will recommend brokers, many, such as Hasbro and Mattel, frequently will, if asked. Make broker list requests to each company's inventor relations department.

Professional toy agents typically expect 50 percent of any advances and royalties. This is fair. But this assumes you have an acceptable looks-like, works-like prototype. If the agent has to further develop your idea, you may have to give up even more of the pie. No up-front money should be required under such an arrangement.

The top agents not only have access to the toy companies at the highest levels, but also are in the loop to know who's looking for what and how to make deals. The best agents are inventors themselves and will enhance your concept. While you may have had the idea, the most successful brokers are inventors with patents and products to their credit. Many top inventors will put on an agent's hat if they spot a promising product opportunity.

Before signing up with a broker, have a face-to-face meeting. Ask to see the products the broker has invented or had a hand in developing or licensing. Talk to inventors the agent represents, and see what they think of the broker.

Oh, by the way, insist that your broker arrange for advances and royalties to be paid directly from the toy manufacturer to you. You want to be a party to contracts. Do not allow a broker to receive your money and then redistribute it. You want the path of least resistance for your advances and royalties. No toy company would deny a request to divide the money and send separate checks and reports. If the broker says the company won't do it, don't believe it. You are outta there.

411

When I need product history, my favorite books include these: *"I Had One of Those": Toys of Our Generation* by Robin Langley Sommer (Crescent Books, 1992) contains more than 160 full-color and 80 black-and-white illustrations; *Toy Bop: Kid Classics of the 50's and 60's* by Tom Frey (Fuzzy Dice Publishing, 1994) contains 180 pages of marvelous product shots and write-ups; and *Toys: Celebrating 100 Years of the Power of Play* by Chris Byrne (Toy Industry Association, 2003) has 279 power-packed pages spanning the years 1903 to 2003.

Prolific inventor Michael Satten, whose hits include P.J. Sparkles, summed up the odds: "Things have to pass through so many people. Imagine. You have to show it to a guy who has to like it; he has to take it back and show it to a group that has to like it; the engineering has to work; it has to work at a cost; it has to be tested with kids and tested with parents; the trade has to see it; the trade has to like it; the agency has to do commercials; the commercials have to be tested with kids and parents who have to like what they see; then the trade has to see the product again and like the commercial. And after all that, there is a problem in China. It's mind-boggling."

Bright Ideas

Experimenting with a highly resilient synthetic rubber, Norman Stingley created the Super Ball. By the mid-1960s, more than 6 million of the high fliers had been sold. Craven Walker invented the lava lamp in the mid-1960s. They can still be found in homes across America. In 1975, Joshua Reynolds created the Mood Ring. As peripheral body temperature increases, which it does in response to emotion, crystals in the ring twist to reflect blue. When a person is excited or stressed, blood flow is directed away from the skin and more toward the internal organs, cooling the fingers, causing the crystals to twist in the other direction, to reflect more yellow.

Questions for Self-Analysis

Before you spend money on a prototype and approach a possible licensee, be sure you've asked yourself some questions. Toy companies do not license ideas or figments of your imagination; they license original, well-developed products that meet certain criteria. Asking yourself these questions—and answering honestly—will save everyone time:

Is your idea original? Talk to seasoned toy store managers. Attend the New York Toy Fair. Read trade magazines. Conduct a patent search (see Part 4). You'll find the answer. All too often, inventors with no memory for a product reinvent something that's been done before. This wastes everyone's time and does nothing to forward your position. David Berko counsels, "Becoming an expert in a category will equalize your position with the people to whom you are presenting."

Does your idea fit the company? Be sure you understand the company's direction and its brands. Companies are eager to see new products that complement their brands. An executive's time is limited. Some companies publish "wish lists" for inventors to keep them focused on the most current needs. (See Part 3 for how to find prospective licensees, get through the door, and make the pitch.)

Does your idea have visual appeal? Hire an industrial designer if you don't possess the skills to design your concept. Toy executives are accustomed to a high level of professionalism. It not only must look good, but it also must have perceived value. (See Part 2 for how to get prototypes built.)

> **Fast Facts**
>
> Slinky was first introduced in 1946 at Gimbel's department store in Philadelphia by its inventor, Richard James. Since then, it has sold more than 300 million units. In 1960, Richard's wife Bettie took over the management of the company when he joined a religious cult and moved to Bolivia. He died there in 1974.

Does your item have play and repeat play value? Child-test a breadboard or mock-up of the item. Be sure it works and can sustain interest. In the case of games, it could take dozens of play sessions to fine-tune a concept.

Does your concept have wide market appeal? Major companies have no interest in small market segments. A small business to a major toy company could be $15 million or $20 million. For a product to make the cut at larger manufacturers, it must have very broad appeal. In other words, it must sell to Toys R Us, Walmart, K-Mart, Target, and other mass-market outlets. If the company cannot sell hundreds of thousands of units the first year and then expand and build the item, it will not license the submission.

Is your product safe? All products selected for manufacture by U.S. or foreign toy makers must meet one or more safety standards. Go to the Safety tab at www.toyassociation.org to see them.

There's also a battery of functional abuse exercises that, depending on the product, can include transit test, aging test, humidity test, drop test, torque and tension test, compression test, abrasion test, adhesion test, and life test.

411

Don't miss the award-winning website www.drtoy.com, an invaluable resource on playthings and the toy industry. The site, founded in 1995, is designed and hosted by Stevanne Auerbach, Ph.D., director of the Institute of Childhood Resources. You'll learn a great deal from the smorgasbord of information she offers.

Can your product be manufactured, and at what cost? You may have to build it or hire someone to figure this out and see if anything would render the concept infeasible. Play value and technical elegance mean little if your concept cannot be made—or made for the right price. No matter how terrific your concept may be, the manufacturer must be sure the product can be manufactured and sold at the right price. It's one thing to make a piece of something, and it's another to make 2.5 million of them. That kind of development work is often just as creative as the idea itself.

Have you come up with a cost guesstimate? In costing toys, we use this rule-of-thumb to reach the whole sale price: hard cost × 4 for nonpromoted items; hard cost × 5 for TV-promoted items.

What competitive products are on the market? Be able to tell your target licensee the category in which you envision your item, as well as the competitive atmosphere. Buy competitive products and tear them apart. Know what makes them tick.

What "wow factors" make your concept unique? Demonstrate to yourself what makes your item unique compared to other products in its category.

Once you have satisfied these issues, then and only then should you embark on building a looks-like, works-like prototype.

Bright Ideas

Barbie, the world's best-selling and most widely recognized fashion doll in history, celebrated her fiftieth birthday in 2009. Since she was introduced in 1959, Barbie has had 108 careers, represented 50 different nationalities, and collaborated with more than 70 different fashion designers. One Barbie doll is sold every three seconds somewhere in the world. To date, over 700 million Barbies and members of the Barbie clan have been sold in 140 countries throughout the world. Mattel has produced 1 billion (estimated) fashions for Barbie and her friends since 1959. The 105 million yards of fabric used to make these fashions makes Mattel one of the largest apparel manufacturers in the world. Barbie is named after the daughter of the doll's inventor, Ruth Handler. Ken is Barbie's real-life brother.

Molding the Deal

Should you be fortunate enough to be extended a licensing agreement by a toymaker, take to heart some words of advice from Howard R. Fine, Esq., of Northbrook, Illinois. Howard is the former senior vice president and general counsel to Tiger Electronics (a division of Hasbro, Inc.) and one of the best and brightest lawyers in the industry.

According to Howard, the most important leverage a toy inventor has is the ability to terminate the license agreement. Consider all the specific tasks you would like the toy company to complete and all the milestones you would like the toy company to achieve, and be sure you can terminate the agreement if they are not met.

Although long-term contracts are acceptable and often desirable for building a brand, be sure they are contingent upon the achievement of ongoing, objectively measurable performance standards, such as annual royalty thresholds or payments.

Although it may be reasonable for a licensee to require 30 or more days to cure some breaches, there is no reason anyone needs this long to write a check that is already late. Limit the cure period for payment breaches to no more than 5 or 10 days, and encourage on-time payments by providing for interest or late fees.

Some licensees will make you beg for your royalties every quarter. To avoid the maddening trap of the "serial breacher," include a provision that waives any cure period and allows you to terminate the agreement immediately after the third or fourth breach.

Limit the number of deductions the licensee may take from its gross receipts when computing your royalties. Your licensee is realizing the vast majority of the income (usually 95 percent of it) and should be absorbing most of the expenses as well.

When you're licensing a toy concept, be sure you get paid on not only the core item, but also any accessories, line extensions, and any other products derived from or meaningfully associated with it.

> **Notable Quotables**
>
> Aren't we lucky to be creative. I really feel that it is the life energy that keeps us all going. I like to tell newcomers that if they have that creative urge to keep going, it can happen; but to learn to love rejection, there is so much of it.
>
> —A. Eddy Goldfarb, inventor, Chattering Teeth and 600 other toys and games

Many successful toy and game brands are expanded into entirely different categories, and even entertainment properties such as movies and associated merchandising. Be sure you participate in the revenue streams for all of them, as none would have existed but for your original contribution.

Try to limit your financial liability as much as possible. Although the ability to do so will vary considerably from deal to deal, at the very least, try to avoid liability in excess of the royalties you will be paid.

If you have partners—more than one person or entity as the "Licensor"—try to limit your individual liability to your proportionate share in the project. Otherwise, you could be liable for 100 percent and have to sort it out among your partners. Likewise, be sure you have an agreement among your partners regarding this issue.

Don't give up your right to sue in court by agreeing to mandatory arbitration. If your licensee is not paying you or is misusing your intellectual property (the two most common problems), you will want to keep all your options open, including the ability to sue. You can always agree to arbitrate later if it is to your benefit.

The Hit Parade

The toy industry's greatest natural resource is the outside, independent inventor, who is responsible for its greatest successes. In an era of intense global competition, the inventor becomes even more important to the health of the industry.

Following are some products that came from outside, although they never would have made it to market and hit pay dirt were it not for the dedicated and talented pros inside the toy companies. The combination of the outsiders and insiders makes it work.

> **Notable Quotables**
>
> Inventor product needs to have at least five out of the following six P's:
> Product: originality; improved adaptation
> Packaging: exciting/impactful point of purchase
> Production: safe; foolproof
> Promotion: consumer awareness
> Price: you can't fool the customers
> Patents: protection from competition
> —Fred Kroll, inventor, Hungry, Hungry Hippos

Battling Tops

Big Wheel

Boggle

Cabbage Patch Kids

Candyland

Clue

Connect Four

Etch-a-Sketch

Frisbee

Furby

Game of Life

G.I. Joe

Giga Pets

Monopoly

Mr. Machine

Mr. Potato Head

Nerf

Othello

Play Doh

Pokémon

Risk

Rubik's Cube

Scrabble

Shelby

Super Soaker

Teenage Mutant Ninja Turtles

Tickle Me Elmo

Trivial Pursuit

Twister

Uno

Upwords

Water Babies

Yomega

Fast Facts

Toy Industry Association publishes the *Toy Inventor/Designer Guide*. For a copy, write to Toy Industry Association, Communication Department, 1115 Broadway, Suite 400, New York, NY 10010, attention: Toy Inventor/Designer Guide; or download a PDF at www.toyassociation.org.

To see a complete list of toy companies, go to www.toyassociation.org and click on Members. Each name in the alphabetical list takes you to another page with links to corporate websites.

The Least You Need to Know

◆ Never get caught with your trends down.

◆ Risk is more than a game.

◆ Color outside the box.

◆ Never grow up. Never give up.

Chapter 23

Inventor Organizations

In This Chapter

- ◆ The benefits of inventor organizations
- ◆ Joining an inventor organization
- ◆ Starting an inventor organization
- ◆ Beware of wolves in sheep's clothing

> A man only learns in two ways, one by reading, and the other by association with smarter people.
>
> —Will Rogers

The best reason to join an inventor organization is fellowship, as it is with any association of people who have common interests and goals. Getting product from your workshop or drawing board to an end user can be a long, tough, and sometimes lonely slog. Isolation is an inevitable drawback of being an inventor, and this can be particularly problematical if you are self-employed and work at home.

Operating on the frontier of an emerging idea is difficult enough. But spearheading the development, licensing, and manufacture of an invention can leave even the most experienced players nonplused. It's nice to have a vibrant social network that is comprised of individuals who share a community and are striving for a similar goal.

Expanding Your Network

We inventors are no different from any other group of people who share a similar purpose. We love to get together; explore professional issues; and share experiences, success stories, heartbreaks, information, personal contacts, methods, techniques, and dreams. Nothing is more satisfying than the camaraderie provided by a club.

> ### Inventions Wanted
>
> According to its website, Kraft, one of the world's largest food and beverage companies, with more than $37 billion in annual revenues, is looking for: "... proprietary, commercially viable products and technologies for our existing categories and for new solutions that will make our products better tasting, better for you, more convenient or more socially responsible." The maker of Oreo, my favorite cookie, is looking for patents and trademarks, joint development deal opportunities, and alliances and partnerships. Check out the details at brands.kraftfoods.com/innovatewithkraft/default.aspx.

Membership can be particularly satisfying in a business like ours that finds people chained to the Wheel of Chance in ways no other enterprise does. Inventing and licensing is one of the most unstable, unforgiving, misunderstood, and risky businesses in the world. It is not for the faint of heart. It is an esoteric field, one in which imagination rules reason. It is understood by so few and fraught with so many hazards. Most people outside the business don't understand it at all, or have very little comprehension of it.

Through association with other inventors, successful and unsuccessful, you will get the benefit of what Hayakawa called "the best possible maps of the territories of experience."

Care to Share?

Membership in an inventor organization connects you to a network of like-minded colleagues, encourages you to exchange ideas and solutions, and gives you access to what's going on within the inventing community locally and, by extension, nationally.

When you are a member of an inventor organization, you can frequently get free advice and information on virtually any aspect of intellectual property (ip) by contacting other members, people who operate on the "if I can't answer your question, I know someone who can" premise. Larger organizations are comprised of memberships that embrace experts in a wide range of specialties, including legal, prototyping, patent searching, drafting, engineering, industrial design, venture capital, Internet, marketing, and so forth.

To meet fellow inventors online, use social networking tools like Twitter, Facebook, and Skype. But these Internet channels should never take the place of meeting people face-to-face and sharing stories over a pizza.

I always remind executives that although on one level independent inventors compete against each other for the placement of product, we are generally very friendly toward each other as a group. We do not perceive each other as competition in the way Walmart considers Target competition or Ford does Toyota. In the toy industry, for example, we inventors help each other with everything from sharing contacts and insights to the best terms available in licensing agreements.

 411

If you want to learn how to start an inventor organization in your area, the Houston Inventors Association, one of the oldest and largest such organizations in America, tells you how at www.inventors.org/invclub/h2start.htm.

I called a friend one day and asked what kind of a deal he received from a certain company. "Let me fax you my agreement," he offered. I frequently do similar favors for friends, if sharing is not prohibited by the agreement. It's one big *quid pro quo*.

Inventor Organizations Thrive on American Soil

Inventor organizations, typically nonprofit, often take root where inventors practice their trade, and there is no more fertile territory than the USA. Seeking to establish relationships among themselves, independent inventors have formed organizations throughout the nation, groups that provide professional and social forums. (For a list of such organizations, see Appendix C. This list was made possible online by the UIA, to which I am grateful. I have not personally contacted and become familiar with each group listed. You'll need to evaluate them yourself.)

These organizations offer all kinds of product development support, guidance, and resources. A common objective is to stimulate self-fulfillment, creativity, and problem solving. Naturally, some inventor groups are more sophisticated than others; some are more organized. But all the legit ones have something positive to offer.

"Inventor organizations are the biggest bargain around for helping inventors to get their invention going, avoid scams, and meet people who have similar interests and have solved similar problems," says Ray Watts, former editor of the *Inventor-Assistance Program News.*

"We've been getting a lot of new members lately due to the economic downfall," Tim Crawley, president of the Inventors Association of Arizona, told *12 News Today.* "People are losing jobs and dredging upon the idea they've had burning in their head for a long time, and they want to get it out there; this is the place to do it."

In Memphis, Mid-South Inventors Association vice president Sammie Riar told Commercialappeal.com, "It's surprising. You can start talking about an invention. By the end of the meetings, you have gotten so many good ideas because other people are thinking like you. The brain thing starts working." Riar's day job is real estate financing.

My old friend Chuck Mullen, former chairman of the board of advisors of Houston Inventors Association (www.inventors.org), told me, "At our regular meetings, when a newcomer stands up and asks for help, there will be at least three or four members that will have the information and experience that he or she needs."

Bright Ideas

Frampton Ellis III of Arlington, Virginia, invented an innovative sole for sports sneakers (U.S. Patent No. 5,317,819), which he licensed to Adidas, who marketed it as the Feet You Wear line. According to an article in *U.S. News & World Report,* Ellis spent 7 years and $30,000 before signing a licensing agreement with Adidas. It took nearly 10 years before he made any money.

On August 1, 2009, the first meeting of the Inventors and Entrepreneurs Club of Rochester, Minnesota, took place. Club president Gary Smith told KAAL-TV that he hopes the club might someday be a feeder system where successful inventors can connect with businesspeople who know how to move the idea from concept to a successful business.

Truth in Packaging—Caveat Emptor

Be especially careful when selecting a national organization. I have found some organizations that are nothing more than wolves (invention marketing companies) in sheep's clothing. The Internet has made it especially easy for unscrupulous vultures with harpy talons to ambush naive inventors. But if you look hard, they are the same old birds of prey. Their con is to get as much money from you as they can without having to deliver any moneymaking results. They'll sell you marketing reports, patent work, insurance, self-published books, ads, expo booths, and even T-shirts. I found one inventor service company running a museum for inventions. They don't, however, deliver wise counsel, honest industry, or the kinds of personal contacts that get inventions licensed.

If you missed my message about such detestable peeps, go to Chapter 2 right now.

If they cannot get your money one way, they'll get it in another way. And the money and what the organization is selling usually gives this away.

Take Your Pick

Now let's look at some organizations I've had more pleasant personal experience with and whose members of the organization's leadership team I know. I cannot, however, vouch for most of the organizations listed, and you should use your own judgment on whether you feel a group meets your personal requirements and on its legitimacy. One of the best ways to qualify an organization is through references by satisfied members. (See Appendix C for a full list of organizations.)

Several kinds of organizations exist:

♦ National

♦ State

♦ Local

♦ Informal

> **Notable Quotables**
>
> Perseverance! Overcome luck through diversity! The more good ideas, the less the need to be lucky.
>
> —Rollie Tesh, inventor, Pente

National Organizations

Two different types of national organizations operate, the United Inventors Association (UIA) and the Intellectual Property Owners, Inc. (IPO).

The UIA claims to represent more than 10,000 inventors worldwide. It was established in September 1990 as an outgrowth of a Department of Energy Conference organized to discuss the needs of our nation's independent inventors.

There is no finer or more impactful group of advocates for the independent inventor than the folks at the UIA. They labor tirelessly on the front lines and behind the scenes, scrupulously watching out for the rights of the independent inventor. The UIA is actively involved in bringing fraudulent invention-marketing companies to the attention of lawmakers, law enforcement agencies, and regulators. I encourage you to visit the UIA website, at www.usuia.org.

Inventions Wanted

You may know 3M best as the maker of Scotch® brand tape and Post-it® notes, but it is a $25 billion, global science-based company that employs 79,000 people in more than 60 countries. And if you have a patented invention appropriate for its lines in health care, highway safety, office products, abrasives, or adhesives, 3M wants to know about it. For details, go to solutions.3m.com/wps/portal/3M/en_US/Submit/YourIdea/?WT.mc_id=www.3m.com/submityouridea.

Intellectual Property Owners (IPO), often at odds with the UIA on issues of patent lawand patent policy, is a fine organization, comprised of many more corporate members than independent inventors. The IPO is not an inventor organization, per se. It is a trade association (read: lobbyists) that serves the needs of owners of patents, trademarks, copyrights, and trade secrets throughout a wide range of industries and fields of technology. Members include Fortune 500 companies, universities, patent law firms, independent inventors, and authors.

The IPO was founded in 1972 by a group of individuals concerned about the lack of understanding of intellectual property rights in the United States. Members include Union Carbide, Monsanto, United Technologies, P&G, AT&T, and more than 300 small businesses, universities, independent inventors, authors, executives, and attorneys.

Herb Wamsley, the IPO's indefatigable executive director, has been at the helm of the organization for as far back as I can remember. While the IPO is definitely not for the casual inventor, it should be given consideration by professional inventors who have interest in up-to-the-minute information about intellectual property issues and who seek contacts within big business. For a full list of the IPO's benefits and services, request a fact sheet and other background material from the organization.

The IPO sponsors the National Inventor of the Year Award. Its purpose is to increase public awareness of current inventors and how they benefit the nation's economy and our quality of life. Its *Daily News*, an awesomely informative summary of current ip news and tidbits, is sent to members via e-mail and is available free to anyone who visits the IPO website at www.ipo.org.

I served two consecutive terms on the IPO's board of directors filling the one seat it had for an independent inventor. It was a great place for making contacts with the gatekeepers of corporate ip. For more information, contact Intellectual Property Owners, 1501 M Street NW, Suite 1150, Washington, DC 20005; 202-507-4500; fax: 202-507-4501; www.ipo.org.

The Value of State and Local Organizations

Don't join a national organization at the exclusion of a state or local group. These organizations complement each other in terms of what they deliver. State and local organizations are typically smaller, warmer, and friendlier. You will be able to attend regular meetings. And because the membership is close by, the information shared will be highly targeted, for example, where to get prototypes made, find competent patent counsel, and so forth. The non-nationals also often have great guest speakers, social events, and recreational activities.

Fred Hart, formerly of the Department of Energy, advises, "Search out the nearest inventors' organization and join. If there isn't one, start one up. It's only through a mutual support group that you can safely get help."

If you need guidance on how to start your own organization, take a look at the advice proffered by the Houston Inventors Association, at www.inventors.org/invclub/h2start.htm.

Informal Organizations

If you don't want to start a formal organization, think about informal get-togethers. A great example of one is what has become known as Toy Inventors Weekend in Vermont every September.

John Hall, a former vice president for R&D at Playskool, and his wife, publishing dynamo Nancy, first organized this weekend back in 1993, and it has become an annual, by-invitation-only event that some 25 people attend. The group takes over a beautiful country inn and spends a fall weekend renewing friendships, sharing business stories and corporate intelligence, and enjoying the beauty of the Green Mountain State.

Toy inventors and their spouses or significant others come from as far away as California and England to attend. The weekend is restricted to independent inventors. No currently employed corporate executives are invited, although some inventors once worked inside.

Palm Beach County, Florida, is home to the Sunshine Santas, a loosely organized band of some 15 toy inventors who work, play, and dine together all year long. Sheryl and I are proud to be founding members of this tightly knit group of elves.

While a licensor might not make a trip to Florida to see a single individual inventor, because the opportunity exists to hear pitches from many different people/teams, there is a steady stream of executives coming in and out from as far away as England, Canada, and California.

The Least You Need to Know

- It's not about giving; it's about sharing.
- There is strength in numbers.
- No man (or woman) is an island.
- Find an organization you like, and sign up.
- Start an organization. It need not be large to be beneficial and enjoyable.

Appendix A

Glossary

The following glossary contains a potpourri of terms and jargon you're apt to hear at some point during the invention, protection, licensing, and manufacturing phases of taking a product from a figment of your imagination to market. It is by no means a comprehensive glossary, which would be impossible given the myriad kinds of inventions, technologies, and methods of production.

I have packed the glossary with words and terms to give you some conversational expertise and send a signal of poise and confidence to those you're working with. It's filled with an array of words and phrases that someone skilled in the high art of glittering repartee can use to convince others into thinking you know what's up.

For example, although you may know nothing about plastics, should a manufacturer ask you for an opinion on which plastic to use for your item, you might suggest ABS, "to give it the durability of a telephone." The idea is to be able to hold your own.

Knowing buzzwords also ensures exact answers to questions and avoids potentially embarrassing semantic ruptures. So if someone asks you to "polish a thumbnail," you will not reach for an emery board. Chances are the person is requesting that a rough pencil drawing of a new concept be tightened and colored with markers.

In the work of product development, the "choke factor" has nothing to do with the Heimlich maneuver; "skews" are not used to barbecue shish kebab; "noodling" is a far cry from pasta; rye is not cut on a breadboard; and N.I.H. are not the initials for the National Institutes of Health.

I hope you'll enjoy and make use of this glossary, a mini-dictionary containing some of the most practical and common terms I come into contact with as an inventor and product developer.

A-price   A manufacturer's wholesale price to the trade, as shown on the company's sell sheets.

abandon   The explicit or implicit relinquishment of a potential patent right. Inaction may render a patent right abandoned.

abandonment   The loss of a patent or trademark application, for failure to file a complete and proper reply as the condition of the application may require within a time period set by the USPTO.

abstract   A one-paragraph description of an invention in a patent.

accelerated aging test   A procedure whereby a product is subjected to extreme but controlled conditions of heat, pressure, or other variables to create over the short haul the effects of long-time use or storage under normal conditions.

accessory   A companion item, adornment, or other component developed for use with an item, the number of which can broaden an inventor's royalty base substantially.

acetal   Thermoset plastic that keeps its shape under extreme pressure. Used in cams, wheels, and other machine parts. Trade names are Celcon and Delrin.

acrylic   Thermoset plastic that takes color easily and offers high clarity. Used in signage, displays, optical lenses, and automotive light domes. Trade names are Lucite and Plexiglas.

acrylonitrile-butadiene-styrene (ABS)   Strong, stain-resistant thermoset plastic. Used in telephones, pipes, wheels, and handles.

add-on   *See* accessory.

administrivia   Too much paperwork.

advance   A negotiated sum of money given to an inventor, frequently against future royalties. It is typically nonrefundable.

age grading   Labeling of products for the appropriate age level of the end users.

agent   A businessperson who represents inventor product and negotiates deals. Agents often work in tandem with an attorney. Also called a broker.

air   (1) A large amount of white space in a layout. (2) Wasted space in a package.

air brush   An atomizer used to spray paint onto models and prototypes to achieve soft gradations and merging of tones.

allylic   Thermoset plastic that resists heat and weather.

arbitration clause   An out-of-court procedure whereby a third party settles a dispute between the inventor and licensee.

"Are you in a hurry to get this back?"   The company wants to keep your concept for review and not pay an option.

assign   To sign over to another person or company.

assignee   One to whom something is assigned.

atomic (to go)   Refers to products that sell beyond anyone's wildest dreams.

audit   Examination of a company's financial records by an inventor or an appointed representative, for the purpose of confirming the accuracy of royalty reports.

B-school   Abbreviation for business school, a place where marketing executives get impractical training.

B-sheet   A preliminary sketch.

BCC   E-mail abbreviation for blind carbon copy. This is to be used only when you want to be sure everyone will read what you've written.

bean counter   An executive who cares more about money than product. A non–risk taker who has no imagination.

beauty shot   A product image on a package that captures an item in its most exciting form.

bench model   A level higher than a test-of-principal (TOP) model. These models are used to prove that a product will perform as expected.

bill of materials (BOM)   List of a product's components.

bird dog   To pay close attention.

blank check   What licensees never give an inventor.

bleed   (1) What inventors often have to do for companies. (2) Image that extends to the outermost edge of a paper or page.

blister   *See* clam shell.

blood supply   New ideas. *See also* managing the blood supply.

blow away   Sell well.

blow molding   A plastic molding process in which a tube of molten resin is inserted into a mold. Compressed air or steam is used to expand the tube, forcing material against a mold's wall, where it is held until hard. Used to produce hollow objects like bottles.

blue-skying   *See* noodling.

boilerplate   (1) Standard language in a licensing agreement. (2) Blocks of repetitive type used and copied over and over again.

brainstorming   Looking for solutions to problems by coming up with many possible answers.

brand equity   The core values consumers associate with a brand.

breadboard   A model that tests the feasibility of a proposed design.

broker   *See* agent.

bullet   A dot or similar marking to emphasize text.

calipers   A calibrated instrument for measuring the thickness of surfaces.

camera ready   Artwork ready for photographic reproduction.

cannibalize   (1) To use parts from an existing product for the purpose of making a prototype. (2) To expand a brand to a point that the extensions erode the market share of the main product.

"Can't wrap my arms around it."   Uttered by an executive struggling to understand a submission.

casting   A sculpture produced from a mold.

cavity   A depression, or a set of matching depressions, in a plastics-forming mold that forms the outer surfaces of the molded articles.

character licensing   (1) Imprinting of a character, image, logo, signature, design, personality, or property on an existing product to heighten awareness and sales. (2) Reproduction of a character, image, logo, signature, design, personality, or property in and of itself as a viable entity.

chip in board (COB)   A silicon IC chip that's mounted directly to an electronic assembly substrate or printed wiring assembly without an intermediate packaging step.

chipboard   A crude form of cardboard used for strength in prototyping.

choke factor   The strongest feature of a new product.

claims   Concise written statements that define the invention covered by the patent application. What falls within that definition is protected by the patent—anything outside it is not protected.

clam shell   Packaging in clear plastic that has been molded to a product's physical profile, hinged in the middle, and snapped around the product for point-of-purchase display.

classic   A product that has been popular with millions of people for more than 25 years.

close-out   Products reduced in price to get rid of remaining inventory.

commercialization   The selling of a product or process for financial gain.

comp   Drawing or model that shows what a product will look like when it's finished. Shortened version of *comprehensive*.

compression molding   The most common method for molding thermoset plastics. Resin powder is put into a mold. Heat and pressure are applied. The plastic sets, and when the mold is opened, a product is released.

Computer Aided Design (CAD)   The process of using a computer in the design process.

Computer Aided Manufacturing (CAM)   The process of using a computer in the manufacturing process.

conception   When you first thought of your invention. Document it with a notebook entry, for example, showing the time and date you had the brainstorm. If you can make a simple sketch, this makes the entry even more efficacious. Sign and date the sketch, too.

Consumer Product Safety Commission (CPSC)   The independent U.S. regulatory agency that helps keep American families safe by reducing the risk of injury or death from consumer products.

contingency (on)   A situation in which a lawyer agrees to represent an owner of a patent or trademark in an infringement suit, in return for a percentage of the proceeds from any out-of-court financial settlement or an amount of money awarded by the court.

control drawing   Drawing with specifications from which model makers can produce working samples.

copyright   Exclusive legal right to reproduce, publish, and sell the matter and form of a literary, musical, or artistic work.

cut steel   To produce a mold for mass production of a product.

"Cute!"   The kiss of death, as in when a prospective licensee says, "That's a cute item."

deal breaker   (1) A proposed contractual stipulation or condition that one party cannot or will not agree to. (2) A lawyer. (3) A product does come in at the right cost.

death by tweakage   When a product fails because of unnecessary tinkering or too many last-minute revisions.

deco   Short for *decoration.*

design   Features of shape, configuration, pattern, or ornamentation that can be judged by the eye in finished products.

design patent   The emphasis of this type of patent is on the design of the invention, not on its functionality. What is important with this type of patent are the invention's unique ornamental and aesthetic properties. Design patent numbers always begin with *D.*

detailed drawings   *See* dimensional drawings.

detent   A device for holding one part in a certain position relative to that of another part.

developer   A person who creates and develops new products.

disclosure form   *See* nondisclosure form.

dog   Slang reference to a product that's dead at retail.

dog-and-pony show   An intricate product pitch.

"Done deal"   Signals the start of negotiations.

double-tooling   Expanding production to meet demand.

draftsman   Person who prepares mechanical drawings, especially for patents.

dropped item   (1) Product that has been withdrawn from consideration. (2) End of an inventor's dream.

dumb it down   Refers to making a product so the masses can understand it.

dumb it up   Refers to making a product just slightly better for the mass market.

Durometer   An instrument used for measuring the hardness of a material.

edutain   To educate through entertainment. Usually refers to science and discovery products.

engineering prototype   An actual working version of a product, system, or process used to gather information on the operation, performance to specifications, and manufacturing requirements.

ergonomics   Science of making buttons and controls fit the product within the limitations of its design.

examining attorney   A USPTO employee who examines (reviews and determines compliance with the legal and regulatory requirements of) an application for registration of a federally registered trademark.

exclusive license   Grants a licensee the sole right to produce and sell certain products in one or more particular product categories, in a territory and/or distribution channel for a certain period of time.

exploded view   A means of showing the relationship of one component against another, drawn in the sequence in which the object would be taken apart.

extruding   A molding process used to produce continuous forms such as pipes, rods, fibers, and wires. Rotating screws force raw material through a heated barrel, in which it melts and is then forced out the other side.

fair use   A court ruling regarding copyright or trademark infringement. It says that under certain circumstances a trademarked or copyrighted material can be used without a license fee or permission.

FedEx   The quickest and most expensive way to get a prototype to key marketing and R&D executives just as they leave on holiday.

file wrapper   The complete PTO file on a particular patent.

first shots   The first plastic pieces out of a new mold.

flashing   Excess plastic not trimmed off during the molding process; caused by poor tool match.

fly on instruments   To work according to instrument readings only, without visual landmarks.

focus group   Formally organized testing of a product by volunteer or paid consumers.

free   No cost, but frequently with strings attached.

free on board (FOB)   A purchase plan whereby a customer can pick up product at its foreign point of manufacture for a lower price than had the goods been delivered to the United States.

gating authority   The key decision maker, especially for new product submissions.

go south   When an idea is dropped by a manufacturer.

gremlins   Obstacles that get in the way of a product's development and success.

guarantee   The minimum sum of money a manufacturer pays to an inventor.

hard cost   A product's full cost, including materials, labor, and packaging. If off-shore, add duty and freight.

hitchhiking   The process of one person's idea producing a similar idea or an enhanced idea from another person.

hype   (1) Promotion of a product through media events. (2) Product claims. (3) Exaggeration of performance or payoff.

"I don't get it."   Signal that you do not want to do business with this individual.

"I don't have e-mail."   Signal that you do not want to do business with this individual.

idea harvesting   The process of gathering ideas.

ideate   To form ideas.

in the review process   Frequently means that your rejection letter has not yet been sent.

indemnification   To hold a party harmless from any claims, actions, or other damages arising from a breach of contract or practices for the licensed technology.

infringement   When someone willingly or unwillingly uses your intellectual property without your permission.

intellectual property (ip)   The property of your mind or intellect. Types of intellectual property include patents, trademarks, designs, confidential information/trade secrets, copyright, circuit layout rights, etc.

inventing community   Catchall for professional inventors.

"It's in the mail."   Your prototype, contract, or check has not been sent yet, but will be now.

joint inventor   An inventor named with at least one other inventor in a patent application, wherein each inventor contributes to the conception of the invention set forth in at least one claim in a patent application.

jump-start a product   To throw a lot of television or media dollars behind a product, in hopes of stimulating consumer sales.

keeper   A new product a manufacturer wants to hold for further review.

kill fee   A negotiated payment made to an inventor by a manufacturer if an agreement is prematurely terminated prior to the start of production.

killer item   A great product.

KISS (keep it simple, stupid)   Refers to an approach to product design.

kitchen research   Informal R&D conducted in a casual manner to get reaction to an idea.

knock-off   (1) Stealing of another person or company's idea by copying it so closely that it embodies the spirit of the original. (2) Nonpromoted copy of a best-selling product at a lower price.

landed costs   Total cost of receiving goods at a U.S. venue, including product costs, transportation costs (e.g., ocean freight, air freight, etc.), brokerage fees, ground freight, insurance, commissions, design costs, duties, payroll taxes, value-added taxes, excise taxes, and other taxes.

lash up   A crude prototype.

Law of Strawberry Jam   The further you spread something, the thinner it gets.

legal scrub   The process of running a contract by a lawyer.

legals   Corporate shorthand for patent, trademark, and copyright notices that go on a package.

"Let me show it to my people."   Music to an inventor's ears.

letter of credit (L/C)   A letter addressed by a banker to a correspondent certifying that the person or company named is entitled to draw a certain amount of money upon the completion of a specific performance, e.g., the manufacture and delivery of so many products to a drop-off point.

license agreement   A contract that gives permission to make, use, or sell a patented product or process. Licensing can be exclusive or nonexclusive, for a specific field of use, for a specific geographical area, or U.S. or foreign. If ownership is transferred, it's called an assignment.

licensed property   Unique character, event, or personality that has proven consumer appeal, which companies incorporate into their products for a royalty.

licensee   The person or company obtaining a right from the licensor to commercialize a concept in connection with a product or service.

licensing   The act of contracting the rights in an invention to a manufacturer.

licensor   A person (e.g., an inventor) or company that owns and/or controls the authority to grant others the right to use or manufacture a property under a license agreement.

life support   Where a product goes just before it is dropped.

line   A family of products typically marketed under the same trademark.

line review   (1) Periodic management meeting to review line development. (2) A bloodbath; often catered.

logo or **logotype**   A trademark.

looks-like prototype   A 3-D model that looks like the final production item, although it may not be made from materials specified for production.

looks-like, works-like prototype   A 3-D model that looks and performs exactly like the final production item, although it may not be made from materials specified for production.

loss leader   A selling technique retailers use, pricing a popular item at or below cost to attract consumers.

managing the blood supply   Keeping new ideas flowing.

marker rendering   An illustration colored with markers.

MBA   Corporate types whose work is too frequently dictated by numbers. They usually carry a calculator, an abacus, or worry beads.

me, too product   A close copy of another product, usually a knock-off of a successful product. *See also* knock-off.

micrometer   An instrument for measuring minute distances, angles, etc.

minimum guarantee   The least amount of money a manufacturer agrees to pay an inventor during a specified period of time.

minimum order quantity (MOQ)   The number of orders required for a manufacturer to produce a product.

mock-up   An experimental model or replica of a proposed product.

model   A clear and detailed prototype.

model makers   Handcrafters of prototypes and models.

mold   A cavity in which a substance is formed.

momentai (phonetic spelling)   Chinese for "No problem." A word heard frequently on factory visits to China.

multicavity mold   A mold with more than one cavity, for molding more than one piece at the same time.

multiple submission   A submission by an inventor of the same concept simultaneously to more than one company. It's a potential survival method used by an inventor to avoid having all eggs in one basket.

neophobia   The fear of anything new.

net sales   Gross sales of licensed articles less allowed deductions such as taxes, returns, or freight.

nice try   An attempt to pay an inventor on a nonroyalty basis. *See also* work for hire.

N.I.H. Syndrome   Not Invented Here Syndrome, a state-of-mind at companies that do not welcome outside submissions of ideas.

"No problem."   Big problem.

nondisclosure agreement (NDA)   An agreement by which inventors share confidential or unprotected information with a potential licensee or people brought in to work on a project.

noodling   Tossing ideas around with other inventors; problem solving.

office action   A letter from the U.S. Patent and Trademark Office providing an assessment of a patent application under review.

one-off   One-of-a-kind prototype.

option agreement   An agreement between an inventor and a potential licensee during which time the company will investigate the patent and market potential of an invention. During this evaluation period, the inventor cannot license to another party. Options often involve holding money.

original equipment manufacturer (OEM)   A factory that produces ready-made elements or products.

parallel development   Similar products from two different creative sources.

patent   The exclusive right to exclude others from making, using, or selling an invention for a specified period of years (usually less than 20), granted by the federal government to the inventor(s) if the device, composition, method, or process is useful, novel, and non-obvious.

Patent and Trademark Depository Library (PTDL)   A library designated by the USPTO to receive copies of patents, CD-ROMs containing registered and pending marks, and patent and trademark materials that are made available to the public for free. The libraries also actively disseminate patent and trademark information and offer Internet access to the USPTO's online collections.

Patent and Trademark Office (PTO or USPTO)   The Department of Commerce agency that examines patent and trademark applications, issues patents, registers trademarks, and furnishes patent and trademark services to the public.

patent attorney   A lawyer who specializes in writing patent applications. The attorney is also frequently an engineer.

patent infringement   *See* infringement.

patent pending   A notice that often appears on manufactured items to signify that someone has applied for a patent on an invention contained in the manufactured item. It serves as a warning that a patent may issue that would cover the item and that people should be careful because they might infringe if the patent issues.

patent troll   A shakedown artist. A person or company that procures active patents from their inventors and uses the patents to bleed money from businesses through lawsuits or the threat of lawsuits for patent infringement.

patentable   Suitable to be patented.

patentee   An inventor.

pattern   The solid form, typically wood, from which a mold is produced.

perceived value   The worth of a product as reflected in its components, packaging, and advertising.

pond (the)   The Pacific Ocean, as in, "I'm going across the pond to visit a factory." Also can be used to refer to the Atlantic Ocean.

preliminary design   (1) R&D department. (2) The breadboard stage of a product in development. *See also* breadboard.

prior art   Relates to existing patents and other sources of information where someone may have already published information about an invention that's similar to an invention you think is patentable.

priority date   A priority date is established for your invention when you first file a patent application that describes the invention in detail. This is used to determine whether your invention is new. If your invention is known to the public before this date, you are not entitled to patent it.

product champion   An executive who wants to license your invention and sell it inside to his or her colleagues.

Promethean   Creative. Derives from Prometheus, a demigod in Greek mythology known for his bold and skillful acts.

prosecution   The proceedings from the initial filing of a patent application in the U.S. Patent and Trademark Office to the issuance of the patent.

prototype   An original model on which something is formed.

"Pull it green"   To take a product off the market before it matures.

push money   Money paid as an incentive to a salesperson.

quality assurance (QA)   Typically refers to a test.

quality control (QC)   The monitoring of production by independent contractors or nonfactory employees.

quarterly reports   Statements from licensees to inventors (a.k.a. licensors) that state how many of any particular items were sold in the previous quarter. Inventors pray that royalty checks accompany quarterly reports.

rapid prototyping   Technologies that additively "grow" a design layer by layer through a process driven by 3-D CAD data. *See also* stereolithography; selective laser sintering.

receptionist   (1) The first stop. (2) Key inventor contact.

red light   (1) Idea that stops traffic. (2) Corporate-speak for "Don't spend any more of our money on that concept."

registered mark (®)   A trademark that has been registered with the USPTO.

rejection   Rehearsal before a big event.

research and development (R&D)   The part of a company tasked to create and develop new product.

rough   The first pencil draft of an illustration.

rough model   *See* breadboard.

royalty   Income based on use (such as percentage of sales) that is returned to the owner of a patented invention by a licensee company. In addition to royalty income, licensees typically pay an execution fee (when they first obtain the license) and an annual maintenance fee (while they are developing the product for marketing). Royalty income replaces the maintenance fee when sufficient sales have been generated.

Rube Goldberg invention   A ridiculously overcomplicated way of accomplishing a simple task.

scale   The size of a picture, plan, or model of a thing compared to the size of the thing itself.

schematic   A diagram that shows the layout of things in a logical manner.

secret   Something everybody is talking about.

sellitus   A disease that overtakes some inventors, amateurs, and professionals who have not sold a product in a while and need the victory (or advance). Sellitus usually results in bad deals.

semiconductors   Conductors of electricity (typically made from silicon) that allow the design and manufacturing of very small, very complicated, yet very inexpensive electrical circuits.

service mark (ˢᴹ)   The same as a trademark, except that it identifies and distinguishes the source of a service rather than a product.

servo   An automatic device that uses a sensor and a motor to control a mechanism.

ship air   To pack a product improperly so the package is oversized for the dimensions of the contents, thereby using excess space.

shots   Molded plastic pieces.

Shtikmeister   (root: Yiddish) A showman.

skew   A product in retail inventory, a stock-keeping unit.

small entity status   Status of an independent inventor that qualifies the inventor for a 50 percent discount on USPTO fees.

"Sorry, I gotta take this call."   Take a deep breath and be prepared to wow 'em. You have two more minutes.

split royalty   When two or more inventors divide the pie.

staple   Product that sells year in and year out.

state of the art   An engineering term implying the state of knowledge available in a field of science or engineering.

stock-keeping unit   *See* skew.

submission form   *See* nondisclosure agreement.

SWAG   The abbreviation for "sophisticated wild-ass guess."

sweat equity   The estimated value of uncompensated labor.

template   A pattern or guide for creating something.

think box   The human brain.

thumbnail   A rough sketch.

thunderbolt thinking   Flashes of insight.

tissues   Rough pencil or charcoal sketches.

tooling   Steel molds with which to produce plastic components.

trade dress   The unique packaging, design, silhouette, or shape of a product that gives it a level of recognition and distinguishes it from other products.

trade secret   A secret method, formula, or device that remains unpatented to keep it a secret.

trademark (™)   A word, phrase, symbol, or design; or a combination of words, phrases, symbols, or designs, that identifies and distinguishes a source of the goods of one party from goods of others.

trademark troll   *See* patent troll and substitute *TMs* for *patents.*

utility patent   A patent granted to an inventor of any new and useful process, machine, article of manufacture, or composition of matter, or any new and useful improvement thereof.

vacuum-forming   A manufacturing process in which a heated sheet of plastic is drawn into or over a mold by way of a vacuum.

Valley of Death   Where products die after transitioning from public to private financing.

vampire project   A project capable of sucking the blood out of anyone associated with it.

visual punctuation   Decoration.

WAG   Abbreviation for "wild-ass guess."

wannabe   (1) Product that is not fully or accurately defined—it wants to be something else. (2) An amateur inventor, usually a part-timer who wants to play in the big leagues.

waste mold   A mold from which only one cast can be taken.

"We've already done that."   (1) No interest. (2) Take a lower royalty.

"Whatever you say."   You have too much control over the company's project. Get ready to take a fall.

white knight   *See* product champion.

"Who has seen this?"   "Which one of our competitors has passed on this, and why?"

wooden stake letter   A rejection letter.

work for hire   Work produced either by an employee within the scope of employment or by an independent contractor under a written agreement. If the work is produced by an independent contractor, the parties must agree expressly in writing that the work will be a work for hire. The employer or commissioning party owns the intellectual property.

works-like prototype   A model that works exactly like the production model of an item will work, although it need not be made from production materials.

worm-eaten   A product that has been seen and rejected by many companies.

WOW factor   The strongest and most promotable feature of a new product.

X   The spot on a license agreement where the inventor signs.

X-acto   A brand of cutting instruments that hold a variety of blades.

yawn   A boring product.

"You're kidding, right?"   It's downhill from here. Take out your next idea and start pitching it.

"You're the genius."   All the pressure is on you.

yum-yum   A tasty, wonderfully innovative product.

zookeeper   An inventor-relations executive.

Appendix

Agreement Templates

The agreement templates in this appendix are not final documents and should be used only as references. Please consult an attorney before you sign any license document or agreement.

Invention License Agreement Template

AGREEMENT made this _____ day of _____, 20_____, by and between _____, located at _____ (hereinafter referred to as LICENSOR) and _____, located at _____ _____ (hereinafter referred to as LICENSEE).

Witnesseth:

WHEREAS, LICENSOR represents and warrants that it is the creator of _____ (hereinafter referred to as the ITEM).

WHEREAS, LICENSOR hereby warrants that, to the best of its knowledge, information and belief, it is the sole and exclusive owner of all rights in the ITEM; that, to the best of its knowledge, information and belief, it has the sole and exclusive right to grant the license herein; and that it is not engaged in litigation or conflict of any nature whatsoever involving the ITEM; and

WHEREAS, LICENSEE is in the business of making and selling (<u>enter type of product, e.g., shoes, faucets, toys, etc.</u>); and

WHEREAS, LICENSEE wishes to obtain the sole and exclusive rights to manufacture and sell the ITEM (<u>enter territories, e.g., worldwide, U.S. and its possessions, Europe, etc.</u>)

NOW, THEREFORE, for and in consideration of the sum of One Dollar (US$1.00) and other good and valuable consideration, receipt of which is hereby acknowledged, and for the performance of the mutual covenants hereinafter to be performed, it is agreed as follows:

DEFINITIONS:

Item: As used in this Agreement, the term ITEM refers to the ITEM described hereinabove, and any Improvements, Accessories or Extensions thereto, whether developed by or for LICENSEE.

Improvements: As used in this Agreement, the term *Improvements* means any design or technical refinements or advances made by or for LICENSEE and reflected in the ITEM as marketed.

Accessories: As used in this Agreement, the term *Accessories* means any products making use of the ITEM, as well as equipment developed by or for LICENSEE designated for use with the ITEM.

Extensions: As used in this Agreement, the term *Extensions* means any products that are sold independently by LICENSEE under the ITEM trademark, i.e., products that trade on the name of the ITEM but are not necessarily marketed as accessories to the ITEM.

Collateral Merchandise: As used in this Agreement, the term *Collateral Merchandise* means products that are sold under the ITEM trademark or trade on its goodwill.

Note: You may not want to grant these rights. If not, omit this reference. Or you might want to allow for certain collateral merchandise and not others. If so, spell it out here. Collateral Merchandise could range from T-shirts to tennis rackets.

1.(a) LICENSOR hereby grants to LICENSEE the sole and exclusive right, privilege, and license to make, reproduce, modify, use and/or sell; to have made, reproduced, modified, used, and/or sold; and to sublicense others to make, reproduce, modify, use and/or sell the ITEM and any images, representations, and material associated with the ITEM, as well as the subject matter of a patent application which is to be filed on the ITEM pursuant to Paragraph 2(a) hereof.

(b) All rights and licenses not herein specifically granted to LICENSEE are reserved by LICENSOR and, as between the parties, are the sole and exclusive property of LICENSOR and may be used or exercised solely by LICENSOR. Included within this understanding is the right of LICENSOR to use whatever trademark LICENSEE markets the ITEM under; however, it is understood and agreed between the parties that

LICENSOR will not license the concept to a third party for a product that would compete with the ITEM as marketed by LICENSEE.

(c) This Agreement shall continue for as long as the ITEM upon which royalties would be payable to LICENSOR, under provisions of this Agreement, shall continue to be manufactured or sold by LICENSEE.

2.(a) LICENSOR agrees to use its best efforts and to bear the expenses of obtaining patent protection in the USA, and any and all such patents will be in the name of and remain the property of LICENSOR during and following any termination or cancellation hereof.

(b) To the best of LICENSOR's knowledge, information and belief the ITEM does not infringe any patent rights.

3.(a) LICENSEE shall pay LICENSOR (<u>insert number</u>) percent (_____%) of the "Net Sales" of the ITEM and its Improvements, Accessories, or Extensions. As used in this Agreement, "Net Sales" are defined as sales computed on prices charged by LICENSEE to its customers for the ITEM, less a deduction not to exceed seven and a half percent (7.5%) which provides for freight allowances, sales allowances actually credited, customary trade discounts (but not cash discounts), volume discounts (not to exceed usual industry practices), to the extent taken, directly applicable to the sale of licensed products, and less returns (but not for exchange) which are accepted and credited by LICENSEE. No deduction shall be made for noncollectible accounts. No costs incurred in the manufacture, sales, distribution, exploitation or promotion of the ITEM, its improvements, accessories or any adaptations thereof shall be deducted from any royalties payable by LICENSEE to LICENSOR, nor shall any deductions from due royalties be made for taxes of any nature. LICENSEE cannot barter or trade or do so-called "charge-backs" on the ITEM without computation of full royalties.

(b) In event LICENSEE sells FOB direct from a foreign manufacturing location, LICENSEE shall pay LICENSOR (<u>insert number</u>) percent (_____%) of all Net Sales, as defined hereinabove, of the ITEM.

(c) LICENSEE may grant foreign manufacturing sublicenses on the ITEM upon any terms and conditions which it wishes to grant and establish so long as said terms and conditions are competitive and market prevailing; and provided that in the event LICENSEE does grant such sublicenses to manufacture and market the ITEM, LICENSEE shall pay to LICENSOR fifty percent (50%) of any and all moneys received, including, but not limited to royalties (which shall be no less than two and a half percent [2½%] of the sales of the ITEM), advances, guarantees, mold or pattern lease or rental fees, etc. as received by LICENSEE from any such sublicense or grant. LICENSEE agrees to send a copy of any sublicense agreement, or shall otherwise promptly inform LICENSOR in writing about the terms of the sublicense to manufacture the ITEM.

(d) In the event LICENSEE sells the ITEM as a premium, the royalty rate shall be (insert number) percent (____%) of the revenue derived by LICENSEE from the sale of the ITEM as a premium. For purposes of this Agreement, the term *premium* shall be defined as including, but not necessarily limited to, combination sales and free or self-liquidating items offered to the public in conjunction with the sale or promotion of a product or service other than the ITEM, including traffic building or continuity visits by the consumer, customer, or any similar scheme or device, whose primary purpose in regard to each of the sales described above is not directed at the sale of the ITEM itself and the prime intent of which is to use the ITEM in such a way as to promote, publicize, and/or sell the products, services, or business image of the user of such ITEM rather than the ITEM itself.

(e) All royalties payable by LICENSEE to LICENSOR based upon LICENSEE's sales of the ITEM shall accrue upon LICENSEE's shipment and invoicing of the item.

(f) If payments are made to LICENSOR from a foreign country, LICENSEE assumes sole responsibility for procuring any permits and documents needed to make all payments under any exchange regulations, and all such royalties shall be made by LICENSEE to LICENSOR in U.S. dollars at the then prevailing rate of exchange as used by (insert name of major bank).

4.(a) Upon execution of this Agreement, LICENSEE shall pay to LICENSOR the sum of $____, as a nonrefundable, guaranteed advance against royalties. In no event shall such advance be repaid to LICENSEE other than in the form of deductions from payments due under Paragraphs 3 and 9 hereof.

(b) Should LICENSEE, for any reason, and at any time, decide not to manufacture the ITEM, or if in any calendar year the ITEM fails to generate $____ in royalties for LICENSOR, LICENSOR shall have the right to terminate this Agreement. And should LICENSEE cease to manufacture said ITEM, or should this Agreement be terminated for a breach of conditions by LICENSEE, then all rights to the development work done on the ITEM on behalf of and/or paid for by LICENSEE (e.g., breadboards, models, etc.) shall belong to LICENSOR free-and-clear and LICENSEE shall have no further claim to the ITEM.

(c) The receipt or acceptance by LICENSOR of any written statements furnished pursuant to this Agreement or of any payments made hereunder (or cashing of any checks paid hereunder) shall not preclude LICENSOR from questioning the correctness thereof at any time.

5. LICENSEE agrees to introduce the ITEM on or before (date). LICENSEE agrees that during the term of this Agreement it will diligently and continuously manufacture, sell, distribute, and promote the ITEM, and that it will make and maintain adequate arrangements for the distribution of the ITEM and satisfy demand for the ITEM.

6. LICENSEE has the right to change the form of the ITEM as submitted by LICENSOR, and to produce and sell it under new form(s), provided, however, that all the provisions of this Agreement shall apply to said new form(s) of the ITEM.

7.(a) LICENSEE shall mark the ITEM and its packages, containers, and display cards with the words "Patent Pending" if advised that a patent application is pending and until advised that a patent has been issued on the ITEM, at which later time LICENSEE shall mark the ITEM, containers, and display cards with the specific patent number.

8.(a) LICENSEE shall annually furnish LICENSOR, free-of-charge, (<u>enter number</u>) samples of each ITEM and its packaging prior to its availability at retail for purposes of quality control. In the case of the ITEM as made by LICENSEE's foreign sublicensees, LICENSEE shall annually furnish, free-of-charge, to LICENSOR (<u>enter number</u>) samples of each and its packaging.

9.(a) The rights to sublicense the ITEM in foreign countries covered by this Agreement are conditioned upon introduction of the ITEM on or before (<u>enter date</u>). In the event LICENSEE has not entered into a fully executed sublicense agreement or made formal, documented arrangements to sell the ITEM through a distributor in a foreign country prior to (<u>enter date, usually one year after domestic release</u>), all rights with respect to such foreign country shall automatically revert to LICENSOR. However, LICENSEE shall be entitled, after expiration of any manufacturing sublicense agreement or distributor arrangement in any foreign country entered into prior to (<u>enter cut-off date</u>) to enter into a new agreement or arrangement in such foreign country.

(b) When either party considers it necessary or desirable to obtain patent protection in a foreign country covered by this Agreement (other than the USA), it shall notify the other party of that decision and, upon the agreement of said other party, LICENSOR shall, if obtaining the foreign patent protection is not barred by prior use or publication, promptly file such foreign application and the expenses thereof shall be shared equally by both parties. In the event the parties do not agree to share the expense of obtaining such patent protection, the party requesting the foreign patent protection may proceed alone, at its own expense, and all rights obtained shall belong to that party alone, notwithstanding any other provisions of this Agreement. If LICENSEE has not timely requested the filing of a patent application in a foreign country, LICENSOR is under no obligation to file such foreign application, and in the event that neither party has filed a patent application in a particular foreign country, or the parties have agreed not to file an application or have agreed to discontinue an application or patent, then the royalties for such foreign country shall be payable to LICENSOR as if the patent protection had been obtained in that country and the expenses shared equally by the parties.

(c) LICENSEE may sublicense its rights hereunder to use the ITEM on Collateral Merchandise under the terms and conditions it wishes to grant and establish as long as they are competitive and market prevailing; and provided that, in the event LICENSEE grants such sublicenses, LICENSEE shall pay to LICENSOR the sum of (<u>insert number</u>) percent (_____%) of any and all moneys received, including, but not limited to, royalties, advances, guarantees, and consultation fees it may receive.

(d) In the case of sublicenses of Collateral Merchandise, LICENSEE shall ensure that sublicensees cause the above trademark notices, if one or both trademarks are used by LICENSEE, to appear on all collateral merchandise, its packaging, containers, advertising, etc.

10.(a) LICENSOR agrees to indemnify, defend, and save harmless LICENSEE against actions brought against LICENSEE with respect to any claim or suit that LICENSOR is not the originator of the Item.

(b) LICENSOR agrees to indemnify LICENSEE against losses, claims, and expenses with respect to losses, claims, or expenses that arise only from an act or omission by LICENSOR that is done in bad faith.

(c) LICENSOR shall not indemnify LICENSEE on claims whereby LICENSEE has been said to have been previously shown an ITEM similar to the ITEM by the claimant. LICENSEE warrants that it has never seen an item similar to the subject ITEM.

(d) LICENSOR agrees to indemnify and hold harmless LICENSEE from and against any claim of infringement of trade secrets arising out of LICENSEE's sale of the ITEM.

(e) LICENSEE will conduct its own patent, copyright, and trademark searches and satisfy itself that the ITEM does not infringe anything in any of these fields, and once satisfied, LICENSEE agrees to indemnify, defend, and save harmless LICENSOR from and against all damages, costs, and attorney fees resulting from all claims, demands, actions, suits, or prosecutions for patent, copyright, or trademark based upon use of the ITEM or its components and all forms of the ITEM as produced and sold by LICENSEE, its subsidiaries, affiliates, and sublicensees. LICENSEE shall be given prompt notice of any claim against LICENSOR and shall have the right to defend such claim with counsel selected by LICENSEE. LICENSOR agrees to cooperate with LICENSEE in connection with the defense of any such claim.

(f) LICENSEE agrees to indemnify, defend, and save harmless LICENSOR from and against all damages, costs, and attorney fees resulting from all claims, demands, actions, suits, or prosecutions for personal injury or property damage. LICENSEE agrees to cover LICENSOR under its product liability insurance, with an insurance company providing protection for itself and LICENSOR against any such claims or suits relating to personal injury, product manufacture, property damage, or materials failure, but in no event in amounts less than (<u>enter number</u>) million dollars or the limits of its policy, whichever is greater, and within thirty (30) days before manufacture of the ITEM, LICENSEE will submit to LICENSOR a certificate of insurance naming LICENSOR as an insured party, and covering LICENSOR requiring that the insurer shall not terminate or materially modify such without written notice to LICENSOR at least twenty (20) days in advance thereof.

(g) In the event of infringement of any patent that may be issued to LICENSOR on the ITEM and upon notice thereof from LICENSEE, LICENSOR shall, within thirty (30) days, notify LICENSEE of its election to prosecute or not prosecute a suit for infringement. If LICENSOR prosecutes said suit, it may select legal counsel and pay legal fees and costs of prosecution subject to being reimbursed therefore from any recovery in said suit. The balance of any recovery shall be divided equally between LICENSOR and LICENSEE. If LICENSOR elects not to prosecute any infringement suit, LICENSEE may do so after notice to LICENSOR of that intention. LICENSEE may then select legal counsel and shall bear all the legal fees and costs subject to reimbursement therefore from any recovery in said suit. The balance of any recovery shall be distributed as follows: one-fourth (¼) to LICENSOR and three-fourths (¾) to LICENSEE.

11. LICENSEE shall, within thirty (30) days following the end of each calendar quarter, starting with the month following the quarter in which sales of the ITEM commence, submit to LICENSOR a report covering the sales of the ITEM during the preceding quarter, and LICENSEE shall therewith send to LICENSOR payment of the amount due under Paragraphs 3 and 9 hereof. Such quarterly statements shall be submitted whether or not they reflect any sales.

12.(a) LICENSEE agrees to keep full and accurate books of account, records, data, and memoranda respecting the manufacture and sales of the ITEM in sufficient detail to enable the payments hereunder to LICENSOR to be determined, and LICENSEE gives LICENSOR the right, upon notice, at its own expense, to examine said books and records, only insofar as they concern the ITEM and not more often than twice in any calendar year, for the purpose of verifying the reports provided for in this Agreement. In the event LICENSOR shall examine the records, documents, and materials in the possession or under the control of LICENSEE with respect to the subject matter, such examination shall be conducted in such a manner as to not unduly interfere with the business of LICENSEE. LICENSOR and its representative shall not disclose to any other person, firm, or corporation any information acquired as a result of any such examination; provided, however, that nothing herein contained shall be construed to prevent LICENSOR and/or its duly authorized representative from testifying, in any court of competent jurisdiction, with respect to the information obtained as a result of such examination in any action instituted to enforce the rights of LICENSEE under the terms of this Agreement.

(b) In the event that LICENSEE has understated Net Shipments or underpaid royalties by five percent (5%) or more for any contract year, LICENSEE shall forthwith and upon written demand also pay to LICENSOR all reasonable costs, fees, and expenses incurred by LICENSOR in conducting such audit.

(c) Payments found to be due LICENSOR as a result of a delay or an examination shall be paid immediately at the prime rate quoted by (insert name of major bank) at the close of business on the due date plus (enter number) percent (_____%) per annum until paid.

13.(a) LICENSEE agrees to send all payments and reports due hereunder to LICENSOR at address noted in this Agreement's preamble.

14.(a) If LICENSEE shall at any time default by failing to make any payment hereunder, or by failing to make any report required under this Agreement, or by making a false report, or for cause, and LICENSEE shall fail to remedy such default within ten (10) days for money, and thirty (30) days for reports, after notice thereof by LICENSOR, LICENSOR may, at its option, terminate this Agreement and the license granted herein by notice to that effect, but such act by LICENSOR shall not relieve LICENSEE of its liabilities accruing up to the time of termination. In the case of subsequent default, the time period which to remedy the default shall be reduced to fifteen (15) days.

(b) Should a third default take place, LICENSOR may, at its option, terminate this Agreement.

15. It is understood and agreed that if LICENSEE does not introduce the ITEM on or before (enter date) or does not sell the ITEM for a period of ninety (90) consecutive days or more except as provided in Paragraph 16 hereof, LICENSOR may give notice to LICENSEE of its desire to terminate this Agreement for that reason, and if LICENSEE does not within thirty (30) days resume producing and selling of the ITEM, this Agreement and the license granted herein shall terminate as of the end of that thirty-day (30) period.

16. It is understood and agreed that in the event an act of government, or war conditions, or fire, flood, or labor trouble in the factory of LICENSEE, or in the factory of those manufacturing parts necessary for the manufacture of the ITEM, prevents the performance by LICENSEE of the provisions of this Agreement, then such nonperformance by LICENSEE shall not be considered a breach of this Agreement and such nonperformance shall be excused, but for no longer than a period of six (6) months on any single occurrence.

17. This Agreement shall continue for as long as the ITEM covered by this Agreement shall continue to be manufactured by LICENSEE, or unless sooner terminated under the provisions of this Agreement.

18. LICENSEE agrees that if this Agreement is terminated under any of its provisions, LICENSEE will not itself, or through others, thereafter manufacture and sell the ITEM, and all rights to the ITEM and to any patents filed hereunder shall revert to LICENSOR.

19.(a) LICENSOR agrees that LICENSEE may assign this Agreement to any affiliate corporation, provided, however, that such assignee shall thereafter be bound by the provisions of this Agreement.

(b) LICENSEE may not assign this Agreement, or any part thereof, without the expressed written permission of LICENSOR, which shall not be unreasonably withheld, unless it is selling its entire business as a going concern, and the same restriction shall be binding upon successors and assigns of LICENSEE.

(c) Should LICENSEE wish to sell its rights in the ITEM or transfer this Agreement to any person or corporation that does not plan to purchase LICENSEE's entire business as a going concern, but has an interest only in said ITEM, then said prospective buyer will have to strike a separate deal with LICENSOR for its consent to the sale.

20.(a) In case of the Receivership or Bankruptcy of LICENSEE, by reason of which LICENSEE is prevented from carrying out the spirit of this Agreement, after written notice thereof by LICENSOR, LICENSOR may, at its option, terminate this Agreement and the license granted herein by notice to that effect, but such act shall not relieve LICENSEE of its liabilities accruing up to the time of termination.

(b) If LICENSEE, at any time after the execution of this Agreement and prior to and during the preparation of said ITEM for production, display, and offering for sale, shall elect not to produce, display, offer, or produce said ITEM, which election shall be in writing sent by Registered or Certified or Express Mail to LICENSOR, then LICENSOR's sole and exclusive remedy shall be to keep the advance against royalties, as provided for in Paragraph 4 hereof, for breach of this Agreement, and such Agreement shall thereafter be of no further force and effect, and the license shall be deemed canceled and neither party shall have claim against the other.

(c) Immediately upon expiration or termination of this Agreement, for any reason whatsoever, all the rights granted to LICENSEE hereunder shall cease and revert to LICENSOR, who shall be free to license others to use any or all of the rights granted herein effective on and after such date of expiration or termination, and to this end, LICENSEE will be deemed to have automatically assigned to LICENSOR upon such expiration or termination, all copyrights, trademarks and service mark rights, equities, goodwill, titles, designs and concepts, and other rights in or to the ITEM. LICENSEE will, upon the expiration or termination of this license, execute any instruments requested by LICENSOR to accomplish or confirm the foregoing. Any assignments shall be without consideration other than mutual covenants and considerations of this Agreement. In addition, for whatever reasons, LICENSEE will forthwith refrain from any further use of the trademarks or copyrights of any further reference to any of them, direct or indirect.

(d) In the event of termination of this Agreement, for any reason other than for failure to pay or make reports due hereunder to LICENSOR, LICENSEE shall have the right to dispose of its existing inventory for a period of 60 days. Further, upon termination of this Agreement, LICENSEE agrees to assign to LICENSOR the right to receive directly any royalties due to LICENSOR from any collateral merchandise sublicensee of the ITEM.

21. All notices wherever required in this Agreement shall be in writing and sent by Certified Mail, Registered Mail, or Express Mail to the addresses first above written.

22. If any provisions of this Agreement are for any reason declared to be invalid, the validity of the remaining provisions shall not be affected thereby.

23. This Agreement shall be binding upon and inure to the benefit of the parties hereto and their successors and assigns as herein provided and said successors and assigns shall be libel hereunder. LICENSOR may assign its rights to receive royalties under this Agreement.

24. It is expressly agreed that LICENSOR is in no way the legal representative of LICENSEE and has no authority, expressed or implied, on behalf of LICENSEE to bind LICENSEE or to pledge its credit.

25. (Optional) It is a condition of this license that, if LICENSEE decides to market the ITEM under LICENSOR's trademark, (insert trademark), LICENSEE shall cause the following notice to appear on the ITEM and its advertising, promotional, packaging, and display materials therefore:

> (insert trademark) is a ™ of (insert name of trademark owner)

> Used with permission. All Rights Reserved.

26. This Agreement shall be construed in accordance with the laws of the State of _____.

IN WITNESS WHEREOF, the parties have executed this Agreement in duplicate originals the day/year first hereinabove written.

LICENSOR: _____

By: _____

LICENSEE: _____

By: _____

Option Agreement Template

THIS AGREEMENT made as of this _____ day of _____, 20_____ between _____, located at _____ (hereinafter "LICENSOR"), and _____, located at _____ (hereinafter "LICENSEE").

WHEREAS, LICENSOR has invented a _____ (hereinafter "Item"), and

WHEREAS, LICENSOR has presented the Item to LICENSEE for evaluation and possible licensing; and

WHEREAS, LICENSEE wishes to review and evaluate the Item;

It is therefore agreed between the parties as follows:

LICENSOR agrees that LICENSEE may examine and evaluate the Item for a period commencing on the date of this Agreement and ending on (insert date) ("Review Period"). LICENSOR represents that, to the best of its knowledge, information and belief, it has such rights in and title to the Item as to enable it to grant LICENSEE an exclusive license for its manufacture and sale. LICENSOR agrees that it will not license or disclose the Item or similar items during the Review Period to any other person, firm, corporation, or other entity that would compete with LICENSEE.

LICENSOR agrees that should LICENSEE wish to license the Item, LICENSOR will enter into a mutually satisfactory licensing agreement for the exclusive use in the _____ (define territory, e.g., United States, Europe, worldwide, etc.) of the Item with LICENSEE or a subsidiary or affiliate designated by LICENSEE.

In consideration of the foregoing, LICENSEE agrees to pay to LICENSOR the sum of $_____, along with other good and valuable consideration, the receipt of which is hereby acknowledged. If LICENSEE decides to license the Item, it will so notify LICENSOR by a written confirmation sent to LICENSOR at the address specified above, e-mailed or faxed no later than the last day of the Review Period, and both parties agree to negotiate a licensing agreement within thirty (30) days thereafter. In that event, LICENSEE may apply the above-referenced paid consideration against any royalties payable under the executed license agreement. In the event that LICENSEE does not elect to use the Item, it is agreed that LICENSOR shall be entitled to retain the entire sum payable hereunder.

IN WITNESS WHEREOF, the parties have executed this Agreement as of the date first written above.

LICENSOR: _____

Title: _____

LICENSEE: _____

Title: _____

Trademark License Agreement Template

THIS AGREEMENT, made and entered into as of the _____ day of _____, 20_____, by and between _____, with a principal place of business at _____ _____, (hereinafter referred to as "Licensor"), and Licensee, Inc., a corporation organized and existing under the laws of the state of _____, and having its principal office at _____ (hereinafter referred to as "Licensee").

WITNESSETH:

WHEREAS, Licensor is the sole and exclusive owner of the rights being licensed herein with respect to United States trademark registration No. _____ for (insert mark), and all associated rights arising through common law in the United States, including all associated goodwill, (the "Licensor Trademark"); and

WHEREAS, Licensee is, among other things, in the business of manufacturing and selling _____ (insert product definition) _____ _____; and

WHEREAS, Licensor and Licensee foresee a mutually beneficial use of the rights being licensed herein; and Licensor is willing to grant the exclusive license specified below to Licensee; and Licensee is desirous of obtaining the rights to manufacture, promote, and sell (insert type of product) bearing the Licensor Trademark to promote such sales.

NOW, THEREFORE, for and in consideration of the mutual covenants and agreements contained herein and for other good and valuable consideration, receipt of which is hereby acknowledged, it is hereby agreed as follows:

Grant of License. Licensor hereby grants to Licensee (including its subsidiaries and affiliates) the exclusive right and license to use the Licensor Trademark in connection with the manufacture, marketing, distribution, and sale of (name product) (hereinafter referred to as the "Licensed Products").

Marketing Rights. The marketing rights granted in Section 1 shall include, but not be limited to, the right to use the Licensor Trademark in connection with advertising, packaging, and promotional materials, including, but not limited to, promotional posters, and shall be exploited in all forms of media, including, but not limited to, the Internet and World Wide Web.

Territory and Distribution. The foregoing license shall be for the United States and shall extend to all channels of distribution without limitation.

Note: If you own TM rights beyond the United States and want to include said rights, #3 above is where to list them.

Right to License. Licensor hereby expressly warrants that it possesses all the rights and authority necessary to enter into this Agreement, that it has the right to convey the licenses granted herein, that is has granted no other license with respect to the Licensed Products, that Licensee is not required to obtain further approvals from any third party in order to exercise the rights granted to Licensee under this Agreement, and, further, that it is not engaged in any litigation or conflict of any nature whatsoever involving its rights in and to the Licensor Trademark. Licensor agrees that during the term hereof, it will not give any other person, firm, association, or corporation a license or right to manufacture or sell in the Territory any items similar to the Licensed Products.

Consideration.

As consideration for the rights granted herein, Licensee agrees to pay Licensor a royalty at the following percentage of the "Net Wholesale Selling Price" on sales of the Licensed Products by Licensee. The royalty rate shall be (insert number) percent (_____%).

As an advance against such royalties, Licensee shall pay Licensor the nonrefundable sum of $_____ upon execution of this Agreement.

As used herein, "Net Wholesale Selling Price" is defined as the gross wholesale selling price on all sales of the Licensed Products after deductions for customary trade discounts, returns that are accepted and credited by Licensee, and markdown allowances. For sales direct to consumers, the Net Selling Price shall be the gross wholesale selling price (regardless of the direct-to-consumer price) less returns actually received, shipping, and handling expenses. No royalties shall be paid on "close-out" sales, which are defined as any sale at a net selling price of less than seventy-five percent (75%) of Licensee's usual price to its customers, and made in contemplation of ceasing sales of the Licensed Products.

Note: The terms in "c" above are negotiable and may vary by industry and product.

In the event the Licensed Products are sold in sets with other products that do not incorporate the Licensor Trademark, royalties shall be paid only on that portion of the Net Wholesale Selling Price of the set attributable to the Licensed Products. The dollar amount of royalty per unit paid to Licensor from sales to customers affiliated with Licensee shall be the same sum as paid on sales of the same item to unaffiliated customers, regardless of the actual Net Wholesale Selling Price to such affiliated customer. Also, if two or more

Licensed Products are sold together as one product with a single SKU, one royalty shall be paid on such sale.

<u>Term.</u> The term of this Agreement shall commence on the date first above written and shall continue through _____ 20_____. Licensee shall have an option to extend the term hereof for an additional three (3) years, commencing upon the expiration of the preceding term and continuing through _____ 20_____. This option shall be exercised, if at all, by written notice given to Licensor at least thirty (30) days prior to the expiration of the then current term, provided that Licensee pays Licensor $_____ on January 1 of each year extended by the option (e.g., January 1, 20_____; January 1, 20_____; and January 1, 20_____). Upon expiration of this extended term, if any, Licensee shall have a continuing, perpetual option to extend the term for additional one-year (1) periods, commencing upon the expiration of the preceding term. Each such option shall be exercised, if at all, by written notice given to Licensor at least thirty (30) days prior to the expiration of the then current term, provided that Licensee pays Licensor $_____ on January 1 of each year extended by the applicable option.

<u>Termination.</u>

<u>Licensor Breach.</u> In the event Licensor breaches any representation or warranty made in this Agreement or breaches any material obligation under this Agreement, Licensee may give written notice to Licensor calling attention to such breach and stating Licensee's intent to terminate this Agreement unless Licensor remedies such breach within five (5) days after receipt of such notice. If the breach is not remedied to Licensee's reasonable satisfaction, Licensee may serve written notice immediately terminating the Agreement and seek all legal remedies to which it is entitled under the law, or at equity.

<u>Licensee Breach.</u> In the event Licensee breaches any material obligation under this Agreement, Licensor may give written notice to Licensee calling attention to such breach and stating Licensor's intent to terminate this Agreement unless Licensee remedies such breach within five (5) days after receipt of such notice. If the breach is not remedied to Licensor's reasonable satisfaction, Licensor may serve written notice immediately terminating the Agreement and seek all legal remedies to which it is entitled under the law.

<u>Licensee Default.</u> In the event Licensee should at any time default by failing to make any payment hereunder, or fail to make any report required under this Agreement and thereafter fail to remedy such default within seven (7) days after notice thereof by Licensor, then Licensor may, at its option, terminate this Agreement and the license granted herein by notice to that effect, but such act shall not relieve Licensee of its liabilities accruing up to the time of termination.

Effect of Termination.

Subject to the disposal of inventory provisions of Section 9, upon and after termination of this Agreement, all rights granted to Licensee hereunder shall forthwith revert to Licensor, and Licensee will refrain from further use of the Licensor Trademark in connection with the manufacture, sale, or advertising of the Licensed Products and goods similar to the Licensed Products.

Notwithstanding termination or expiration of this Agreement and the licenses granted herein, the obligations in Section 12 shall survive such termination for a period of three (3) years.

Sell-Off. In the event of expiration or earlier termination of this Agreement, except for nonpayment of financial obligations to Licensor, Licensee shall have the right to dispose of its existing inventory of the Licensed Products, whether completed or in the process of manufacture, for a period of three (3) months after expiration or such early termination, and may do so: (a) at prices less than its normal wholesale price; and (b) through its normal marketing efforts and distribution channels. Royalty payments shall continue, unless such sales are on a close-out basis. Notwithstanding the aforementioned rights to dispose inventory, Licensee acknowledges that it shall have no rights to sell any Licensed Products that materially deviate in quality from the samples approved by Licensor.

Intellectual Property

Trademark Ownership. Licensee shall have the right, in its discretion, to obtain trademark and copyright protection that will adequately protect the Licensed Products from competition worldwide, except for the United States, and, if such protection is sought by Licensee, then Licensee shall bear the expense of obtaining such protection. It is the express understanding and agreement of the parties that Licensee shall be the sole owner of any and all trademarks and copyrights which are designed, invented, developed, or acquired by or for Licensee and used in connection with the Licensed Products, with the exception of the Licensor Trademark. Licensor acknowledges and agrees that Licensee is the sole owner of all right, title, and interest in and to the Licensee Trademarks (as defined in Section 10[b]), and all associated goodwill and other interests.

No Derogation of Licensee's Rights. Licensor shall not: (a) do anything that might harm the reputation or goodwill of the trademarks, trade names, service marks, logos, designations, or marks owned, registered, or licensed to Licensee, or that may be owned, registered, or licensed to Licensee (collectively, the "Licensee Trademarks"); (b) take any action inconsistent with Licensee's ownership of the Licensee Trademarks; or (c) challenge Licensee's rights or interest in the Licensee Trademarks, or attempt to register the Licensee Trademarks or any mark or logo substantially similar thereto. Licensee's use of the Licensee Trademarks inures solely to the benefit of Licensee.

Further Assurances. Licensor agrees to cooperate with Licensee and take all reasonable actions required to vest and secure in Licensee the ownership rights and appurtenant interests as provided in this Agreement, and shall also assist Licensee to the extent necessary to protect and maintain the Licensee Trademarks, including but not limited to: (a) giving prompt notice to Licensee of any known, actual, or potential infringement of the Licensee Trademarks; and (b) cooperating with Licensee in the preparation and execution of any documents necessary to register the Licensee Trademarks.

Quality Approval.

In the manufacture, sale, and distribution of the Licensed Products, Licensee shall maintain standards of quality that conform to those quality standards used at present by Licensee with respect to the manufacture, distribution, and sale of Licensee's goods and those high-quality standards evidenced by the samples of Licensee products furnished to and inspected by Licensor.

In order to ensure that the high level of quality standards described above are maintained, Licensee shall furnish to Licensor one (1) sample of each category of the Licensed Products for Licensor's inspection and approval, which approval shall not be unreasonably withheld. Licensor shall be deemed to have approved any sample unless written rejection thereof is sent to Licensee, directed to the attention of the Licensee Product Legal Department, within ten (10) days of receipt of the sample by Licensor.

(c) Licensee shall utilize a continuous quality-control system to ensure that high quality standards are maintained. Furthermore, upon reasonable notice and no more than twice during any one calendar year, Licensee's facilities for the manufacturing, sale, and distribution of Licensed Products shall be subject to inspection during reasonable business hours by Licensor or its duly authorized representative.

Indemnification.

Licensor agrees to indemnify and save harmless Licensee from and against claims, demands, damages, costs, and attorney's fees involving any breach of the representations and warranties contained herein and from any claim alleging that the Licensor Trademark infringes the rights of any third party. If any third party brings a lawsuit or makes a claim alleging that Licensee's use of the Licensor Trademark constitutes an infringement of the rights of such third person, Licensee shall give Licensor notice of such claim or lawsuit. Licensor shall defend any such lawsuit or claim, and any and all expenses thereof and all liabilities resulting therefrom shall be borne solely by Licensor. After notice has been received by Licensee, Licensee shall be entitled to escrow all royalties accrued thereafter to defray costs incurred and damages assessed until such time that the infringement charge is settled or otherwise disposed of. Any excess in such escrow account shall be paid to Licensor. Such indemnity shall be in addition to any other remedy available to Licensee.

Licensee agrees to indemnify and save harmless Licensor and undertakes to defend itself and Licensor against and hold Licensor harmless from any claim, suits, loss, and damage, including Licensor's reasonable and necessary attorneys' fees arising out of any allegedly unauthorized use of any patent, process, idea, method, or device by Licensee in connection with the Licensed Products or arising out of alleged defects in the Licensed Products.

Product Liability Insurance. Licensee confirms that it has and will maintain, at its own expense, product liability insurance from a recognized insurance company providing coverage in the amount of at least two million dollars ($2,000,000.00) for any such product liability claim. As proof of such insurance coverage, upon request, Licensee shall provide Licensor with a certificate of insurance showing Licensor as an additional insured party, which certificate shall obligate insurer to provide ten (10) days written notice to Licensee of any termination or reduction of coverage confirmed by such certificate.

Royalty Reports. Licensee shall, within (insert number) (_____) days following the end of each calendar quarter, starting with the month in which sales of the Licensed Products commence, submit to Licensor a report covering the sales of the Licensed Products during the preceding quarter, and Licensee shall therewith transmit to Licensor payment of the amount due under Section 5 hereof.

Books and Records. Licensee agrees to keep full and accurate books of account, records, data, and memoranda respecting the manufacture and sales of the Licensed Products in sufficient detail to enable the payments hereunder to Licensor to be determined, and Licensee further gives Licensor the right, at its own expense, to examine said books and records on prior written notice of at least ten (10) days, insofar as they concern the Licensed Products and not more often than once in any calendar year, for the purpose of verifying the reports provided for in this Agreement. In the event that Licensor examines the records, documents, and materials in the possession or under the control of Licensee with respect to the subject matter, such examination shall be conducted by an independent auditor selected by Licensor and approved by Licensee, such examination being conducted in such manner as to not unduly interfere with the business of Licensee. Licensor's representatives shall not disclose to any other person, firm, or corporation any information acquired as a result of any such examination, provided, however, that nothing herein contained shall be construed to prevent Licensor and/or its duly authorized representatives from testifying in any court of competent jurisdiction with respect to the information obtained as a result of such examination, in any action instituted to enforce the rights of Licensor under the terms of the Agreement.

Excused Performance. It is understood and agreed that in the event of an act of government; war; fire; flood; interruptions of transportation; embargo; accident; explosion; act of terrorism; inability to procure or shortage of supply and materials, equipment, or production facilities; prohibition of transportation of the Licensed Products; strike, lockout, or other labor trouble interfering with the production or transportation of such goods or with the supplies of raw materials entering into their production; or an Act of God; or other cause beyond the control of Licensee, Licensee shall not be liable for failure of performance hereunder, and such nonperformance shall be excused while, but no longer than, the conditions described herein prevail.

No Waiver. A failure by either party to enforce any of the provisions of this Agreement or rights or remedies with respect thereto or to exercise election therein provided shall not constitute a waiver of such provision, right, remedy, or election, or affect the validity thereof or of this Agreement.

Assignment. Licensee may assign or sublicense this Agreement to any subsidiary or affiliate corporation, provided, however, that such assignee or sublicensee shall thereafter be bound by all provisions of this Agreement.

Note: You may deny the right to sublicense.

Notices. All notices wherever required in this Agreement shall be in writing and sent by certified mail and shall be deemed given when mailed or, alternatively, shall be given by facsimile with receipt notification, and shall be deemed given upon receipt of notification when given to the respective addresses/facsimile numbers of the parties as set forth below:

If to Licensor:

YOUR NAME: _____

Address: _____

If to Licensee:

Licensee name: _____

Address: _____

Validity. If any provision of this Agreement is for any reason declared to be invalid, the validity of the remaining provisions shall not be affected thereby.

Binding Nature. This Agreement shall be binding upon and inure to the benefit of the parties hereto and their successors and assigns.

Choice of Laws. This Agreement and each and every one of its provisions shall be interpreted under the laws of the State of (insert your state).

Confidential. Each party to this Agreement agrees to consider the terms of the Agreement as confidential and not to divulge the business terms and conditions of the Agreement without the prior written consent of each other party.

<u>Entire Agreement.</u> This Agreement represents and expresses the entire agreement of the parties and supersedes all prior agreements, representations, and understandings (written or oral) between the parties concerning the subject matter hereof. An amendment or modification of a term or condition of this Agreement must be in writing duly executed by both parties.

IN WITNESS WHEREOF, the parties have hereunto set their hands to this Agreement:

Licensor: _____   Licensee, Inc.: _____

By: _____   By: _____

Name: _____   Name: _____

Title: _____   Title: _____

Agreement to Hold Secret and Confidential Template

The below described invention, idea, or concept (hereinafter referred to as INVENTION) is being submitted to _____ of _____ (hereinafter referred to as COMPANY) by _____ of _____ on _____, 20_____, (hereinafter referred to as INVENTOR) who is the inventor of record. The undersigned, in consideration of examining said INVENTION, with a purpose to opening negotiations to obtain a license to manufacture and sell said INVENTION, hereby agrees on behalf of himself/herself and said COMPANY that he/she represents, that:

1) He/she (during or after the termination of employment with said COMPANY) and said COMPANY, will keep said INVENTION, and any information pertaining to it, in confidence.

2) He/she will not disclose said INVENTION or data related thereto to anyone except for employees of said COMPANY, sufficient information about said INVENTION to enable said COMPANY to continue with negotiations for said license, and that anyone in said COMPANY to whom said INVENTION is revealed shall be informed of the confidential nature of the disclosure and shall agree to hold confidential the information and be bound by the terms hereof, to the same extent as if they had signed this Agreement.

3) Neither he/she nor said COMPANY shall use any of the information provided to produce said INVENTION until agreement is reached with INVENTOR.

4) He/she has the authority to make this Agreement on behalf of said COMPANY.

It is understood, nevertheless, that the undersigned and said COMPANY shall not be prevented by the Agreement from selling any product heretofore sold by said COMPANY, or any product in the development or planning stage, as of the date first above written, or any product disclosed in any heretofore issued U.S. Letters Patent or otherwise known to the general public.

The terms of the preceding section releasing, under certain conditions, the obligation to hold the disclosure in confidence does not, however, constitute a waiver of any patent, copyright, or other rights which said Inventor or any licensee thereof may have against the undersigned or said COMPANY.

IN WITNESS WHEREOF, the parties have signed this Agreement on the respective dates hereinafter written.

The INVENTION is generally described as follows:

Discloser: _____

Company Representative: _____

Date: _____

Resources

Here are some resources I encourage you to become familiar with. Go to the cited websites and snoop around. You never know what invaluable information or contacts you may stumble upon.

Patent and Trademark Depository Libraries

A Patent and Trademark Depository Library (PTDL) is a library designated by the U.S. Patent and Trademark Office (PTO) to receive and house copies of U.S. patents and patent and trademark materials, to make them freely available to the public, and to actively disseminate patent and trademark information. For more information, see www.uspto.gov/web/offices/ac/ido/ptdl/ptdlib_1.html.

Federal Laboratories

The Federal Laboratory Consortium for Technology Transfer (FLC) is the nationwide network of federal laboratories that provides the forum to develop strategies and opportunities for linking laboratory mission technologies and expertise with the marketplace.

The FLC was organized in 1974 and formally chartered by the Federal Technology Transfer Act of 1986 to promote and strengthen technology transfer nationwide. Today more than 250 federal laboratories and centers and their parent departments and agencies are FLC members. The government may grant nonexclusive, partially exclusive, or exclusive licenses to its technologies. For more information, see www.federallabs.org/labs/results.

State and Local Inventor Organizations

It's impossible to keep an up-to-date, accurate list of state and local inventor organizations, their officers, telephone numbers, e-mail addresses, and websites in a book of this nature. So please refer to what appears to be the most comprehensive list available, the United Inventors Association's (UIA) list at www.uiausa.org/Default.aspx?page=81.

You can also click through to state-by-state organizations from *Inventor's Digest* at www.inventorsdigest.com/?page_id=164.

If your group isn't mentioned on the list, I encourage you to contact UIA and register.

Toy and Game Manufacturers

The toy industry has a tremendous appetite for new product, and most companies welcome outside submissions. According to the Toy Industry Association, each year between 6,000 and 7,000 new products are introduced at its American International Toy Fair in New York City.

What was once a stable list of potential licensees for your concepts has become destabilized by the current economic upheaval and paradigm shifts in business models. So rather than provide a list of companies, many of which could be gone by the time this book is published, I refer you to the Toy Industry Association's website for the names and addresses of its members: www.toyassociation.org.

Index